W9-CKQ-010

WITHDRAWN

EDUCATION IN SCHOOL
AND NONSCHOOL SETTINGS

EDUCATION IN SCHOOL
AND NONSCHOOL SETTINGS

Eighty-fourth Yearbook of the
National Society for the Study of Education

PART I

By

THE YEARBOOK COMMITTEE

AND

ASSOCIATED CONTRIBUTORS

Edited by

MARIO D. FANTINI AND ROBERT L. SINCLAIR

Editor for the Society

KENNETH J. REHAGE

19 **NSSE** 85

Theodore Lownik Library
Illinois Benedictine College
Lisle, Illinois 60532

Distributed by THE UNIVERSITY OF CHICAGO PRESS ● CHICAGO, ILLINOIS

370. 6
N21
v. 84
pt. 1

The National Society for the Study of Education

Founded in 1901 as successor to the National Herbart Society, the National Society for the Study of Education has provided a means by which the results of serious study of educational issues could become a basis for informed discussion of those issues. The Society's two-volume yearbooks, now in their eighty-fourth year of publication, reflect the thoughtful attention given to a wide range of educational problems during those years. A recently inaugurated series on Contemporary Educational Issues includes substantial publications in paperback that supplement the yearbooks. Each year, the Society's publications contain contributions to the literature of education from more than a hundred scholars and practitioners who are doing significant work in their respective fields.

An elected Board of Directors selects the subjects with which volumes in the yearbook series are to deal, appropriates funds to meet necessary expenses in the preparation of a given volume, and appoints a committee to oversee the preparation of manuscripts for that volume. A special committee created by the Board performs similar functions for the Society's paperback series.

The Society's publications are distributed each year without charge to more than 3,000 members in the United States, Canada, and elsewhere throughout the world. The Society welcomes as members all individuals who desire to receive its publications. For information about membership and current dues, see pages 279-80 of this volume or write to the Secretary-Treasurer, 5835 Kimbark Avenue, Chicago, Illinois 60637.

The Eighty-fourth Yearbook includes the following two volumes:

Part I: *Education in School and Nonschool Settings*
Part II: *Learning and Teaching the Ways of Knowing*

A complete listing of the Society's previous publications, together with information as to how earlier publications still in print may be obtained, is found in the back pages of this volume.

Library of Congress Catalog Number: 84-062253
ISSN: 0077-5762

Published 1985 by
THE NATIONAL SOCIETY FOR THE STUDY OF EDUCATION

5835 Kimbark Avenue, Chicago, Illinois 60637
© 1985 by the National Society for the Study of Education

No part of this Yearbook may be reproduced in any form without written permission from the Secretary of the Society

First Printing, 6,500 Copies

Printed in the United States of America

Officers of the Society
1984-85

(Term of office expires March 1 of the year indicated.)

HARRY S. BROUDY

(1985)
University of Illinois, Champaign, Illinois

MARGARET EARLY

(1986)
Syracuse University, Syracuse, New York

ELLIOT W. EISNER

(1986)
Stanford University, Stanford, California

JOHN I. GOODLAD

(1987)
University of California, Los Angeles, California

A. HARRY PASSOW

(1985)
Teachers College, Columbia University, New York, New York

RALPH W. TYLER

(1987)
*Director Emeritus, Center for Advanced Study in the Behavioral Sciences
Stanford, California*

KENNETH J. REHAGE

(Ex-officio)
University of Chicago, Chicago, Illinois

Secretary-Treasurer

KENNETH J. REHAGE

5835 Kimbark Avenue, Chicago, Illinois 60637

The Society's Committee on
Education in School and Nonschool Settings

MARIO D. FANTINI

(Cochairman)
Professor and Dean, School of Education
University of Massachusetts
Amherst, Massachusetts

ROBERT L. SINCLAIR

(Cochairman)
Professor of Education
Director, Center for Curriculum Studies
School of Education
University of Massachusetts
Amherst, Massachusetts

A. HARRY PASSOW

Jacob A. Schiff Professor of Education
Teachers College, Columbia University
New York, New York

RALPH W. TYLER

Director Emeritus, Center for
Advanced Study in the Behavioral Sciences
Stanford, California

Associated Contributors

GERALDINE JONCICH CLIFFORD

Professor, School of Education
University of California at Berkeley
Berkeley, California

BURTON COHEN

Assistant Professor of Education
Jewish Theological Seminary of America
New York, New York

JAMES P. COMER

Associate Dean, Yale Medical School
Yale University
New Haven, Connecticut

MARVIN FELDMAN

President, Fashion Institute of Technology
New York, New York

EDWARD L. FRICKEY

Professor, Cooperative Extension Service
Purdue University
West Lafayette, Indiana

WARD J. GHORY

Director of Curriculum and Instruction
Walnut Hills High School
Cincinnati, Ohio

JOHN I. GOODLAD

Professor, Graduate School of Education
Director, Laboratory in School and Community Education
University of California at Los Angeles
Los Angeles, California

MARY CONWAY KOHLER

Founder, National Commission on Resources for Youth, Inc.
New York, New York

DIXIE LEA

President, Lea Associates
Pacific Beach, California

ASSOCIATED CONTRIBUTORS

HOPE JENSEN LEICHTER

Director, Elbenwood Center for the Study of Family as Educator
Teachers College, Columbia University
New York, New York

JOSEPH LUKINSKY

Associate Professor of Education
Jewish Theological Seminary of America
New York, New York

BONNIE PITMAN-GELLES

Associate Director for Programs
Seattle Art Museum
Seattle, Washington

NEIL POSTMAN

Professor, Department of Communication Arts and Sciences
New York University
New York, New York

Acknowledgments

The Editors of this volume are extremely grateful to all who have participated in its preparation, most especially to the several contributors for the time and talent they have given to the preparation of their manuscripts. We are also indebted to others who have had important parts in this project: to Jeanne Masson Douglas, who assisted in the development of the original proposal to the National Society for the Study of Education; to Laura Holland and Paul Houts for help with research and technical matters; to Cindy Gula for superb secretarial support; and to Nancy Kominski for most competent administrative and organizational help. Marvin Feldman graciously hosted meetings of the Advisory Committee. That Committee, consisting of Ralph W. Tyler and A. Harry Passow, gave valued advice, support, and professional leadership throughout, as well as providing for liaison with the Board of Directors of the Society.

To all these individuals we extend our sincere appreciation for their very considerable efforts.

Mario D. Fantini
Robert L. Sinclair

The Board of Directors of the National Society for the Study of Education acknowledges with deepest gratitude the work of all who have contributed to the development of this volume. Special recognition is due the Editors, Mario D. Fantini and Robert L. Sinclair, who devoted long hours and considerable thought to this project from its inception more than four years ago to its completion. The preparation of a NSSE Yearbook is an enormous task. It requires a deep professional commitment, which Messrs. Fantini and Sinclair have exhibited in the fullest measure. It is this kind of commitment from editors and contributors that makes possible the production of the Society's series of Yearbooks, to which this volume makes a distinguished contribution.

The Society is also grateful to Eunice Helmkamp McGuire who has assisted with the reading of proof for this volume and has also prepared the indexes.

Kenneth J. Rehage
Editor for the Society

Preface

The formal school setting is not the only place in which children and youth learn and are taught. We have always known, for example, that the family is a powerful educational setting and that parents are important educators of their own children. The workplace also has educational consequences, as do various religious institutions. Television, computers, and museums are all "educators" in their own way, influencing us even while we attend school. An "educational system" is, in fact, composed of a network of learning environments, and the schools, as important as they are, cannot and should not attempt the total job of educating alone. The school is a major agency for learning, but it is only one among many potential educators. It is time for the school, as an institution, to redefine its role in the context of contemporary society. This clarification will undoubtedly include a meaningful association between schools and other educational settings in the community.

American society, through its policymakers, has found it convenient to delegate increased responsibilities to the schools. For example, when the expanding needs of this industrialized nation became apparent, the schools were expected to keep pace by serving as the manpower instruments of society. The school system responded to this expectation with a pattern of add-ons. However, in the decades of the 1960s and the 1970s, the school system became unwieldy. Witness, for example, the symptoms occasioned by the ponderous nature of the "add-on" approach to changes that tinkered with more and more additions rather than tackling basic reforms. The rapid changes in the larger society outpaced the ability of the schools to respond. The result was a growing institutional obsolescence characterized by increasing public dissatisfaction and a serious loss of confidence in the schools.

Society may have expected too much from the public schools and too little from other educative institutions. Delegating ever-increasing responsibilities to the schools led to an overload and an eventual compromise of quality education. Clearly, other institutions must now share the increasing responsibilities of the school. The public is slowly coming to support policies aimed at strengthening the role of these community agents in the overall educational process. Perhaps the persistence of accountability during the 1960s and 1970s has served to clarify the role of schools in the context of the larger educational enterprise. Public demands have helped the schools realize that they are now indeed complementary to an array of learning environments in the larger community.

The school is now beginning to take inventory of what it can and should do while seeking associations with other educational institutions. Hence, it is timely for professional educators and citizens alike to consider future educational arrangements—formal and nonformal—and to plan sensibly for the school and community to modernize through a carefully interconnected system of educational services.

The purpose of this Yearbook, then, is to reexamine school and nonschool education, and to suggest directions for clearing the present confusion about the educational responsibility of various institutions. Part One provides a base for understanding the importance of moving responsibility for education beyond the formal school setting. Part Two considers the present and future contributions of various educating institutions to the learning of children and youth and makes clear the potential for learning inherent in key institutions in the community. Part Three explores issues central to making decisions for linking school and nonschool settings in more effective ways and considers the realities to be faced when building a closer association between schools and other educational environments.

Our democratic society is rapidly being transformed. We are becoming an information-based economy in an interdependent world. The process by which we educate our people must effectively promote this transformation. At the heart of necessary changes is the need to connect school and nonschool settings into a system that promotes equal and quality education for all children and youth.

American society has awakened to a new call for excellence in education. However, the national attention span for serious educational reform is short. Thus, educators, and responsible citizens must attend to this newfound expression of public interest by acting constructively to advance public education in ways that will meet the challenges of these times. This Yearbook establishes a perspective for increasing coordination among various learning environments and advances proposals for the delivery of effective education in our contemporary society.

MARIO D. FANTINI
ROBERT L. SINCLAIR

January, 1985

Table of Contents

PAGE

THE NATIONAL SOCIETY FOR THE STUDY OF EDUCATION iv

OFFICERS OF THE SOCIETY, 1984-85 v

THE SOCIETY'S COMMITTEE ON EDUCATION IN SCHOOL AND
NONSCHOOL SETTINGS vi

ASSOCIATED CONTRIBUTORS vii

ACKNOWLEDGMENTS ix

PREFACE xi

Part One

A Perspective on School and Nonschool Collaboration for Learning 1

CHAPTER

I. THE SHIFTING RELATIONS BETWEEN SCHOOLS AND NONSCHOOL
EDUCATION, *Geraldine Joncich Clifford* 4

II. RETHINKING WHAT SCHOOLS CAN DO BEST, *John I. Goodlad* . . . 29

III. STAGES OF LINKING SCHOOL AND NONSCHOOL LEARNING ENVIRON-
MENTS, *Mario D. Fantini* 46

IV. COMBINED EFFORTS: MODELS FOR NONSCHOOL SETTINGS FOR
LEARNING, *A. Harry Passow* 64

Part Two

The Other Educative Settings 79

V. FAMILIES AS EDUCATORS, *Hope Jensen Leichter* 81

VI. THE WORKPLACE AS EDUCATOR, *Marvin Feldman* 102

VII. MUSEUMS AND SCHOOLS: A MEANINGFUL PARTNERSHIP, *Bonnie
Pitman-Gelles* 114

VIII. RELIGIOUS INSTITUTIONS AS EDUCATORS, *Burton Cohen* and *Joseph
Lukinsky* 140

IX. YOUTH-SERVING AGENCIES AS EDUCATORS, *Mary C. Kohler, Edward
L. Frickey,* and *Dixie Lea* 159

X. MEDIA AND TECHNOLOGY AS EDUCATORS, *Neil Postman* . . . 183

Part Three

PAGE

Relating School and Nonschool Settings 201

CHAPTER

XI. CONDITIONS FOR EFFECTIVE LEARNING, *Ralph W. Tyler* . . . 203

XII. CURRICULUM CONNECTIONS: COMBINING ENVIRONMENTS FOR LEARNING, *Robert L. Sinclair* and *Ward J. Ghory* 230

XIII. DEMAND FOR EXCELLENCE AND THE NEED FOR EQUITY, *James P. Comer* 245

XIV. LINKING SCHOOL AND NONSCHOOL EDUCATION: PUBLIC POLICY CONSIDERATIONS, *Mario D. Fantini* and *Robert L. Sinclair* . . . 264

NAME INDEX 273

SUBJECT INDEX 276

INFORMATION ABOUT MEMBERSHIP IN THE SOCIETY 279

PUBLICATIONS OF THE SOCIETY 281

Part One
A PERSPECTIVE ON SCHOOL AND NONSCHOOL COLLABORATION FOR LEARNING

Introduction

A remarkable number of recent reports on schools has turned the nation's attention once again to public education. Though these reports did not always bring us cheering news, they served a valuable purpose. They rekindled the country's interest in its schools after over a decade of neglect. They gave us new insights into the strengths and weaknesses of our educational system, and they offered us a bevy of often useful recommendations for improving schools.

Schools are not, however, the only institutions in our society that educate. Moreover, we believe that they cannot be studied in isolation if we are to develop a coherent and modern plan for educational reform. We must examine schools and other educative institutions in tandem, and within the context of the society they serve. That context is a dramatically altered one.

1. In less than a century, we have moved from being an agrarian society to an industrial society to an information society. At the turn of the century, farmers represented one-third of the work force. Today, they represent less than 3 percent, fewer than the total number of people now employed in our universities. The shift in the industrial sector has been even more dramatic over the last quarter century. Twenty-five years ago, almost 50 percent of our work force occupied blue-collar jobs. Currently, fewer than one out of three jobs is in the goods producing sector, whereas over 50 percent are in the information sector. Indeed, more than half of our gross national product comes from developing, storing, processing, and disseminating information. This change in the nature of work is a shift from the menial to the mental.

2. Our current society is not only an information one but a learning society as well. Students graduating from high schools today

1

can expect to change jobs 6.6 times during their lifetime. Many of these jobs will require entirely new sets of skills. By one estimate, for example, 75 percent of all jobs by 1985 will involve computers in some way. Clearly, in the years ahead, students will need a sturdy capacity for adaptability plus abundant opportunities for education and reeducation, training and retraining. Schools will be only one of numerous settings providing these opportunities.

   3. Our economy has shifted from a national to an international one. We no longer occupy a preeminent and self-sufficient place in the world's economy. We buy steel in Korea to manufacture cars in Japan to be assembled and distributed in the United States. Between 1960 and 1980, the United States share of world manufacturing slipped from 25 to 17 percent. Less than 50 percent of consumer electronics sold in the United States were manufactured here. Moreover, we now depend on countries strung about the globe for many of our most essential resources. The global society has become a reality; isolation is an impossibility. As Marshall McLuhan has observed: "There are no passengers on the Spaceship Earth. We are all crew."

   4. We have moved into a scientific and technological era. As a result, public policy issues have become highly complex, requiring specialized knowledge. As citizens, we are called upon to ponder the merits of new weapons systems, debate disarmament proposals, and make judgments on numerous global issues, often without having the necessary knowledge to participate effectively in the debate. Indeed, so omnipresent is science in our society that we can no longer pinpoint it on our cultural map. In less than two decades, science and technology may well in fact have become our primary culture. It has now become vitally important to produce a generation capable of making its way successfully in a scientific society, of making intelligent and informed decisions relating to science and technology and the public issues they permeate. "Ignorance of science and technology," warns Jeremy Bernstein, "is becoming the ultimate self-indulgent luxury."

   5. Young people today are at the receiving end of more information than ever before in human history. At the touch of a button or the flick of a switch, they are bombarded with information from television, calculators, computers, and word processors, not to mention the print media. Television presents a dramatic case in point. The average child has watched over 5,000 hours of television before entering school. By

the time of high school graduation, television viewing has consumed more of the student's life than any activity except sleep. Clearly, information is increasingly available to students from many sources other than the schools. Much of this information, however, is provided to students in relatively passive and undemanding forms; much of it is random and disconnected; much of it is meretricious. What are students to make of these visual patches and data pockets? We may wonder, in T. S. Eliot's words, "Where is the wisdom we have lost in knowledge? Where is the knowledge we have lost in information?"

All of these changes have profound implications for education now and in the years ahead. Such dramatically shifting patterns in the fabric of our society raise totally new questions about the purposes of education, what is important to know, and who shall teach it.

As the chapters in this section point out, these are not new issues; for generations Americans have been asking these questions about education in their time. And each generation has devised its own solutions. One such solution for our own time, we believe, is in building more constructive associations between schools and other settings of educational importance. While schools will continue to be a positive force in our society, increased collaborations (as this section makes clear) will become a necessary and rewarding way of life that can result in a richer, more effective education for American society in the years to come.

CHAPTER I

The Shifting Relations between Schools and Nonschool Education: A Historical Account

GERALDINE JONCICH CLIFFORD

Introduction

This Yearbook is itself a phenomenon of contemporary history. Looked at as a historiographic puzzle, it can be considered a product of three related events: (a) the erosion of the coalition supporting American public schools; (b) the deeply felt wish to save and enhance the public schools as a distinctively American institution; and (c) the emerging scholarship that has contributed to a growing recognition that many agencies, besides schools, have shared the responsibilities of education.

For 150 years, public schooling flourished in America under the protection and in the interests of middle-class and main-line Protestantism. This same coalition sustained the more general movement of institution building that created other "problem-solving" and educating organizations: orphanages and asylums, prisons and reform schools, hospitals, libraries, youth organizations, coordinated charities. In time, new groups joined the coalition on behalf of schools: freed blacks, Jews, and aspiring immigrants. They did so partly to secure perceived benefits for their children and partly to establish their status as "real" Americans.[1]

Like other institutions, today's schools are shaken by a crisis of confidence and withdrawals of financial support. Skepticism about the benefits or fairness of schooling has unravelled its consensus and undermined the schools' political footing. "De-schoolers" like Ivan Illich rode a rising tide of rhetoric demanding the deinstitutionalization of society. The advocacy of home-birth, probation for convicted offenders, half-way houses, and support groups represent a general distrust of institutions and the professionals who staff them.

Professionals have a stake in fighting these tendencies. In their self-interested need to preserve the public school as the chief instrument of publicly financed education, public school professionals still have allies: in the remnants of their political alliance, in a "cultural memory" of once effective schools, in a preference for known over "untried" solutions. One way to "save the schools," moreover, is to place them in a different perspective: to create a public opinion that would relieve schools of "inappropriate burdens" and reduce expectations of what they should attempt to do.

In the past quarter-century, educational research has often unwittingly stressed the limitations of schooling. James Coleman's *Equality of Educational Opportunity* (1966) and Christopher Jencks's *Inequality: A Reassessment of the Effect of Family and Schooling in America* (1972) reported pessimistic conclusions about the schools' ability to reduce academic and social differences between groups. Works of historical analysis like *The Imperfect Panacea* (1968), *Class, Bureaucracy and Schools* (1971), and *The Sorting Machine* (1976) tipped their hands by their titles. Diane Ravitch even warned that such interpretation could strengthen assaults on the public schools: from the political right, Christian fundamentalists, taxpayers in revolt, academic conservatives, and antibusing groups.[2]

However, for those who remain convinced of the positive accomplishments of public schools, help was at hand in another kind of historical revisionism: the concept of "configurations of education" developed by Lawrence Cremin. Impressed by Bernard Bailyn's critique of traditional school-centered histories of education, and by Bailyn's rediscovery of the primacy of family-as-educator in colonial America,[3] Cremin began a three-volume history that would put schools alongside—not overshadowing—other educators: families, churches, work experience, libraries, museums, agricultural fairs and other facilitators of self-education, benevolent and fraternal societies, political institutions, labor organizations, and the mass media of communication.

Cremin proposed that *relationships* among schools and nonschool educators alter over time. He also emphasized that their specific configurations of education may vary among given individuals and groups. Thus, religious leaders remained important educators of Orthodox Jews and, while apprenticeship lost ground to university book-learning for many professionals, it retained its centrality for skilled crafts. Cremin's reminder that education always goes on in many settings offers us opportunities to reassess the past role of schools alongside and in interaction with other educators, and for school professionals and policy makers to consider greater future integration of educational efforts. He writes, for example, that "the real message of the Coleman and Jencks studies of equal educational opportunity [is] not that the school is power*less* but that the family is power*ful*."[4] Thus, while seeming to diminish the school in educational history, Cremin in fact protects it by acknowledging the proper weight of other educators.

Defining Education and Educators

Social science and historical research show that the family, community, television networks, churches, and employers are among the agencies that both influence what schools do and are themselves educators. They educate, as well as socialize, because they supply information and meaning to children and adults, teaching what is important and what is not, what to do and what to avoid. Under the influence of such research, the definitions of educating have changed. To distinguish education from the anthropologist's "enculturation"— all the learning that makes one a full member of one's society by coming to share its culture—James Axtell's definition includes deliberate and conserving requirements: education is "the *self-conscious* pursuit of certain intellectual, social, and moral ideas by any society, from the family to the nation, that wishes to *preserve and transmit* its distinctive character to future generations."[5] Although Cremin acknowledges that incidental learning can be powerful, he also emphasizes *intention* in his definition of education as "the deliberate, systematic, and sustained effort to transmit or evoke knowledge, attitudes, values, skills, and sensibilities."[6] Both historians recognize that the formation of character and personality is present in all manner of educational settings, even when their surface concern appears limited to imparting skills ranging from conjugating verbs to installing engines.

The "teachers" of the Slovak immigrants of Homestead, Pennsylvania, around 1910 included a well-patronized butcher shop that sold meat but also gave advice and translations; along with "the mill" and foreign-language newspapers and parishes, it was a unit in an educational network.[7] In the case of the Homestead schools and most families, however, education was their primary and sustained task.

All educational agencies have components of the kinds just suggested, but of differing intensity. The educating intention may range from primarily "informing" (in the case of newspapers or documentary cinema) to "shaping" (in the case of churches). Educating may vary from being casual or capricious (when a neighbor corrects a child's street behavior) to sustained (as with a family's unremitting attention). Educating may be a secondary concern (as often happens in the workplace, hospital, or recreational agency) or the organization's essential function (as in schools and colleges). It may range from self-managed (in independent study in the library) to being directed by others (as in the Great Books Program). Education may be undifferentiated in its audience (as with the electronic media) or have an age-specific or otherwise designated clientele (as in the educational programs of the Future Farmers of America or the League of Women Voters). The school or college lies on the extreme end of the continuum in each of the above components—it is shaping in intent, deliberate in design, with instruction as its intrinsic function; a managed system, with a designated population.

In the nineteenth and twentieth centuries, schools proliferated in Europe and North America—reaching more children, with more regular attendance, and for more years of their youth; with better articulated courses and materials; with better trained teachers and more insistent administration. In the process, such traditional educators as the family, church, labor organizations, and employers became less deliberate, systematic, sustained, and self-confident in *their* instruction. In nineteenth-century America, especially, ecological relationships among educational institutions were altered. Thus, "families spent less time systematically teaching reading as they increasingly assumed that schools . . . would do so, and apprenticeships in law and medicine carried less of an educational burden as law schools and medical schools became more widely available."[8] Many churches, Protestant and Catholic, probably counted on reaching more children through their schools and youth organizations than through traditional religious services.

The Ascendance of the School

The oldest documents of Western civilization record the use of schools. Originating as irregularly supplied and fitfully attended *ad hoc* institutions, as complementary extensions of other institutions, schools have slowly become central to many educational systems. Their enhanced status is a consequence, an indicator, and a contributor to the congeries of technological, political, social, and attitudinal changes sometimes called "modernism."[9] We will now examine some of these kinds of shifts and indicate how they altered the status of schools and colleges in the network of educational agencies.

TECHNOLOGICAL CHANGE

We readily associate books with schools. Although, as Patrick Suppes reminds us,[10] it took more than three centuries from the invention of printing for books to challenge seriously the oral teaching methods of schools and colleges, the print medium spread the opportunity and, hence, the need for literacy. Traditional prohibitions against scribes teaching reading and schoolmasters teaching writing collapsed. As commerce grew and made numeracy a more valued skill, the "Three Rs" gradually emerged as the essential curriculum of elementary schooling.[11] Today we hear speculations that television, the "talking" computer, the telephone, and the calculator are making older skills obsolete as universal requirements for participation in society—and that they will eventually reshape education more than did the invention of printing. Nevertheless, the last 300 years of the history of education, especially of schooling, is a story of extending literacy through the population in one society after another.

Universally men demonstrate higher literacy rates than do women, and such was the case in colonial New England. The Puritan compulsion to read the Bible theoretically enlarged the importance of literacy, for both sexes. Greater recourse to schools by males apparently came in the period 1710-1760, when modest increases in population density made schools cheaper to supply and there was more "need" for literacy across occupations. The rise in adult male literacy went from

68 percent to 82 percent. The corresponding figures for women were only 40 percent and 44 percent, not surprising when we consider that publicly supported town schools excluded females and perceptions of women's roles did not add new demands on their literacy.[12] Eventually political and economic events would make basic literacy and numeracy skills imperative for both men and women. In the meanwhile, as schools grew to meet these pressures, the statistical definition of literacy changed: from the ability to sign one's name, to the ability to read and write, to the current standard of the U. S. Census Bureau—the completion of five years of schooling.

THE PROTESTANT REVOLUTION

Given that "for two thousand years, the public values of the West had been thought about and articulated via the language and categories of religion,"[13] education had to be animated by the Protestant insistence that everyone, not merely the clergy, read directly of God's words and works. Lutherans in parts of Germany and Scandinavia and the Calvinists in Old and New England, Scotland, and Switzerland led the way in promoting the instruction of children and adults—by teaching them to read, preaching in churches (and later in camp meetings), and catechizing in Sunday schools. This effort produced an outpouring of religious books and magazines, and mission and Bible societies spread. Unlike the Roman church, Protestantism spurred on the vernacular languages. This stimulated more book production and eventually led to academic studies in the grammars and literatures of German, English, and other languages once neglected because of the near monopoly of Latin as the language of scholarship and of the professions. The printing of secular books, pamphlets, and magazines gained from these movements, and much of this literature was didactic: advising people how to govern their families, cure their ailments, improve their farms, and make scientific observations.

The individualism that lies at the core of the Protestant revolution resulted in its fragmentation into new sects. While Baptists and Methodists did not initially accept the Calvinist emphasis on learning, as such groups matured they founded their own schools, colleges, and theological seminaries. More important, in the United States, they collaborated locally with other Protestants in supporting free and compulsory public schooling. This united effort among Protestant denominations also inspired Catholic efforts in religiously divided lands. While some American Catholics initially kept their children out of overtly Protestant public schools, an increasing number began to send their children to these schools or they patronized new parish schools. Religious differences have accommodated to other pressures, thereby reducing pluralism in the interests of a common culture. In the United States the "Americanization" of the Catholic Church and of Catholics eventually created strong resemblances between parochial and public schools in the same community[14]—and between different church-sponsored youth leagues.

THE MODERN NATION-STATE

Attention to education is a recurring theme in the independence movements that founded new nations after World War II. State-controlled radio and television, mass literacy programs, health and population agencies, as well as schools, are considered essential to securing a new political identity. This may require weaning groups from tribal or regional idioms in favor of a national language and supplementing social and religious customs with modern political codes of behavior, as well as the more obvious uses of education and training to advance economic development.

The revolutions of the eighteenth and nineteenth centuries also spawned their plans for systems of education appropriate to the new polity. The American Revolution generated thinking about the educational requirements for a self-governing people. The French Revolution produced elaborate schemes with centralization as its distinguishing permanent legacy. New education laws, with attempts to upgrade and coordinate schools, followed the unifications of the Italian states and the German principalities. The Russian Revolution attempted even more thorough-going educational reform.

In the new United States of America, it was argued that a republic with a democratic social and economic system required a high degree of "civic literacy." A government of laws, a polity built on the consent of the governed, made high educational demands of its citizens. For example, while not admitted to full citizenship, women had to be educated to be qualified first-teachers of their sons, "young republicans."[15] In the late years of the eighteenth century, therefore, New England town schools began to admit girls on equal terms with boys. Patrons were found to sponsor private girls' schools, and female seminaries spread in the next century. These and subsequently normal schools, women's colleges, and coeducational colleges justified advanced schooling for women on the grounds of their civic contributions as future wives and mothers, as volunteers in social betterment campaigns, and as school teachers. These last roles were extensions into the public sphere of what was considered women's "natural" function as educator in the home.

Citizenship, then, supplemented other claims on education, in schools and elsewhere. Because American citizenship promised equality, freed blacks demanded access to schools in order to realize that pledge and to take advantage of economic and social opportunities associated with political freedom. Other groups—Orientals and Jews, for example—asserted their own educational rights. Although admission to schools and colleges was central, these groups also sought access to industrial and union-sponsored job training, as part of the same process.

COMMERCIAL AND INDUSTRIAL DEVELOPMENT

Economic developments have influenced schools in various ways. Rather than being used to expand the apprenticeship system, the surplus capital produced by economic growth was invested heavily in founding or expanding private and public schools, colleges, and universities, and also in research institutes, libraries, museums, art galleries, and other educational settings. Relative prosperity enabled more families to prolong their children's schooling in lieu of putting them to work. In America, though not in Europe, secondary schools grew enormously; the very fact that others enrolled their children caused the status-anxious lower-middle class to do the same.[16]

Economic contractions also stimulated school attendance as schools became more available. This happened to American public high school enrollments during the severe depression of the 1890s and to high schools and colleges in the 1930s. Recessionary economics also produced nonschool training programs, and in recent years promoted more education in the military and in government programs to create jobs. A great deal of occupational training and work socialization continued to take place at the job site, especially for unskilled and semiskilled factory workers and clerical and domestic workers. Nonetheless, expanded demand for labor has encouraged women, ethnic and racial minorities, the handicapped, and other once educationally marginal populations to seek more general education or job-related training thought necessary even to compete for employment. Their wages were, in turn, often used to purchase further or better schooling and other educational advantages for themselves or their children.

In the United States, the federal legislation that created the land-grant colleges of agriculture and mechanic arts (the Morrill Act of 1862) and the vocational education programs in high schools (the Smith-Hughes Act of 1917) explicitly recognized the links between formal education, occupational preparation, and national economic development; so did the junior and community colleges. In this century the association of school attendance with employment became commonplace in the mind of the consumer or policy maker. Henry Steele Commager has put it well: "Education was his religion, and to it he paid the tribute both of his money and his affection; yet, as he expected his religion to be practical and pay dividends, he expected education to prepare for life—by which he meant, increasingly, jobs and professions."[17] Attention receded from the earlier recognized functions of schooling: to attest to one's inherited social superiority, to indulge rare academic talent, to save one's soul, to prepare for the few learned professions. Increasingly, formal schooling became more closely linked to entering the wage-labor force at a more advantageous level or competing more effectively for any job in economic hard times.

Another historic school function had been custodial: relieving parents or guardians of some or all of the care of youth for largely private reasons like children's incorrigibility or temporary dislocations due to family illness or death. Changes in the work world have diminished the proportions of self-employed shopkeepers and artisans, agricultural, and unskilled factory labor. These, in turn, caused occupational training, formerly given in the family, to lose importance and reduced the need for youthful labor generally, especially where adult immigrants constituted a labor pool. Organized labor lobbied to keep youth in school as a means of protecting adult wages. The custodial function of schooling grew apace. In "postindustrial" societies, the principal explanation for almost universal school attendance in the late years of adolescence is not so much that schools supply explicit work skills as that they buy time for the labor market to absorb young workers. Manpower specialists in the developed countries now speak of permanent rather than cyclical youth unemployment; this will further challenge the whole educational system.[18]

High schools have been called "state supported social service centers for adolescents at loose ends." And "having invented the adolescent," writes British sociologist Frank Musgrove, "society has been faced with two major problems: how and where to accommodate him in the social structure, and how to make his behavior accord with the specifications."[19] Despite curricular adjustments, relaxed academic and behavioral standards, and the extracurriculum, custodial secondary schools and even some colleges have experienced a loss of morale and threats of disruption.

CHANGES IN CHILDHOOD AND THE FAMILY

Entering school has become a *rite de passage* for virtually every child in Western societies; it is also spreading through the less developed nations of the second and third worlds. Our understanding of the elevation of schools in the educational configurations of Europe and North America was reordered by Philippe Ariès's examination of shifts in attitudes and practices in sixteenth- and seventeenth-century French families.[20] Nuclear family solidarity and its self-conscious concentration upon character formation, socialization, and instruction of children originated in the upper classes of Western societies and spread slowly downward to encompass most families. Fueled by complicated interactions of ideational and demographic changes, the child assumed a new standing; modern concepts of "childhood" and "adolescence" were being invented. Instead of considering children innately evil and interchangeable, the new view stressed each child's innocence and uniqueness. Improvements in nutrition and sanitation that lowered infant mortality rates undoubtedly contributed to this change. The growing importance of the family-as-educator also benefited schools because schools served to endorse the family's mission and strengthen its competence. By attending to the advice of the schoolmen, experts in the instruction of youth, and by patronizing schools, a family showed its regard for its educational obligations.

Despite their converging histories and some common goals, families and schools may also become adversaries, as some sociologists have observed. "Parents and teachers are natural enemies, predestined each for the discomfiture of the other."[21] Parents have particularistic and sometimes indulgent expectations for their children; the schools' are universalistic and more impersonal. While schools act legally *in loco parentis*, teachers and administrators have distinctive as well as overlapping interests with parents. The very processes of institutionalization caused inevitable tensions. The upper-class boarding schools of nineteenth-century England, for example, increasingly regarded themselves "as actually superior in the management of the lives of young persons than home life could ever be."[22]

Differences in social status often bedevil the relationships of home and school. Families of higher social status may look down upon teachers, as they earlier scorned the governess and tutor.[23] Poor families, especially if racially or culturally different, have been labelled *inattentive* to their children's interests—thus justifying compulsory school attendance, compulsory vaccination, and other programs—or merely *inadequate* in instilling proper values and habits.[24] The stresses of immigration, the massive entry of mothers into the labor force, divorce and other signs of family "pathology" have repeatedly generated educational remedies—some aimed at recreating a home-like environment in the school. In the United States, kindergarten was first popularized for the children of the "troubled and incompetent poor"; its home visits, interactions with parents, and emphasis on play, however, were gradually transformed by academic pressures. Daycare, nursery schools, and other preschool programs have been similarly affected.

The Special Place of Schools in the United States

One of many indicators of the schools' growing centrality among educational agencies was that, between 1820 and 1850, estimates of dollars spent in book production showed schoolbooks' share growing from 30 percent to 44 percent.[25] It is not surprising, then, that a Norwegian immigrant writing from Beloit, Wisconsin, in 1851 would comment:

The Americans are a most educated people. On the whole, I do not think that one will find anywhere a more educated people than here. Much attention is given to the educational system. Both children and adults go to school.[26]

Two factors created a reputation for America's public schools that cast other educational agencies into relative obscurity: the inclusiveness of American schooling—relative even to European leaders like Prussia, France, and England—and undoubtedly exaggerated accounts of schools' effects on individual social mobility and national wealth. By 1950, when the boom in college enrollments was beginning,[27] American schooling was already called the "Eighth Wonder of the World."

As early as the 1830s, in some regions schools outnumbered churches, and a Catholic bishop in 1842 advised his co-religionists that, "I think the time is almost come when it will be necessary to build the schoolhouse first, and the church afterward." This enhanced status of schools was a phenomenon of the nineteenth century that the United States shared with northwestern Europe.[28] In retrospect, however, there were crucial reasons why the American system diverged. Public schools came to replace the diversity of school types that had brought about high literacy levels and general, if erratic, attendance at schools before public schools were made free or school attendance became compulsory. In Europe, generally, public and private schools existed in closer parity for a longer period; schooling was not so massive or ambitious a part of any nation's educational system. From the early expectations of New England Puritans—that they would found their New Jerusalem to regenerate Protestantism—to the ideas of Manifest Destiny, Americans dreamed grandly. And, notes Joseph Adelson, "the utopian tendencies in the American mind were to some large degree invested in the schools, in the notion of perfectability through learning."[29]

That the desired learning included becoming a *Christian* American was an urgent objective—one threatened by the religious diversity that grew with the immigration of Catholics, Jews, and agnostics, and with the multiplication of Protestant denominations. However much they competed through their publishing houses, tract societies, Sunday schools, and preaching circuits, the Protestant churches increasingly found it wise to unite. To preserve what Lawrence Cremin calls the Protestant *paidea*, they encouraged public schools and such compatible crusades as the temperance movement. Suffused with political meaning this Protestant *paidea* grew into what has been called the "civil religion" or the religion of the "American Way of Life."[30] Public and nonpublic schools, their books and ceremonies, helped forge a common culture in this pluralistic society.

In the words of the editor of *Century* magazine, and first president of the New York Kindergarten Association, the kindergarten gave the nation "our earliest opportunity to catch the little Russian, the little Italian, the little German, Pole, Syrian, and the rest and begin to make good American citizens of them."[31] In addition, political parties, workplaces, unions, the press (even the foreign-language press) carried on elements of Americanization. Catholic and Lutheran schools indoctrinated students in American patriotism and promoted the need to master the English language.[32] They were less sure about assimilation into "Anglo-Saxon culture", and some parochial schools tried to maintain Polish, German, or Norwegian languages and customs for the sake of their first-generation clientele. With time such efforts usually withered away.[33]

While recent historiography reveals that Americanization was imposed on unwilling Native Americans, this was not necessarily the case with white and yellow immigrants. As Timothy Smith has argued, many immigrants were predisposed to adopt the American way of life and valued the opportunity to use American institutions like the public schools. Immigrant enrollment rates support this thesis, although nationality groups differed in these and other particulars.[34] Schooling was a prize and most immigrants, blacks, and women competed for it, using their political strength of numbers and recourse to the courts to gain access to it where they could.[35] Nonetheless, many ethnic neighborhoods and their newspapers, benevolent and social organizations, churches, even ethnic union locals, long persisted and performed *their* own roles in the educational process.

Local government has been the essence of American politics and administration. From the beginning schooling fit that dominant pattern of localism. Before public schools became the mode—in Massachusetts by around 1830, in Mississippi over a half-century later—school arrangements were determined by local circumstances, initiatives, requirements, and prejudices. If the local mix of transitory subscription schools, endowed or tuition academies, church-connected instruction— each sometimes tax-aided—was not suitable, one labored in the community to add options and, failing that, acquiesced or moved elsewhere. As more communities chose to petition their states for school-district status and a share of the state's common-school fund, public schools proliferated and grew to a dominant position. This happened locally *without* the need to establish a *national* consensus to found tax-supported schools, then to make them free, enforce attendance, decide for or against coeducation of the sexes, add or subtract subjects, decide on teacher qualifications, select an architecture, or choose schoolbooks.

Franklin, Indiana, illustrates a common accommodation to, and enlargement of, local tradition. Its public school was organized in 1866; its school board was composed of the pastors of the local churches—Baptist, Methodist, and Presbyterian—that had formerly operated schools in town. In 1868, these board members were succeeded by the local doctor, leading merchant, and county judge: a trio that looked after the schools for many years, to the evident satisfaction of the community majority.[36]

Since local pride and "boosterism" were powerful forces in expanding schooling, state governments usually restrained themselves in recommending some improvement or compelling certain standardizations. In 1907, Indiana was the first state to require that all state-licensed teachers be high school graduates, but it did not require that all districts hire only licensed teachers. Recently, in this same tradition, California passed a minimum-competency requirement for high school graduation, leaving it to each of 1,042 school districts to set its own standard.[37] The community's control over school policy had come to symbolize the health of citizen participation in government generally.

Only recently federal initiatives have imposed administrative and fiscal pressures upon schools. Local mores and national goals are now forced to compete. Federally funded and mandated programs are often being fought over by a historically decentralized system. That programs like Head Start and the "mainstreaming" of handicapped youngsters require parent advisory councils or negotiated agreements between parents and school personnel reflects less a historic commitment by the federal government to local citizen involvement than it reveals the "watchdog mentality" of the consumer and ecology movements. A profound hostility to experts and institutions, the assumption of adversarial relationships, and legal protectionism have entered the politics of education.[38] It remains to be seen whether or not the federal role will diminish and judicial activism abate. Nevertheless, there is no question that the slow accumulation of Washington's "bewildering hodgepodge of enactments strewn across dozens of federal agencies and congressional subcommittees"[39] has put sufficient strain on schools—enough to call into question the continued workability and logic of traditional educational arrangements in the United States.

Challenge to the Hegemony of the Schools

"Conceived as the prime instruments of individual self-realization, social progress, and economic prosperity," schools were surrounded by euphoria.[40] In the United States, that elan has now dissipated. Europe is also questioning the value of its schools; it is witnessing the disinterest of policy makers, the erosion of financial support, and the talk of declining standards—trends that characterized North American education, especially during the 1970s.

The too evident fallibility of the sixteenth-century Catholic Church brought about *its* loss of authority. So it now appears with the "state religion" of the United States: the public school. Once triumphant, it is now diminished, with its best friends considering how its authority and responsibilities can be shared. One explanation for its present troubles is that Americans have discovered that the schools' past successes were never as great as imagined: "The schools achieved their reputation *when they did not have to succeed*, when there were educational alternatives—the farm, the shop, the apprenticeship—and when there were other routes to economic and social advancement."[41]

Another view is that schools have broken down under the burden of conflicting tasks added to their agenda since 1950. "It is now fairly clear that the schools took on too much," Adelson writes, "and by doing so without sufficient caution or demurral, they were implicitly promising more than they could fulfill."[42]

Among the pressures on schools was the challenge to ensure equality of opportunity for minority and marginal groups—to be verified, some thought, by equalizing outcomes. Equality of opportunity was to be accomplished without losing the confidence of those conventional supporters of public education: those more privileged families that wished to preserve *their* children's relative advantage. The health of public schooling was further assaulted by an electronic popular culture that undermined educators' self-confidence, by demographic shifts that eroded the school's political and economic base, and by an assault on bureaucracy from the left and on secular modernism from the right—these in the name of individual potential and family rights respectively.

A RISING CONSCIOUSNESS OF CLASS

Unlike traditional European systems, where both duration of schooling and type of school quite rigidly matched a social hierarchy, America's system was widely considered to be an open system—suitable to a society with permeable class lines. Americans went so far as to proclaim theirs to be classless schools in a classless society. But the exposés of chronic poverty in America that launched federal programs in health, housing, occupational training, community organizing, and schooling were joined by new fears of technologically created unemployment of youth and minorities. The spectre grew of a permanent underclass of the unemployable, persisting even in economic upturns. Education was the obvious answer to technological unemployment, as well as to remediating old inequities.

Measured by greater persistence in completing high school and higher college-going rates, progress *was* made in reducing group differences. But educational research, declining test scores, high absenteeism among students and teachers, complaints from business and the military about functional illiteracy among high school graduates, and employment and income statistics raised doubts about the efficacy of schools in promoting social and economic democracy—however hard they tried. In the mere effort, however, schools were politically damaged. "White flight" revealed a heightened class consciousness that refused to trust racially desegregated local schools. Much of the early history of public schools had been driven by the need to make them attractive enough to the middle class that it would abandon private institutions. Now, traditional support was being withdrawn to suburban or nonpublic schools; some of those who could not move sullenly voted "No!" on taxes, repudiating the social goals mandated by congressional statutes, executive orders, and court directives. An adversarial culture suffused school board politics. The business and professional men (or their wives) who formerly controlled school boards had little stomach for the emerging politics of confrontation and invective. Unionized teachers and the students' rights movement were other new ingredients in the politics of schools.

By 1980, school governance was a mare's nest of competing claims for academic quality and equality, distrust of professionals and divisions within their ranks, budget cuts, and demoralizing regulations. Elements of status anxiety, class-based and racially based antipathies, struggles between entrenched privilege and empowered claimants may not add up to class warfare. But an unblushing analysis shows schools brought lower by the strengthened realization that they were not, and evidently could not become, all things to all people. And they were clearly *not* "above politics," as many had once believed.

THE COMPELLING CULTURES OF TECHNOLOGY

In technological change, all educational agencies confront the difficulties of preparing people to deal creatively with its effects on such matters as occupational dislocation, human relationships within the work world, and environmental preservation.[43] The microelectronics revolution is expected to affect further how humans communicate, acquire and process information, learn and relearn, and instruct others. The assumption that youth is the period for acquiring the permanent base of habits and skills of a lifetime no longer suffices; the importance attached to schools wanes accordingly. While continuing education could happen in schools, there are competing possibilities: corporations, labor exchanges, unions, proprietary schools, professional associations, and other organizations. Business and industry already invest more in instructional programs than the states spend on higher education.[44] "It is inevitable that as the development and maintenance of human capital becomes more important, the responsibility for this task becomes increasingly disaggregated," writes Ernest Lynton. "No one system and no single set of institutions can or should retain the monopoly for education and training."[45]

The foregoing poses a technological culture of the future, centering on work, in which the schools' role is uncertain. But technology has already affected schools by its effects on leisure. A culture of play and consumption has spread efficiently through the electronic media. It is a counterculture to the school culture, treating *all work* as a "middle-class hang up." The school has been devalued as imparter of literacy, custodian of high culture, authoritative source of information, inculcator of values, and general socializer. Spread through and hardened to dogma by the peer group, the lessons of popular culture deny the authority of traditional educators, including teachers, families, churches, and youth organizations. Of the reductionist and undifferentiating impact of television, for example, Neil Postman observes:

Mainly I think it is disastrous because it makes problematic the future of the school, which is one of the few institutions still based on the assumption that there are significant differences between children and adults and that adults therefore have something of value to teach children.[46]

Some families and schools have chosen not to fight these influences but to "go with the flow," adapting as best they can. In so doing, they have opened themselves to the same charges of irresponsibility that they level at the mass media.

THE DEMOGRAPHIC STRAITS

The schools' response to the "baby boom crisis" contributed to faith in schools in the 1950s. While the new "numbers game" could mean smaller classes and more individualization of instruction, the short-range implications are not encouraging. Schools face absolute numerical declines in the youth to be educated. Moreover, a larger proportion of their clientele will be poor and native or immigrant minorities. The nonwhite population, 15 percent of the fourteen-to-seventeen age group in 1974, will be nearly 20 percent in 1990.[47] Demographic shifts also include larger numbers of students from single-parent households: by 1990, only one household in two will contain a married couple. This situation promises an increase in numbers of children raised in relative poverty and the need for more services as mothers continue to enter the workforce. Funds for these services could be withdrawn from schools.

When shrinking enrollments and budgets force school closures, citizen support is again tested and often found wanting. Consolidated districts receive less loyalty from their publics. Reduced mobility in and out of teaching means an older corps of teacher, with higher median salaries. With inflation and union contracts, this keeps instructional budgets higher than the public may accept, given the presence of fewer students. Decreasing birth rates and improvements in health have changed the age-profile of Western nations. The larger population of older citizens represents those without children (or even grandchildren) in schools, but who have their own compelling needs for costly services. Schools are, therefore, competing intensely with other agencies for public resources. They are competing among themselves for students and funded programs.

THE CLAIMS OF INDIVIDUAL AND FAMILY RIGHTS

A compelling image of the public schools since the middle 1960s is that of "a kind of lightning rod, attracting many of the disaffections, agitations, and utopian attitudes gathering in American society."[48] Passionate campaigns against racism and poverty were joined by opposition to the Vietnam War, by the environmental protection movement, and constitutional repudiation of a presidential administration. Personal life-styles became another societal issue in which schools were enmeshed: drug use, homosexual rights, teenage sex and its concomitants of open access to birth control and abortion. The public school curriculum and culture—its behavioral standards and pedagogical styles—rehearsed a larger cultural struggle: the values of the adversary culture confronting the common culture of traditional America. The counterculture was a creature of the mass media, the sports and entertainment industries, and the intense and protracted association of youth with their peers in schools and colleges. It was then re-presented to middle-America in television news and magazine features, disclosing schools as places where hard drugs and soft pedagogy flourished together.

To their critics among students, and to adult romantics like John Holt and Paul Goodman, schools remained too traditional: rigidly bureaucratic, subservient to discreditable national policies and to economic elites. Schools were called colonial institutions, violating freedom and individual rights and ignoring human potential as the government violated human rights and popular sovereignty in domestic and international affairs. Continued high dropout rates, apathy, absenteeism, school vandalism—all were considered evidence of youthful alienation. Yet, in their often very modest efforts to be "hip," "authentic," "relevant," more "laid back," the schools alarmed many patrons who proclaimed their own adherence to traditional values, respect for authority, and patriotism. They eschewed relativism in favor of distinctions between absolute rights and wrongs. Uncomfortable with many elements of the modernist spirit, these critics protested on behalf of family rights and invoked the help of conservative churches. Opposition to sex education and the perennial effort to establish public school prayer were other signs of patronal disaffection.

One way to recapture parental rights relinquished to the state is to challenge compulsory school attendance in the name of home instruction; a small but growing number of families has done so. Another is to patronize private schooling; the spread of fundamentalist Protestant schools was especially notable. Efforts to legislate voucher systems and tuition tax credits, sometimes described as promoting a "healthy diversity," also represent a desire for a less pluralistic and less tolerant America. Other signs of cultural alienation included lowered public interest in public education, weakened parental participation, and reluctance to fund schools. While the public school once stood for and captured the essence of "community," the withdrawals of the recent past indicate a narrowing sense of association and of the public interest.

Some Final Considerations

The environment of the future is not knowable but, as Eric Ashby points out, "we already know what its heredity will be like."[49] To study the past of anything, then, is to be less surprised by tomorrow's events and by what has excited them. The history of education has been driven by private interests joined to some agreement about the public weal. Not facts but values, and conflicts over values, have shaped the histories of all kinds of educational agencies. This is obviously the case of families and churches but is true also for the curriculum of professional societies, assembly lines, and press syndicates. Even the most clearly specialized instrumentalities for educating are not *purely* so. Thus, individuals patronize schools or colleges not solely, nor always primarily, for instruction—but as a badge of status, a place for making social contacts, and to acquire credentials.

Since decision making in education is better apprehended as a political than a technical process, rational planning for distributing instructional responsibilities must be compromised by interest groups and divergent ideologies. It might, for instance, be rather readily agreed that: (a) schools cannot "do everything"; (b) they should concentrate upon general education, teaching basic skills like "learning how to learn"; (c) technological advances and obsolescence dictate that expensive and job-connected training will not be attempted in schools; and (d) profit and not-for-profit enterprises will train and retrain for occupations and avocations, perhaps in financial partnership with government. This agreement would not prevent some schools from teaching technical operations on costly equipment to gratify an ambitious, advantage-seeking constituency. It would not preclude a social studies or science curriculum from developing critical thinking by debating divisive issues like the virtues of work and leisure, thrift and consumerism, government regulation and nationalization of certain industries, worker participation in management, the moral and political implications of resource development and international economic competition—and perhaps raising tensions between worker consciousness and the mechanized workplace.[50]

Those who ponder desirable changes in the configurations of education might consider trying to conserve two characteristics of public schools in their heyday: one, the schools' concern for the common culture and for social cohesion and, second, their objective of advancing some measure of equality of access. The separate educational agendas of industry, the military, families, the mass media, and voluntary organizations guarantee fragmentation; short-range goals and specific needs will guide most of their programs. A large remaining task for schools might be preparing for the larger possibilities of American life and reestablishing a sense of common purpose— admittedly difficult but all the more essential for a pluralistic, restless America. Do we wish the mass media of communication, and those who run them, to provide and shape the *only* shared, sustained experience of future Americans?

Although much recent emphasis has been placed on the shortcomings of schools in the pursuit of equality, they have helped break the monopolies of knowledge that once excluded various ethnic and racial groups, the dependent and laboring classes, and one sex from much learning and from the concomitant opportunity to lead personally gratifying and socially useful lives. Access to household computers is more likely to reproduce inequities in family income, education, sophistication, and other resources than will happen through public school-based programs—even given the schools' vulnerability to social class influences and community wealth. Gender biases may limit opportunity more in families, churches, and the labor market than in schools. There is good evidence that "formal education must be regarded as the most important institutional support for women's quest for expanded opportunities in the nineteenth and twentieth centuries."[51]

John Dewey believed that society's educational progress required widened perspectives: what "the best and wisest parent wants for his own child," that must become what "the community wants for all of its children."[52] If, as seems the case, the willingness to expand opportunities for others requires being secure that one's own opportunities are wide, then the emerging design of future relations among educational settings must attend consciously to that psychosocial requirement.

1. Paul E. Peterson, "Urban Politics and Changing Schools: A Competitive View" (Paper prepared for the National Institute of Education, July 1980), esp. pp. 9-13.

2. Diane Ravitch, *The Revisionists Revised: A Critique of the Radical Attack on the Schools* (New York: Basic Books, 1978).

3. Bernard Bailyn, *Education in the Forming of American Society* (Chapel Hill: University of North Carolina Press, 1960).

4. Lawrence A. Cremin, *Public Education* (New York: Basic Books, 1976), p. 68.

5. James Axtell, *The School Upon a Hill: Education and Society in Colonial New England* (New Haven: Yale University Press, 1974), pp. xi-xii. Emphasis added.

6. Lawrence A. Cremin, *American Education: The Colonial Experience, 1607-1783* (New York: Harper and Row, 1970), p. xiii.

7. "Schooling in Homestead" (Research prospectus, College of Education, Pennsylvania State University, January 1981), p. 15.

8. Lawrence A. Cremin, *American Education: The National Experience, 1783-1876* (New York: Harper and Row, 1980), p. 12.

9. Richard D. Brown, *Modernization: The Transformation of American Life, 1600-1865* (New York: Hill and Wang, 1976).

10. Patrick Suppes, "The School of the Future: Technological Possibilities," in *The Future of Education: Perspectives on Tomorrow's Schooling*, ed. Louis Rubin (Boston: Allyn and Bacon, Inc., 1975), p. 146.

11. David R. Olson, "Introduction," in *Media and Symbols: The Forms of Expression, Communication, and Education*, ed. David R. Olson, Seventy-third Yearbook of the National Society for the Study of Education, Part I (Chicago: University of Chicago Press, 1974), p. 4.

12. Kenneth A. Lockridge, *Literacy in Colonial New England* (New York: W. W. Norton, 1974), esp. pp. 61-77, 146-47.

13. Cremin, *American Education: The National Experience*, p. 18.

14. Marvin Lazerson, "Consensus and Conflict in American Education: Historical Perspectives," *History of Education* 7, no. 3 (1978): 200.

15. Linda Kerber, *Women of the Republic: Intellect and Ideology in Revolutionary America* (Chapel Hill: University of North Carolina Press, 1980), esp. pp. 185-288.

16. Robert L. Church and Michael W. Sedlak, *Education in the United States* (New York: Free Press, 1976), esp. pp. 181-86.

17. Henry S. Commager, *The American Mind* (New Haven: Yale University Press, 1950), p. 10.

18. Jennifer A. Mundy, "Science and Technology in Schools and Working Life: Are We Aiming in the Right Direction?" *Comparative Education* 14 (June 1978): 109-20.

19. David K. Cohen and Barbara Neufeld, "The Failure of High Schools and the Progress of Education," *Daedalus* 110 (Summer 1981): 83; Frank Musgrove, *Youth and the Social Order* (Bloomington, Ind.: Indiana University Press, 1964), p. 33.

20. Philippe Ariès, *Centuries of Childhood: A Social History of Family Life*, trans. Robert Baldick (New York: Alfred A. Knopf, 1962).

21. Willard Waller, *The Sociology of Teaching* (New York: Russell and Russell, 1932; John Wiley, 1965), p. 68. See also Sara Lightfoot, *Worlds Apart: Relationships between Families and Schools* (New York: Basic Books, 1978), esp. pp. 20-42.

22. Sheldon Rothblatt, "Failure in Early Nineteenth-Century Oxford and Cambridge," *History of Education* 11, no. 1 (1982): 11.

23. In the small city (Berkeley, California) that she studied, Mary Metz found that poorer families (most of them black) distrusted the schools for lack of competence and interest in educating their children. College-educated, professionally employed parents communicated their own feelings of superiority to their children, who constantly challenged teachers. The middle class, the most supportive group, is not numerous in this school community. See Mary Metz, *Classrooms and Corridors: The Crisis of Authority in Desegregated Secondary Schools* (Berkeley: University of California Press, 1978).

24. Charles Burgess, "The Goddess, the School Book, and Compulsion," *Harvard Educational Review* 46 (May 1976): 199-216. See also Carole E. Joffe, *Friendly Intruders: Childcare Professionals and Family Life* (Berkeley: University of California Press, 1977).

25. Cremin, *American Education: The National Experience*, p. 301.

26. Reprinted in Theodore C. Blegin, *Land of Their Choice: The Immigrants Write Home* (Minneapolis: University of Minnesota Press, 1955), p. 272.

27. Although their systems of higher education are not closely comparable, Europe persuaded itself to imitate the United States by increasing the university sector of postsecondary education. In 1950, the percentage of the college age group (eighteen to twenty-one) attending college in the United States was already 27 percent; the university figures (ages twenty to twenty-four) for Western Europe averaged around 4 percent. In 1970, the United States figure was 45 percent and European university enrollments ranged from 12 percent in Ireland to 24 percent in Denmark. Philip H. Coombs, *The World Education Crisis* (New York: Oxford University Press, 1968); Torsten Husén, *The School in Question: A Comparative Study of the School and Its Future in Western Societies* (New York: Oxford University Press, 1979), p. 64.

28. Cremin, *American Education: The National Experience*, pp. 139, 168, 388.

29. Joseph Adelson, "What Happened to the Schools," *Commentary* 71 (March 1981): 36.

CLIFFORD   27

30. Robert N. Bellah, "Civil Religion in America," *Daedalus* 96 (Winter 1967): 1-21; Will Herberg, *Catholic-Protestant-Jew: An Essay in American Religious Sociology* (New York: Doubleday and Co., 1960).

31. Richard W. Gilder, "The Kindergarten: An Uplifting Social Influence in the Home and District," *Addresses and Proceedings of the National Education Association, 1903*, pp. 390-91. Quoted in *Children and Youth in America: A Documentary History, vol. II: 1866-1932*, ed. Robert H. Bremer (Cambridge: Harvard University Press, 1971), p. 1459.

32. Three nuns from the parochial school came to his home around 1950 to ask Richard Rodriguez's parents to help their children practice English at home; Spanish immediately ceased to be the parent-child medium of private communication. See Richard Rodriguez, *Hunger of Memory: The Education of Richard Rodriguez* (New York: Bantam Books, 1983), pp. 20 ff.

33. Heinz Kloss, "German-American Language Maintenance Efforts," in *Language Loyalty in the United States*, ed. Joshua Fishman (The Hague: Mouton and Co., 1966).

34. Timothy Smith, "Immigrant Social Aspirations and American Education, 1880-1930," *American Quarterly* 21 (Fall 1969): 523-43; idem, "New Approaches to the History of Immigration in Twentieth-Century America," *American Historical Review* 72 (July 1966): 1272-73; Michael R. Olneck and Marvin Lazerson, "The School Achievement of Immigrant Children: 1900-1930," *History of Education Quarterly* 14 (March 1974): 453-82.

35. Peterson, "Urban Politics," esp. pp. 7-12.

36. Patricia A. Graham, "America's Unsystematic Education System," in *A Nation of Learners* (Washington, D.C.: U.S. Department of Health, Education, and Welfare, 1976), p. 18. A lengthier account can be found in her *Community and Class in American Education, 1865-1918* (New York: John Wiley and Sons, 1974), pp. 30-58.

37. Gene I. Maeroff, *Don't Blame the Kids: The Trouble with America's Public Schools* (New York: McGraw-Hill Book Co., 1982), p. 45. In 1983, a new law set state-wide minimum curriculum requirements for graduation, again leaving some discretion in implementation in local hands.

38. Guy Benveniste, "Democracy and Technology in Education: The Case of PL 94-142" (Unpublished paper, School of Education, University of California, Berkeley).

39. Jack H. Schuster, "Out of the Frying Pan: The Politics of Education in a New Era," *Phi Delta Kappan* 63 (May 1982): 584.

40. Husén, *The School in Question*, p. 9.

41. Peter Schrag, "End of the Impossible Dream," *Saturday Review* 53 (September 1970): 68. Emphasis added.

42. Adelson, "What Happened to the Schools," p. 40.

43. Tom Whiston, Peter Senker, and Petrine Macdonald, "Introduction" to *An Annotated Bibliography on the Relationship between Technological Change and Educational Development* (Paris: International Institute for Educational Planning, UNESCO, 1980), pp. 9-24.

44. Robert L. Craig and Christine J. Evers, "Employers as Educators: The Shadow Educational System," in *Toward Higher Education and Business Alliances*, ed. Gerald G. Gold (San Francisco: Jossey-Bass, 1981); *Chronicle of Higher Education* 23 (October 1981): 13.

45. Ernest Lynton, "The Interdependence of Employment and Education" (Paper prepared for the Alden Seminar in Higher Education of the University of Massachusetts and the Association of Independent Colleges and Universities of Massachusetts, April 22, 1982, p. 9.

46. Neil Postman, "The Day Our Children Disappear," *Phi Delta Kappan* 62 (January 1981): 386; idem, "Engaging Students in the Great Conversation," *Phi Delta Kappan* 64 (January 1983): 310-16.

47. Shirley Boes Neill, "The Demographers' Message to Education," *American Education* 15 (January-February 1979): 7.

48. Joseph Adelson, "Battered Pillars of the American System: Education," *Fortune* 91 (April 1975): 141.

49. Eric Ashby, "Ivory Towers in Tomorrow's World," *Journal of Higher Education* 38 (November 1967): 427.

50. Michael Maccoby, "Introduction" to Harold L. Sheppard and Neil Q. Herrick, *Where Have All the Robots Gone? Worker Dissatisfaction in the Seventies* (New York: Free Press, 1972), p. xxxi; Mundy, "Science and Technology in Schools and Working Life."

51. Susan B. Carter, "Access to Skills Versus Access to Jobs: The Nineteenth and Twentieth Century Cooeducation Movement Evaluated" (Paper presented to the Conference on Equitable Education, Skidmore College, March 11-12, 1983), p. 5.

52. John Dewey, "The School and Society" (1899), in *Dewey on Education*, ed. Martin S. Dworkin (New York: Teachers College Press, 1959), p. 34.

CHAPTER II

Rethinking What Schools Can Do Best

JOHN I. GOODLAD

A Plethora of Expectations

Schools perform functions beyond cultivating the tools of thought. For example, they provide an enormous, cheap, and reasonably safe child-sitting service. School personnel tamper with this function at considerable peril. It probably is easier to make changes in the social studies curriculum than to release pupils early one day each month to accommodate teachers' meetings. To assume that schools exist solely to advance academic or intellectual matters is to err.

Perennialists may define education as the same in every time and in every place. But schooling and education are not the same thing. The functions of schools vary from time to time and place to place, whatever we perceive education to be.

History bears out this observation. What was expected of schools and what went on in them broadened steadily in this country from the early beginnings.[1] By the end of the nineteenth century, curricula included in some form most of the major domains of knowledge and some kind of both vocational and citizenship education. These changes were pushed onto schools by events. They were not planned by visionaries and effected by engineers.

Yet, philosopher-visionaries and social engineers play a significant part in determining what schools do. The progressive social and political reform movement emerging in America at the turn of this century would have found its way into schools without John Dewey. But Dewey, probably more than anyone else, provided the shift in thought about the function of schools: education not only for responsibility (to be a good mother, father, worker, and citizen[2]), but to live life to the fullest.[3]

29

In the mid-1920s, most educational practitioners were blissfully unaware of a weighty effort to give clearer direction to their work. A dozen leading professors of education and twenty associated contributors were endeavoring to think and write their way through the meanings of their place and time for school curricula. The product of their work was the Twenty-sixth Yearbook of the National Society for the Study of Education. Some sentences in the foreword read as though the group's chairman, Harold Rugg, contemplated a synthesis that might outlast the century:

In fifty years of curriculum-making, the greatest need has been for a comprehensive overview of the currents of American life and education, appraisal of all the factors in the educational situation. Rarely—and then only by fast striding pioneers—have the child, American civilization, and the school been considered together.[4]

The curriculum that Rugg and his associates would throw out was rooted in Britain and the classics and not focused "upon youth understanding American life. . . . Silas Marner, The Iliad, The Odyssey, The Vicar of Wakefield, The Lady of the Lake ('sitting comfortably in the high-school curriculum for seventy-five years') usurped the place which should have been devoted to creating an insight into the stirring movements in the new industrial America."[5] Rugg and his associates could not have foreseen the economic collapse of 1929 (extending with some periods of recovery to World War II) that brought into the secondary schools large numbers of youth who otherwise would not have been there, and whose presence highlighted the need for curricular reform far beyond what any scholarly report might do. But they interpreted their time and place, and contributed, for better or for worse, to the ways in which the larger progressive trends took on meaning and found their way into the schools.

Most of what the pedagogical progressives promoted in the 1930s and 1940s was out of fashion by the mid-1950s. "The 'great debate' about American education continued to rage until the fall of 1957, when the Russians orbited Sputnik, the first space satellite. . . . Neither the Russians nor the critics killed progressive education. It died because it was, ironically, no longer relevant to the times."[6]

Few periods in American history were as replete with provocative ideas about education and schooling as "The Education Decade" following Sputnik. Research and heuristics on individual differences, the structure of knowledge, intuitive learning, and the ability of young children to learn influenced school organization, curriculum development, pedagogy, the creation of Headstart, and more. The reform movement of the 1960s was aided as never before by presidential rhetoric, government strategies, and federal dollars.

Again, great movements in the United States and particularly in the world economy proved dominant in determining the course of schooling. Administrators spent their time discussing the meaning of public policy regarding desegregation and implementing both their own interpretations and those of the courts. Teachers, particularly in urban areas, struggled with the classroom problems brought on through enrollment of diverse pupil populations. The changing place of the United States in economic productivity had an impact not only on resources made available to schools but also on how we felt about ourselves as a people. During the 1970s, there was a marked drop in confidence regarding virtually all of our institutions. Schooling was not excluded. The momentum of school improvement that had been focused centrally on curricular and instructional matters was replaced by a regressive back-to-basics movement. The supposed innovations of the 1960s were seen by many as contributing to the ills of schooling.

There is no doubt that the disaffection regarding schooling, building steadily in the 1970s, would have found some highly visible means of expression without *A Nation at Risk*, the explosive report of the National Commission on Excellence in Education.[7] The report served the nation in 1983 as Sputnik had done earlier. It linked mediocre schools with the state of the economy and with a declining place for the United States in world affairs. Nothing short of excellence in schooling would suffice. The rhetoric echoed the "hard and tough" theme in American life and education identified by William James at the beginning of the century. According to the Commission's recommendations, excellence is to be achieved through a longer school day and year, more homework and discipline, higher standards, and the like—all reminiscent of the rhetoric following the launching of Sputnik in 1957.

When the hard and tough theme is excessively dominant, history reminds us, the "soft and tender" will not be far behind. What *A*

Nation at Risk has done for us is to open up another intensive debate over what our schools are for and what we should do to improve them—a debate largely missing from the late 1960s into the early 1980s. This is healthy. What the report did not do was to analyze the circumstances within which schools now function, the conditions mediating expectations for schools and determining, for example, the degree to which they rise above their custodial functions to perform educational ones. We examine some of these circumstances in the next section.

The central point to be drawn from this brief, sweeping review of several episodes in the development of schooling in this country is that events, more than ideas, shape what schools do. But this observation must be tempered by another: after schools have lived for a time with the aftermath of rapid change in their circumstances (for example, explosive growth in secondary school enrollments; desegregation), they tend to open up to alternative ways of dealing with conditions that were once crises. Consequently, the ideas for curriculum and instruction (the heart of a school's educational function), which find their way through the social-political structure, do indeed matter. A longer school day, for example, mandated by the state legislature, may complicate rather than assist teachers in their effort to hold the attention of restless junior high school students. A better solution might be more intensive student encounters with humankind's knowledge and ways of knowing over a shorter school day. The latter way of thinking opens our minds to educational alternatives outside the schools and perhaps to sharper thinking about what schools are for.

The Context of Schooling Today

We are in a period of transition from a declared crisis in schooling to serious consideration and some implementation of a wide range of inevitably conflicting ideas for improvement. Several hundred state-level commissions are being watched and listened to by legislatures fashioning and acting upon bills designed to have an impact on school curricula, teachers' salaries, the education of teachers, and much more. At least three books on the contemporary high school are well known to both educators and lay citizens, especially school board members.[8] During the 1984-85 school year, tens of thousands of educators came together in local, state, and district meetings to discuss strengths and weaknesses of the schools and what to do about perceived short-comings.

The positive side of this flurry of interest in our schools is the likelihood, barring the emergence once again of a crisis likely to shift attention away from schooling and particularly the educational function of schools, of creating a productive tension between ideas and practice. The negative side is the possibility of using a large reservoir of human time and energy in activities reflecting a poor interpretation of our time and place. For time and energy to be most productively employed, these analyses of present circumstances must include the following: (a) our society's assumptions about the role of schools in educating for responsibility, (b) parental assumptions about the contribution of schools to the growth and development of their children, (c) the degree to which schools meet or fall short of both sets of expectations, and (d) the extent to which the shortfall in what schools do suggests school reform or the transfer of functions to other agencies and institutions. This last analysis in particular should lead to a sharper conceptualization of what schools can do best. It is dealt with in a separate section. Clearly, these analyses call for the juxtaposition of data and values (or interests).

SOCIOPOLITICAL EXPECTATIONS FOR SCHOOLS

The news media rarely present a balanced picture; if they did, it would not be news. The news stories reaching European shores earlier in this century convinced many readers that the chances of being killed by gang warfare on the streets of Chicago were very high. News stories about schools in the 1980s convinced many readers that schools had virtually abandoned the teaching of reading, writing, and arithmetic, that there was widespread dissatisfaction with schools,[9] and that many parents would opt for a return to the McGuffey Readers and other artifacts of an earlier era. Simultaneously, however, state bodies endeavoring to determine what was fundamental and therefore worthy of financial support, were discovering that learnings extending well beyond the three R's were expected of schools by large numbers of people.

In the course of a comprehensive study of elementary and secondary schools in seven regions of the United States, entitled "A Study of Schooling,"[10] my colleagues and I also examined expectations for schools in a number of ways. A historical analysis revealed the steady expansion of goals to encompass ultimately academic, vocational, and personal development of the young and education for citizenship. A parallel analysis of documents sent to us by all fifty states most certainly did not convey the impression that, by the end of the 1970s, at the height of our most recent back-to-basics movement, the last three of these four sets of goals had been pushed aside. Quite the contrary. Thirty-seven of the fifty states endorsed them quite specifically, even to the point of specifying and being in general agreement on six or eight subgoals in each category. Most of the rest concurred, although in more obscure language. These findings and others reported below led me to conclude that "we want it all" with respect to our society's expectations for schools.[11]

But the state documents on expectations did not stop here. Many specified equity regarding access to what these goals convey with respect to knowledge, skills, and values. An assumption rising clearly out of these pages is that the school to be commonly attended and commonly completed, *circa* 1980, is the high school, not the common elementary school of the beginning decades of the twentieth century.

We see emerging out of these sociopolitical documents, then, the implicit expectation that education for responsible citizenship and economic productivity means comprehensive secondary schooling for all. Even though we cannot predict the disjunctures in realizing this expectation to be caused by economic and social upheavals, we can be confident that our standards of excellence for schools will increasingly reflect such criteria as their holding power to graduation, the comprehensiveness of the education provided, and equity regarding access to knowledge. We already begin to see such criteria reflected in the search for "quality indicators" going beyond achievement test scores.

The implications for the subject of this chapter are many. For example, if equal access to knowledge is increasingly to be called for, how do we justify continuing to divide secondary school students into tracks in which they encounter markedly different content in English, mathematics, and the like? Or, can we continue to defend vocational training programs that accommodate and, indeed, encourage students to leave high school before graduation?[12] Increasingly, studies are supporting the conclusion that the kind of education required for students leaving high school to enter the work place is very similar to that considered appropriate for higher education.[13] And surely we do not want kinds of citizenship education for persons who work primarily with their hands to differ from citizenship training for those who work primarily with their heads.

I repeat a point made earlier. We may debate with gusto concepts of what education is and how schools should educate in the light of our beliefs. But what schools do depends in large part on combinations of events and on interpretations of major currents, both long- and short-term, in the surrounding society.

PARENTAL EXPECTATIONS FOR SCHOOLS

But interpretations of what our society needs in its citizens and workers fall short of giving schools the guidance they need to assure satisfied clients. The messages coming down through the educational system to principals and teachers tend toward being hard and tough. It is difficult to soften the factory-like tone of the requirement that schools must attend to the nation's humanpower needs. Parents provide, in general, a softer message. They want their children to be known and safe at school, to be given individual attention. Even the parent at a public meeting who rails at the school's perceived inattention to the fundamentals usually presents a much softer front in talking with his or her child's teacher the next day.

We queried the 8,600 parents in our sample about their goal preferences for schools.[14] Overwhelmingly, they gave "very important" ratings to the four major goal areas cited earlier. Surprisingly, when forced to choose among them, only 50 percent selected academic goals. The remaining 50 percent chose other major goals—personal, vocational, or social. Indicators such as scores on the SAT are very important to policy makers and university professors in considering the quality of education in schools. But, clearly, parents have additional things in mind.

In Chapter 8 of *A Place Called School*, I sort out an array of characteristics serving to differentiate the schools at each level (elementary, junior high, senior high) identified as most (top quartile) or least (bottom quartile) satisfying to students, teachers, and parents whose responses were combined to form a single satisfaction index. The qualitative differences between the most and least satisfying groups of schools can be summed up quite accurately in three words:

the human connection. The most satisfying schools were perceived by those most closely associated with them as having teachers who were demonstrably concerned about their students' learning (as perceived by students), as having a trusting relationship between the principal and the teachers (as perceived by both), as having positive relationships among teachers (as perceived by teachers), and as having teachers who were accessible to parents (as perceived by parents), to cite just a few examples.

What comes through in our data is the need for maintaining a reasonable balance among the school's several functions. When a school was seen by parents as providing for the academic function, parents would give more attention to the personal. When parents viewed the academic program to be in some disarray (with shortcomings particularly in offerings in English, language arts, and mathematics), they would shift more emphasis to this area. Needless to say, the degree of variance from expectations likely to cause concerns is itself a variable, with the press for attending to one dimension of schooling over another differing from community to community.

However much our definitions of education stress knowledge and cognitive processes, it becomes apparent that schools will not pass the test of excellence with a good many parents if they are perceived to be uncaring with respect to the personal welfare of their students. The "rising tide of mediocrity" in our schools identified in words of alarm by the National Commission on Excellence in Education may set off a wave of attention to academics. But only a short time will elapse before worry about the impact of pressure on students will surface and pull in other directions.

Realities of Schools and Classrooms

If we assume that perceptions of students, teachers, and parents reflect extant emphases in schools, it becomes apparent that schools differ markedly in their attention to the human connection. Satisfaction among these groups varied surprisingly closely with differences in such things as school climate, class climate, principal-teacher relationships, school-community relationships, and so forth. Although we compared schools with those constituting the sample and, therefore, had no yardstick to help us determine whether they were performing well or poorly in attending to students as persons, those of us working with large bodies of data (some of which were distributed on scales of quality) were forced to conclude that only a few schools functioned at a high level in this area. Put differently, we had a more difficult time identifying exemplary schools than we did below-par schools, whatever the criterion employed.

The implication to be drawn from this conclusion is that there probably are many schools in the nation that will not be judged satisfactory by their clients even if they come out quite well on academic criteria currently in vogue: new curricular requirements for graduation, especially in English and mathematics; a heavier distribution of academic subjects in the junior and senior year; improved performance on standardized achievement tests, and the like. It is well and good to say that our schools must educate the young and provide encounters with the academic disciplines. But those closest to schools—students and teachers as well as parents—want more than this.

Indeed, it is becoming increasingly clear from studies of the school as a social system or culture[15] that most schools will not be able to place academics high in school life unless they first address the ambience of school and classroom. In several of the secondary schools in our sample, the quality of the relationship between the school and its community and between teachers and students was such that those schools barely performed their custodial function.

But let us concentrate here on the academic function, generally perceived to be the most important side of schooling. Many critics of the schools would push aside any competing claims for school attention. Out, then, with vocational education, extracurricular activities, and athletics. This now focuses school attention on what is centrally educational.

But does it? The goals for schools articulated in the states' documents include in the academic area mastery of basic skills, the ability to solve problems and apply principles of logic, the ability to make judgments and decisions, the understanding of concepts from the subject fields, creative thinking, and the like. We documented practices in 1,016 classrooms, simultaneously gathering data on topics taught, the content of textbooks in use, paper-and-pencil tests used, and more. We found an enormous sameness and narrowness in pedagogy and in the structure or form of the instructional curriculum. From the upper elementary grades through the senior high schools, teachers spent their time almost exclusively lecturing, telling, and questioning the total class or monitoring some form of seat work including quizzes. Beyond the primary grades, we rarely encountered teachers using some of the dozen or more other procedures available to them; there were few surprises.[16] The passivity observed in students did not square with definitions of education going much beyond the acquisition of the more mechanical aspects of learning. Their encounters with the subject fields appeared to emphasize topics, not concepts from the academic disciplines.

We found somewhat more evidence of students participating actively (in activities going beyond listening, reading textbooks, and taking quizzes) in the arts, vocational education, and physical education—the three subjects reported consistently as being the most interesting and best liked by students. And it appears that participation in extracurricular activities such as student government, the yearbook, clubs, and so on assures some opportunities for making decisions, exercising creativity, and assuming responsibility[17]—something not as often provided in academic classes.

To assume, then, that exposing students to more courses in English, mathematics, science, and social studies will take us closer in schools to the essence of education and, therefore, to what schools should do, is to be overly idealistic. Adler and his associates regard it essential that classroom instruction and learning go well beyond didactics, coaching, and supervised practice to the socratic questioning and discussion that bring an "enlarged understanding of ideas and values."[18] Adler would virtually reverse the amounts of classroom time now devoted to didactics on the one hand and discussion on the other.

But effecting such a reversal will be extraordinarily difficult for several reasons. First, the pedagogy we found in most of the classrooms studied is the kind of teaching to which future teachers had been exposed from the time they first attended school as students. Further, their classes in pedagogy employ largely didactics. The instructor may refer to Dewey's model of inquiry, but future teachers rarely have experience with it. Second, the student teaching part of teacher education—usually reported by beginning teachers as the most useful part—does not provide countervailing practices. Indeed, it virtually assures inculcation of the conventional wisdom. Third, as Sizer insightfully points out,[19] the circumstances under which teachers teach reinforce the dominant pedagogy described earlier—pedagogy well suited to controlling a class in a small box-like space and not disturbing those in the box next door.

So far as I am able to determine, there is no strong press within the teaching profession, including that part engaged in teacher education, to change what is described above. Our data on the in-service activities in which the teachers in our sample were engaged lead to the conclusion that conventional practice was being reinforced rather than challenged. They saw lack of student interest as a major problem in their schools but not bad or boring teaching. Nor did the students and parents rank teaching high as a problem. Further, although I expressed considerable concern about curricula organized and presented in such a way as to highlight facts and topics rather than concepts, parental satisfaction with the curricula of their schools was high. Because of the sameness of instructional and curricula practices in schools, we were not able to arrange the schools according to quality indicators in this area and then to correlate quality with the overall index of satisfaction. All we can conclude from these data is that the pedagogy and curricular arrangements we found in schools appear to be a far cry from what the educational process ideally is supposed to be. And yet, this perceived discrepancy appears not to be creating a driving force for change either from the community or within the education profession.

The Function of Schools from an Ecological Perspective

I have argued that our schools are expected at any given time to perform an array of functions—from child-sitting to cultivation of the intellect. I have argued, also, perhaps more implicitly than explicitly, that the essence of this functioning is educating, whether in the academic, social, vocational, or personal domain. This implies some definition of what education is and, therefore, of what schools essentially are for. Regardless of the sometimes considerable differences among definitions, the similarities are substantial. They all go beyond mastery of mere mechanics to include exercising critical judgment, developing aesthetic sensibilities, and sometimes even acquiring individual style—"the ultimate morality of mind."[20] Many definitions include something about a process that is deliberate and systematic over time.

If schools were held together by an internalized and articulated sense of what education is—or, better, by an ongoing critical inquiry[21] into what education is and what practices best reflect the fruits of this inquiry—they would be less caught up in the contradicting messages coming from their contextual circumstances, less pushed first this way and then that by declared crises in the teaching of foreign languages and international understanding, or the humanities, or mathematics and the natural sciences, or in regard to the condition of schooling generally. Such inquiry is not characteristic of schools. Yet, ironically, this shortcoming rarely is included in attacks on schools.

Let us leap over the logistics of creating this inquiring ambience in schools, formidable though they are. Institutions perform functions desired by society and, if they are to survive, demonstrate both the uniqueness and the quality of that performance. When functions being performed are no longer needed or when institutions compete in serving similar functions, the need for reappraisal and change increases. An overarching postulate should guide the necessary process of inquiry: the school should do only what individuals and their society clearly need but is not done or could not readily be done by other agencies and institutions. The functions of schools must be considered, then, in the light of present and potential roles of other institutions.

Even a cursory look quickly reveals rapid change in both the home and the workplace, change that must have implications for the school. Regarding the home, there is no need to recount here the fast-changing statistics on working mothers, one-parent families, and the like—conditions producing increasing numbers of latch-key children who come home to no adults. A simplistic answer is to keep them in school longer. But schools operate according to concepts and principles geared more to a prescribed curriculum than to what may be best for students who already have been exposed to a school day averaging 150 minutes of talk, most of it teacher talk.[22] There are other alternatives. (In focusing so narrowly on the school, the National Commission on Excellence in Education virtually ignored the possibility of an ecology of educating institutions when it proposed to increase the hours of schooling rather than considering other options.) There are lessons to be learned from other countries[23] and we certainly do not lack visions of what might work well in American communities.[24]

The importance of looking at alternatives beyond the school is not merely to avoid adding to an already burdened institution, an institution that has grown upwards, downwards, and sideways without careful consideration of the consequences. It also is to reaffirm the postulate stated in reverse: schools should not take on what other institutions could do better. In addition, serious consideration of alternatives to schools often helps to reestablish the role of an important but eroding sister institution. For example, pre-school playgroups in England, involving the active participation of parents and thus increasing the child-parent association, are proving to be a satisfying alternative to private nursery schools.[25] Changing demographics regarding the structure of the family should not necessarily mean the erosion of the home as an institution. More positively, it means reexamining and changing the ecological relationships among institutions and creating new ones if necessary. Such a posture increases the likelihood that schools will spend more time on what is central to their educational function.

Ongoing changes in the workplace suggest that schools should slough off some functions that have become nearly sacred rather than take on new functions. At the senior high school level, more teachers in our sample (24 percent) were assigned to the teaching of vocational subjects than to any other field. In one school, the number equalled the total of all teachers assigned to English, mathematics, science, social studies, and foreign languages. The greater the proportion of the curriculum devoted to vocational education, the greater the likelihood of courses with a training orientation and the greater the rhetoric of support by principals and counselors for the programs' success in preparing nonacademic students for jobs (and the greater the likelihood of a disproportionately heavy enrollment of poor and minority students).

The humanitarian claims for job-oriented vocational education in schools are hard to ignore—until one digs a little deeper. The first question coming to mind is, "What jobs?" Often, they are no longer performed or are filled. The training received frequently transfers poorly to other jobs. Technological change does not increase employment for those trained for yesterday's jobs. It decreases them while simultaneously increasing the cost of training for the new. This observation alone should be sufficient to give us pause whenever we consider the vocational function of schools. The more we justify it by and orient it toward preparation for specific jobs, the less utilitarian it is likely to be. (In *A Place Called School*, I argue for about 15 percent of the curriculum being devoted to vocational education for all students. However, I argue for it as a component of general education, perceived and conducted in the same way one would hope that education in mathematics and science, literature and language, society and social studies, and the arts would be perceived and conducted.)

Perhaps the most invidious aspect of a training-oriented curriculum for some students is the way it seductively distracts us from making the rest of the curriculum more attractive and engaging. Must those English and social studies classes be so dominated by teacher talk and textbooks? Suppose we were to infuse them with activities that students who like to work with their hands will enjoy—not to make of them carpenters or gardeners or plumbers but happier workers, better parents, and more thoughtful citizens. Suppose we were to take seriously the concept introduced earlier that today's common school includes the senior high school. The good school becomes one that carries all its students through a comprehensive general education program to graduation with a high school certificate.

What about job-training, then? If preparation for work and preparation for higher education increasingly are becoming identical, then the school's role in training for specific jobs correspondingly declines. This last becomes more and more the responsibility of those employers who must have workers with certain entry skills. They can provide the training on the job, subcontract for it, or employ the graduates of proprietary schools created to serve a recognized need. The possibilities for business and industry simultaneously collaborating with schools for career education purposes are many and need not be expanded upon here.

Part of the school's problem in seeking to respond to so many different and, often, seemingly contradictory messages is our now traditional tendency to lump so many different kinds of activities under the education label and then equate education, thus defined, with schooling. To some degree, we took advantage of this proclivity in seeking out parents' expectations for schools (in "A Study of Schooling"). Had we posed options for schools, including ways of enhancing the role of home, religious institutions, and the workplace in providing for vocational and personal development, they might have given us a much stronger message regarding the school's responsibility for academic and intellectual development. Instead, the message we received seems to compound the problem of reconstructing our schools without pointing to the potential of our other institutions. A healthy educational ecology is one in which each institution fulfills clear and appropriate functions, none is overburdened, and there is much collaboration in alternative formal, informal, and nonformal ways of educating children and youth.

CODA: Some Guiding Postulates

In thinking about what schools are for, I have been guided by a series of postulates—propositions taken to be axiomatic for the sake of argument. They are presented here explicitly with no further elaboration, as a way of summarizing the foregoing.

1. The more complex and dynamic the society and the greater the number and variety of its institutions, the greater the need for inquiring into and clarifying the function of its schools.

2. The more responsive the schools to specialized interests, the less the likelihood of their satisfying the general polity.

3. The more fragmented the society, varied the interests, and diverse the voices clamoring for attention, the greater the need for schools to seek a common, unifying core.

4. The greater the need for this common core, the greater the need for creative, imaginative ways of making it available to all.

5. The more institutions such as the home lapse in their roles of nurturing the young and the more schools take on these roles by default, the less effective schools are likely to be in performing their educational function.

6. The more specifically and explicitly instrumental schools become, the less well they serve a dynamic, democratic society.

7. The more of their school time students spend encountering civilization's accumulated knowledge and wisdom through all the ways of knowing that civilization has found useful, the better schools serve their educational function.

8. The more educational schools are, the more immune they are to the myriad ways we unwittingly seek to corrupt them.

FOOTNOTES

1. For documentation and further discussion, see John I. Goodlad, *What Schools Are For* (Bloomington, Ind.: Phi Delta Kappa Educational Foundation, 1979).

2. Lawrence A. Cremin, *The Transformation of the School* (New York: Alfred K. Knopf, 1961), p. 122.

3. John Dewey, *Democracy and Education* (New York: Macmillan, 1916).

4. Harold Rugg, "Foreword," in *Curriculum-Making: Past and Present*, ed. Guy M. Whipple, Twenty-sixth Yearbook of the National Society for the Study of Education, Part 1 (Bloomington, Ill.: Public School Publishing Co., 1926), p. xi.

5. Ibid., pp. 25-26.

6. Diane Ravitch, *The Troubled Crusade* (New York: Basic Books, 1983), p. 79.

7. National Commission on Excellence in Education, *A Nation at Risk: The Imperative for Educational Reform* (Washington, D.C.: U.S. Government Printing Office, 1983).

8. Ernest L. Boyer, *High School* (New York: Harper and Row, 1983); Sara Lawrence Lightfoot, *The Good High School* (New York: Basic Books, 1983); Theodore R. Sizer, *Horace's Compromise* (Boston: Houghton Mifflin, 1984).

9. Polls are misleading in that they both survey and *create* public opinion. Parents tend to give their local school rather good marks, especially at the elementary level, but to rate "schooling" or schools in general much lower. Presumably, other polls have convinced them that there must be a lot of bad schools "out there."

10. Reported in John I. Goodlad, *A Place Called School* (New York: McGraw-Hill, 1984).

11. The same conclusion was reached by Boyer, who entitled a chapter of his book, *High School*, as I did: "We Want It All."

12. For a detailed discussion of this and related issues, see Jeannie Oakes, *Keeping Track: How Schools Structure Inequality* (New Haven: Yale University Press, 1985).

13. See, for example, National Academy of Sciences, National Academy of Engineering, and Institute of Medicine, *High Schools and the Changing Workplace* (Washington, D.C.: National Academy Press, 1984).

14. Goodlad, *A Place Called School*, pp. 35-39, 62-69.

15. See, for example, John I. Goodlad, *The Dynamics of Educational Change* (New York: McGraw-Hill, 1975), and Seymour B. Sarason, *The Culture of the School and the Problem of Change*, 2d ed. (Boston: Allyn and Bacon, 1982).

16. For a detailed account, see Kenneth A. Sirotnik, "What You See Is What You Get—Consistency, Persistency, and Mediocrity in Classrooms," *Harvard Educational Review* 53 (February 1983): 16-31.

17. Robert G. Barker and Paul V. Gump, *Big School, Small School* (Stanford, Calif.: Stanford University Press, 1964).

18. Mortimer J. Adler, *The Paideia Proposal* (New York: Macmillan, 1982), pp. 28-31.

19. Theodore R. Sizer, *High School Reform and the Reform of Teacher Education*, Ninth Annual DeGarmo Lecture (Minneapolis, Minn.: University of Minnesota, 1984).

20. Alfred N. Whitehead, *The Aims of Education and Other Essays* (New York: Macmillan, 1929), p. 19.

21. For elaboration of the concept of critical inquiry and its use in the change process, see Kenneth A. Sirotnik and Jeannie Oakes, *Critical Inquiry and School Renewal: A Liberation of Method within a Theoretical Perspective*, Occasional Report no. 4 (Los Angeles: Laboratory in School and Community Education, Graduate School of Education, University of California, 1983).

22. A further finding from analyses of 526 senior high classes observed in "A Study of Schooling." Further realities of classroom life are described and discussed in books on the junior and senior high schools constituting the sample in "A Study of Schooling." See Kenneth A. Tye, *The Junior High: School in Search of a Mission* (Lanham, Md.: University Press of America, 1984) and Barbara Benham Tye, *Multiple Realities: A Study of 13 American High Schools* (Lanham, Md.: University Press of America, 1984).

23. See, for example, Thomas J. LaBelle and Robert E. Verhine, "School-Community Interaction: A Comparative and International Perspective," in *Communities and Their Schools*, ed. Don Davies (New York: McGraw-Hill, 1981), pp. 211-68.

24. One such vision is presented by Nicholas Hobbs, "Families, Schools, and Communities: An Ecosystem for Children," in *Families and Communities as Educators*, ed. Hope Jensen Leichter (New York: Teachers College Press, 1979), pp. 192-202.

25. Norma D. Feshbach, John I. Goodlad, and Avima Lombard, *Early Schooling in England and Israel* (New York: McGraw-Hill, 1973).

CHAPTER III

Stages of Linking School and Nonschool Learning Environments

MARIO D. FANTINI

Our society has labored to create an educational system compatible with our noblest aspirations as a free and just society. This effort has been played out historically in considerably varied ways; each locality has developed in its own way just as each era has called for its own responses to changes in the larger social system. The reaffirmation of civil rights for women, people of color, and handicapped citizens, along with the emphasis on bilingual and multicultural education, responds to the current emphasis on the recognition, respect, and support for the individuality of every person. What has emerged is a tradition of pluralism in schooling and education, characterized by local community control, committed to the twin goals of quality and equality, and struggling with a diversity of means to achieve those goals.

Such efforts reflect the process of modernization. In this process, the public, through governmental structures, establishes policies geared to changing trends and times, while leaders and professionals in all fields have the obligation to put advances in knowledge into practice. Transformations in the socioeconomic nature of the larger society now mandate modernization of our scholastic and educational processes in both school and nonschool settings.

The distinction between schooling and education is, therefore, important. The former relates to activities concerning schools while the latter refers to the total community context, relating all of the learning environments in which and through which people progress.

This chapter provides a historical overview of four stages in the evolution of school and nonschool settings. Each major socioeconomic period provided the context that determined an appropriate model of interaction between school and nonschool environments. However, when we review the evolution of different educational stages, we need to acknowledge that they represent merely summations of tendencies toward varying emphases within locally controlled systems of education. These stages are also overlapping, with the roots of one firmly resting in the previous one and extending into the next, although each became dominant at a particular stage in our socioeconomic history. Of particular interest is the emerging model for the twenty-first century, for it represents the one that most citizens, professionals, and policymakers will be shaping in the years ahead.

Stages in the Evolution of School and Nonschool Settings

It may be useful to view the relationship of school to nonschool settings by examining the major socioeconomic periods through which the nation has progressed. Briefly, the relationship of school to nonschool agencies has changed in accordance with societal transformations as we moved from an agricultural to an industrial to a post-industrial society.

RURAL/AGRICULTURAL ECONOMY: SHARED MODEL

Looking back, we can see that the founding of our country influenced our early educational models and expectations. The early settlers in the New World carried with them seventeenth-century European models of a class society. Formal schools were primarily for the privileged classes. In colonial times, the family was the main unit of the community-based educational system. The pervasive religious flavor of that period made the church a key educative agency, especially in the promotion of ethical and moral attitudes. Parents passed their vocations on to their children. The son of a gentleman was trained, at home and at school, to be a gentleman; the son of a farmer followed in his father's footsteps and became a farmer; and from his parents, the son of a candlestick maker learned the craft of candlestick making. As society became more complex, with the increased specialization of jobs and need for extensive training, more educational responsibilities were delegated outside the home and beyond the direct sphere of the parents' influence.

In the eighteenth and early nineteenth centuries, our socioeconomic structure was mainly agricultural. Communities tended to be homogeneous with similar backgrounds, activities, and values reflected in the home, the church, the workplace, the local governing body, and the schools. Education was home-based with some community support. Parents were the main arbiters of what was taught, where it was taught, and how it was taught. The clergy also exercised a significant degree of authority and accountability within the closely knit community.

Children of all ages and abilities were taught together in a one-room schoolhouse. Curriculum usually emphasized the "3 Rs" of reading, writing, and arithmetic, but the religious and moral values of the community were often incorporated into the curriculum. Each separate agency within the community contributed in its own way to the task of educating and socializing the youth of the community. This stage, rooted in an agrarian economy, could well be called a "Shared Stage of Education": the responsibilities for education are shared by a number of community agencies and institutions. (See figure 1.)

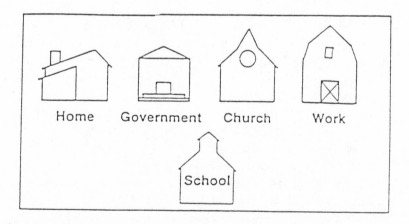

Fig. 1. Shared Stage: Division of Educational Responsibility

Source: Mario D. Fantini, "Changing Concepts of Education: From School System to Educational System," in *Community, Educational, and Social Impact Perspectives*, ed. Donna Hager Schoeny and Larry E. Decker (Charlottesville, Va.: Mid-Atlantic Center for Community Education, University of Virginia, 1983), p. 32. Reprinted with permission.

URBAN AND INDUSTRIAL ECONOMY:
COMPREHENSIVE DELEGATIVE STAGE

As our society changed, however, educational needs altered and new demands and expectations were placed on the schools. With the industrialization and urbanization of the nineteenth and early twentieth centuries, a second educational structure evolved. The rapid economic, political, and cultural changes of the times affected the structure of the community and altered the balance of relationships between all community agencies and institutions. Increased industrialization altered modes of production and changed the structure of the economy. The nineteenth-century shift from a predominantly rural to a heavily industrial society had implications for family patterns and influenced both the effectiveness and the extent of the educational and socializing power of the family unit. Gradually, social and educational services that had formerly been delivered by the family, the church, the workplace, and other community agencies were assumed by the school. This development can be described as a "Delegative Stage of Education": the school's role and responsibilities in society were greatly enlarged. (See figure 2.)

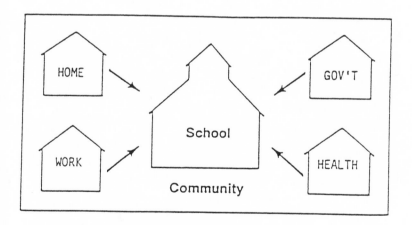

Fig. 2. Delegative Stage: Delegation of
Educational Responsibility

Source: Fantini, "Changing Concepts of Education," p. 33. Reprinted with permission.

Schools grew in size to become more comprehensive. All learning considered important was delivered under the expanding roof of the schoolhouse. Increasingly, schooling was seen as synonymous with education. The primary place of learning was identified as the schoolhouse, and the classroom and *teaching* took on greater significance. The new professionalism of teachers, as evidenced by an increased regard for licensing and certification, underscored the importance of legitimate learning inside the formal structure of scholastic institutions. Advances in the arts and sciences of teaching and learning necessitated not only more education and training for professional educators, but also a separation of the formal schoolhouse from the more informal learning settings of the community. Professional educators were the experts to whom the community delegated responsibilities formerly assumed by various community agents and agencies. The heightened regard for formal learning led to a subsequent deemphasis of the nonformal agencies and educators, including the family. This tendency was especially strong in many nineteenth- and early twentieth-century immigrants, who themselves had little formal schooling.

The need to integrate large numbers of immigrants from diverse backgrounds into the American mainstream—enabling them to participate as citizens and to function effectively in the marketplace—led to greater standardization in the schools. Standardization, even uniformity, was seen as a way to achieve the goal of mainstreaming and offer quality education equally to all learners, however diverse. With large numbers of students streaming into the schools at this time, the concept of mass schooling emerged. The school became similar in structure to a factory, with its own assembly line in the form of an age-graded organization. Since the assembly line was having such a positive effect on increasing productivity in the factories, the reasoning went that the same might be true for schools. Criteria of age and intellectual ability, as measured by test scores, were used as the primary bases for dividing large numbers of children into manageable groups.

With this system of classification, labels and categories also developed. Children who adapted well under the structured conditions of mass schooling were labeled as successful, the "winners." At the same time, children who for a variety of reasons could not adjust to a particular set of norms were frequently labeled unsuccessful, the "losers." Unfortunately, the labels attached to children early in their school experience often served as self-fulfilling prophecies. Those children labeled "winners" were fostered and supported by the expectations of their parents, teachers, and peers, while those students deemed "losers" also tended eventually to act out the implications of their label. Such a system did not accommodate the great variety of human differences. It made scant allowance for the full development of human potential, which began to penetrate the state of the art in educational theory and practice in the latter half of the twentieth century.

As the school's responsibilities expanded, the curriculum also grew. The concept of the comprehensive school developed, with the idea that all the educational resources of the community could be offered within the school. Educational professionals garnered considerable authority and, along with it, accepted a considerable amount of accountability. While parents did not substantially relinquish power over their children's lives, they did delegate increasing responsibilities to the schools, which resulted in an enlarged role for educational professionals. Some school people did respond to nonschool agents and agencies, particularly with the development of community schools. These schools were opened for afternoons, evenings, weekends, and summers and served as a center for various community activities.

INFORMATION-BASED ECONOMY: COORDINATIVE AND FACILITATIVE STAGES

Toward the second half of the twentieth century, a transformation in society—namely, the shift from industrial to high technology—brought about different relationships between schools and their communities. Attempts to reform the public schools elicited community participation and increased policy decisions by elected and judicial officials. As the impact of a knowledge-based economy took hold, business and industry became involved in the debate on school improvement and added important weight to efforts to bring about change. A series of new partnerships and collaboratives began to emerge between the school and the various educational agents in the community.

Advanced technology and further democratization—A coordinative stage. In 1916, John Dewey described the coordinative role within the larger community's system of education:

The school has the function . . . of coordinating within the disposition of each individual the diverse influences of the various social environments into which he enters. One code prevails in the family; another on the streets; a third, in the workshop or store; a fourth, in the religious association. As a person passes from one of the environments to another, he is subjected to antagonistic pulls, and is in danger of being split into a being having different standards of judgment and emotion for differing occasions. This danger imposes upon the school a steadying and integrating office.[1]

Nearly seventy years later, Dewey's words are still timely and, in fact, adumbrate a role that may well be developing for professional educators in the future. Serving as the linchpin between community institutions and guiding the entire process of educational linkage and interconnection, the school in Dewey's vision assumes a special, central, and difficult role. In the late twentieth century, rapid technological developments, increasing urbanization, and significant social changes have undermined the interlocking system of social institutions and made the central role of the school even more crucial.

With the decade of the 1960s came a rediscovery of the importance of diversity and a recognition of the value of pluralism in society and in the schools. There was, above all, strong concern for developing a series of legitimate options in education. Turning from bigness to smallness, from centralization to decentralization, from mass schooling to individualization, from chance to choice, this major shift combined economic, political, and pedagogical developments. Community participation in governance and in other matters of schooling became a more active, vocal, and visible affair. Educators, in turn, began to perceive the community as a resource for the school, making use of community facilities and welcoming volunteers working at all levels and in many capacities within the schools. Increased flexibility in the schools was matched by the expansion of learning environments outside the school. Business and industry began to develop programs to serve their own needs. As technology and telecommunications opened up more avenues of communication, a variety of new learning environments emerged. Increasing numbers of parents reclaimed total responsibility and chose to educate their children at home.[2]

Home education is only one of a range of educational options in which parents seek increased and occasionally direct control. Alternative schools, magnet schools, thematic schools and programs, both in the public and private sectors, began and then burgeoned in cities and towns across the country. With the recognition that each individual is unique in terms of psychology as well as physiognomy, a new emphasis was placed on different learning and teaching styles, and, further, on the development of techniques to bring about a more refined match between the learner and the learning environments.[3] The use of computers in education, moreover, flourished with educational software packages developed by the computer companies and by professional educators.

The Community Schools and Comprehensive Community Education Act of 1978, which adds several new titles to the Elementary and Secondary Act of 1965, recognizes the school's potential as the center of a community-wide system of educational resources. The Act states: "As the primary educational institution of the community, the school is most effective when it involves the people of that community in a program to fulfill the educational needs of individuals of the community."[4] These developments, with the expansion of educative environments centrally coordinated by the school, can be described as the "Coordinative Stage." (See figure 3.)

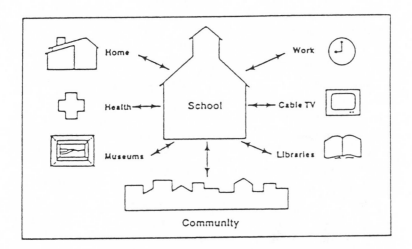

Fig. 3. Coordinative Stage: Coordination of
Educational Responsibilities
Source: Fantini, "Changing Concepts of Education," p. 35. Reprinted with permission.

Faced with diminishing resources during the 1970s and 1980s, the schools and school personnel began to reach out to the educative resources of the community. Partnerships with business and industry spread throughout the country. In Boston, the Boston Compact tied the public schools and the business community together to serve mutual interests. In Chicago, a school adoption program was initiated with the business community. In San Francisco, an educational foundation was developed by the private sector in concert with the public schools of that city. Partnerships with human service agencies, with colleges and universities, and with community agencies also flourished, becoming at times a part of new state legislative policy. (In many states, school-based advisory councils, in which representatives from the Commonwealth participated, were provided.)

Partnerships for Excellence were mounted by elected officials. In Lowell, Massachusetts, for example, U.S. Senator Paul Tsongas led a process called "The Lowell Model for Educational Excellence" involving the cooperation of various community agencies including business and industry. In Springfield, Massachusetts, the Mayor spearheaded a "Partnership for Excellence" project, again including a cross section of community agencies involving local business and industry and the colleges and universities in the area. The Boston Compact, for example, represents a formal collaborative involving the school department, the government, and the business community in working together to improve learning. A common plan of action has been initiated involving such measurable outcomes as: (a) a 5 percent increase per year in the number of students who graduate as compared with the number who entered ninth grade; (b) increased performance by all graduates in reading and mathematics skills necessary for employment; and (c) a 5 percent increase per year in the number of graduates who are placed in jobs or further education. This original compact has been followed by other collaborative initiatives involving the arts community, the human services, and higher education.

During this period, the school began to reconnect with its educative partners, sharing resources during a tight fiscal period and learning once again the benefits of collaboration to the participants and to the learner.

Toward a Facilitative Stage: Lifelong Learning for the Information

Age. As we move toward the next century, our educational system is evolving to meet the changing needs and aspirations, brought about by the massive shifts in our society. We do not have to look far to discover symptoms of the obsolescence of the present comprehensive school stage. Consider declining test scores and concern over student achievement, the high rate of student absenteeism and truancy, the high number of school dropouts, the instances of violence and vandalism in the schools, the evidence of teacher burnout, management-labor conflict, the rapid turnover in school administrators, the politicization of school boards, the exodus of the middle class from the public schools (especially from urban systems), educational malpractice suits, increased public accountability, and concern over the quality of mathematics and science education. All of these point to a serious problem in the ability of our current system to deliver the educational services we now require. An array of nationally visible reviews on the public schools confirms this conclusion.[5] The model that evolved to meet the needs of the nation in the nineteenth century and in the first half of the twentieth century can no longer adequately or appropriately serve our needs now or in the years to come.

Our socioeconomic transformation is resulting in what has been described as the knowledge or information age. Educational activities have become increasingly critical in solving economic and quality-of-life issues. Business and industry, in attempting to keep pace with rapid technological advances, find it necessary to establish their own systems of corporate education. Greater emphasis is given to continuing lifelong education, while greater attention to human rights stresses the need for individualized learning opportunities. At this stage, a confluence of societal forces has brought about the necessity for fundamental reform. Such reforms lead to a basic restructuring of the delivery of educational services. The older reform efforts are viewed increasingly as duplicative, additive in cost, and ineffective. Social policies are increasingly based on the new principles emerging from contemporary world views.

With an ever-expanding variety of learning environments, educators are better able to design and implement individualized programs. Such programs may occur both inside the school and outside the school in nonschool educational settings. In our current situation, quality education does not depend solely on what happens within the school setting during school hours. The concept of quality education now includes learning environments outside the school. Each particular learning environment has its own unique approach, with its own potential strengths and weaknesses. Collaboration and partnerships between and among these learning environments could improve the educational quality of all these settings for all learners.

A coordinated lifelong learning system, therefore, must strive to improve continually through collaboration. The goal is to eradicate those conditions that lead to miseducation, and support those conditions that are conducive to positive learning experiences, that is, education. In terms of pedagogical methods, curriculum and content, and guidance in linking with other agencies, the schools can offer crucial assistance to the other educative agents in the community. People who seek help to improve their parenting skills are a case in point. Similarly, children who express an interest in tutoring peers may need guidance and training. Media specialists in the communities who are able to employ the latest in telecommunications theory may need help from the schools in relating their sophisticated knowledge to the needs and interests of children. Consequently, educators must now work at functional incorporation with various agents and agencies in the community, to strengthen the positive educational impact of parents, peer groups, television, computers, various forms of mass media, and so on.

In an era of rapidly advancing technology, we see the need to increase computer literacy and electronic literacy. In the growth of chronic unemployment, we see the need for education to adapt to new and rapidly changing manpower requirements. Because the schools as presently structured cannot keep pace with the ever-changing demands of high technology, corporations have begun to develop their own in-house educational programs. A new stage for education linking school and nonschool settings—including business and industry—now appears to be evolving, and a new paradigm for human learning is emerging related to the realities of the postindustrial, information age. Learning structures for this new age point toward more flexibility and adaptability, and move away from the standardization accompanying the industrial period. Our society is progressing through a major cultural transformation of enormous consequence.

The Conditions for a New Stage

In overall world view, we have moved from a view of the universe based on Sir Isaac Newton's laws of mechanics to a view defined by Albert Einstein's theory of relativity; where one describes a static state of the universe, with fixed laws, the other describes a universe both dynamic and relative in nature. Similarly, from an emphasis on the importance of heredity, we have moved, with such thinkers as Charles Darwin and B. F. Skinner, to a concept of the importance of the environment. From an emphasis on the cure of obvious ills and inequities in health care, education, and economics, we now attempt to deal with prevention. From a meritocracy, we move more toward a concept of democracy, with the realization that quality education, in order to be truly equal, must be available to and attainable by everyone, and must be more individualized and personalized rather than standardized.

The growing acceptance of the psychology of becoming, combined with the psychology of being, increases the emphasis on individual learning, growth, and potential, which are major criteria for selecting appropriate pedagogical approaches. The labeling of "winners" and "losers" gives way to the notion that every child *can* learn, given appropriate or "least restrictive" environments and conditions for learning. Traditional human categories themselves are perceived as arbitrary, inappropriate, and inadequate terms to describe the complex variations in human learning styles and abilities. Quality education becomes redefined as a right, not a privilege, and access to quality education a matter of choice, not chance. The concept of learner fault implicit in many remedial and compensatory school improvement efforts gives way to a concept of program or institutional fault. Since everyone can learn, given the appropriate setting, if a child does *not* learn, changes in the program rather than adaptation to fixed programs on the part of the child are in order. From a position fostering exclusivity, we move to a commitment to inclusivity; from uniformity, we move to diversity; from centralization, we move to decentralization. These changing and shifting perspectives will eventually result in a different conception of human learning—one that requires a new stage.

The Facilitative Stage and the Educative Community

The information age will require new connections between school and nonschool learning environments. As the industrial stage declines, with its emphasis on standardization and uniformity, more flexible and adaptable formats will emerge. The advent of new tools for learning, such as telecommunications, will increase the capacity of all people to pursue learning regardless of age or background. Education will undergo dramatic redefinitions and more learning resources will be available to the individual than ever before. Learners of all ages may need personal advisors in order to take complete advantage of the full range of appropriate and available resources. Parents and professional educators will assume major responsibility in guiding the young learner to his or her objectives.

Along with these shifts, there are shifts in our educational needs and in our perceptions of the role of professional educators. From an emphasis on teaching, we move to an emphasis on *learning*, wherever, however, and whenever it best occurs. From a dependence on testing as measurement, we move to a use of testing as a means of diagnosis and of guiding growth. From the system of adding-on to the structure of the school in society, we increasingly explore ways to use community agents, facilities, and resources within the larger educational system. And from playing a major role in the direct delivery of educational services, the professional educator shifts to a more coordinative and facilitative role. We can, in fact, sum up the potential of these developments in a "Facilitative Stage for Education." (See figure 4.)

At the individual school and community level, changes in the economy inevitably affect resources, especially resources for the schools since they are locally funded. The bulk of budget cuts due to Proposition 2½ in Massachusetts, for instance, falls on the schools simply because the bulk of property tax revenue goes to fund the schools. Out of necessity, the Massachusetts schools have begun to identify learning resources in the community. Ideally, as the community becomes more directly involved with school affairs, the school, at the same time, will become more actively involved with other educative community organizations, agencies, and learning

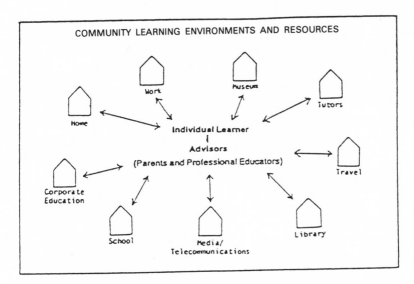

COMMUNITY LEARNING ENVIRONMENTS AND RESOURCES

Work   Museum   Tutors   Home

Individual Learner
Advisors
(Parents and Professional Educators)

Travel   Corporate Education   School   Media/Telecommunications   Library

Fig. 4. The Facilitative Learning Stage: Facilitation
of Community Learning Educational Resources and Services

Source: Fantini, "Changing Concepts of Education," p. 40. Reprinted with permission.

resources. Even now, we can see instances of more volunteers in the school and the community, fuller use of community learning resources, efforts to avoid duplication of facilities and services, and more focused connections or partnerships, between the schools and business and industry.

In his book, *A Place Called School*, where he summarized the results of a comprehensive review of the nation's schools, John Goodlad concludes by pointing toward what he calls Educative Communities— those optimally structured communities that would link the various learning centers of the region into one comprehensive system of education.[6] Another educator, Lawrence A. Cremin, in his book *Public Education*, envisions an "Ecology of Education," which ties together the different educative forces in the community.[7]

The systematic expansion of education into nonschool settings, however, reaffirms the importance of the individual learner, the individual school, and its major advisors including school people and parents. As nonschool settings are developed, the role of the school and school professionals may change, but it will not diminish. Instead of being responsible for the direct delivery of most, if not all, legitimate educational services, professional educators may assume the role of coordinator or orchestrator. The emphasis on the individual school and on school effectiveness and improvement will continue, but will expand to include an emphasis on ways in which the schools and school people are linked to the community. Instead of the family and church serving as primary educational arbiters, we now have a series of agencies cooperatively involved in education. In effect, shifts in family patterns and social structures make education even more important. The schools may be the social institution best able to assist parents in their own parenting efforts and educational activities. In other instances, the schools may refer parents to other appropriate agencies, institutions, and resources in the community. In a very significant sense, the school becomes the great equalizer, and the professional educator assumes an important role in terms of accountability.

The Role of Schools and Professional Educators

Professional educators are in the best position to ensure quality and commitment to equality in each nonschool setting. Both in terms of expertise and accountability, they are most able to serve the best interests of learners. For parents, educators can serve as advisors and become a major resource in planning and carrying out individualized educational programs. With the array of learning agents and environments now available to this generation of learners, the educator's major role will be to serve as a primary resource to help learners plan the best program—one that draws upon a full complement of community resources. The "school" of the past will become the "major educational service" center of the future, facilitating a custom-tailored program of education for each learner utilizing the full complement of learning resources available in the community.

To community institutions, educators can supply pedagogical aid, work to ensure the truly educative quality of each learning environment, and be the major agent for linkage and interconnection. In programs collaborating with businesses and industries, educators may also serve a special role. As more and more corporations develop their own educational programs, they naturally look to serve their own needs and interests rather than the needs of the individual learner. For a corporation, the bottom line may be productivity rather than equality.

But what is best for the corporation may not be best for the individual learner. Therefore, supervision by educators committed to quality and equality becomes even more crucial. Equally essential will be the means of releasing teachers from direct delivery of all educational services to enable them to assume such facilitative tasks. Innovations such as computer-assisted instruction or peer, parent, and community volunteer tutoring can have a positive effect in helping teach the basics. If some of the teachers' former duties were taken on by these alternatives, teachers would then have more time to pursue a major facilitative role. Even now, private corporations[8] and government[9] are making efforts to train teachers in the use of the new technologies. Schools of education will need to prepare a new generation of professionals in concert with their colleagues in the educative environment of the total community.

In this emerging stage of the educational community, professional educators may take on a new facilitative role in the schools and in the community. Educators are not solely responsible for the entire delivery of educational services. But their experience and expertise will be called on as they increasingly serve as the guardians and gatekeepers of quality and equality. Educators will take on the special responsibility for linking learning environments in a comprehensive way and, equally important, for ensuring the quality of learning experiences in all settings. Working as part of a team of learning facilitators—with parents, the church, the peer group, the workplace, and so on—professional educators can become the chief advisors and advocates for the individual educational needs of every learner. As the community, with its diversity of means, works to offer a variety of learning experiences, professional educators can work to ensure commitment to the twin goals of *quality* and *equality*.

Conclusion

Our society is moving toward more emphasis on expanding our environments for *learning* as opposed to a concentration on improving our effectiveness and efficiency of *schooling*. Learning comes to be redefined in our current society as a lifelong activity that starts earlier than kindergarten or even nursery school and continues on, after formal schooling, throughout the individual's personal and professional life through formal and nonformal contexts. With changes in family structures, work patterns, geographic mobility, and economic systems, the importance of quality day care and parenting becomes increasingly crucial. With changes in manpower needs, new literacies, and a rapidly advancing technology, the need for corporate education and human resource development becomes even more apparent. In this century, we have been moving from a *school-based system* of education to a *community-based* system of education. In the former, education took place entirely within the school; in the latter, the school became one of a network of educational learning centers in the community. The growth of formalized school systems has occasioned a perception that schooling and education are virtually synonymous and that the only legitimate learning is that obtained within scholastic institutions. Clearly, learning takes place in many places and in many ways. Parents and families educate; so do peers, media, the workplace, and the like. These institutions educate and miseducate. Yet our overall goal is to help all be fully educated. Consequently, when there is a national agenda aimed at educational reform—but at only one of the educative agencies, albeit a very important one such as the school—we are only focusing on one piece of the educational process. Not to assure that the reform policy covers all of education is to invite failure. To reform education requires attention to all of the educative institutions. Put somewhat differently, if we expect that school reform will lead to educational reform, then we will be disappointed. Most educational reform efforts have not taken a broad view that coordinates a system for human learning. Instead, they have viewed each institution separately and unrelated to the broader process of education. Thus we have a family crisis, a media crisis, a school crisis, with little attention to their interdependence and connection with human learning and education. Now is a time for us to reassess our system of education, regroup our educational resources in the school and in the community outside the school, and systematically link these school and nonschool environments to support learning for all people.

FOOTNOTES

1. John Dewey, *Democracy and Education* (New York: Macmillan Co., 1916), p. 26.
2. John Naisbitt, *Megatrends* (New York: Warner Books, 1982), p. 44; John Holt, *Teach Your Own: A Hopeful Path for Home Schooling* (New York: Delacorte Press, 1981).

3. Rita Dunn and Kenneth Dunn, *Teaching Students through Their Individual Learning Styles: A Practical Approach* (Reston, Va.: Reston Publishing Co.: 1978).

4. The Community Schools and Comprehensive Community Education Act of 1978, Public Law 95-561.

5. Ernest L. Boyer, *High School: A Report on Secondary Education in America*, for the Carnegie Foundation for the Advancement of Teaching (New York: Harper and Row, 1983); John I. Goodlad, *A Place Called School: Prospects for the Future* (New York: McGraw-Hill, 1984); National Commission on Excellence in Education, *A Nation at Risk: The Imperative for Educational Reform* (Washington, D.C.: U.S. Government Printing Office, 1983); Theodore Sizer, *The Dilemma of the American High School* (Boston: Houghton-Mifflin, 1984); Task Force on Education for Economic Growth, *Action for Excellence* (Denver, Colo.: Education Commission of the States, 1983); Twentieth Century Fund, *Report of the Twentieth Century Fund Task Force on Federal Elementary and Secondary Education Policy* (New York: Twentieth Century Fund, 1983).

6. Goodlad, *A Place Called School*, p. 349.

7. Lawrence A. Cremin, *Public Education* (New York: Basic Books, 1976).

8. A number of personal computer companies, including the Tandy Corporation, IBM, and Apple Corporation, are moving with government approval to give computer training to teachers in the schools and in teacher training centers.

9. Two proposed bills, the Tsongas Bill and the Perkins Bill, are in motion and are designed to offer technological assistance to teachers.

CHAPTER IV

Combined Efforts: Models for Nonschool Settings for Learning

A. HARRY PASSOW

Lawrence Cremin has defined education "as the deliberate, systematic, and sustained effort to transmit, evoke, or acquire knowledge, attitudes, values, skills, and sensibilities, and any learning that results from the effort, direct or indirect, intended or unintended."[1] His definition of education includes such concepts as schooling, socialization, and enculturation, but is broader than all of them. In addition to schools and colleges, there is a "multiplicity of individuals and institutions that educate—parents, peers, siblings and friends, as well as families, churches, synagogues, libraries, museums, summer camps, benevolent societies, agricultural fairs, settlement houses, factories, publishers, radio stations, and television networks."[2]

Some of these institutions and agencies maintain schools and classrooms in which the pedagogy, climate, teachers, and resources are not substantially different from those found in elementary and secondary schools or higher education institutions. For example, classrooms in factories, religious institutions, the military, ethnic or racial societies, and 4-H or Future Farmer Clubs clearly educate even though their settings are not those normally associated with "schools." There are "learners" and "teachers" and there are "curricula," some more formal and structured than others. In the case of the Boy Scouts and Girl Scouts, the curricula are specific and detailed as the scout moves through the various ranks and merits achievement awards. For some of the achievements and promotion activities, the scout must relate to the school and to teachers in that school.

Many churches and synagogues maintain schools for direct instruction in the religious tenets, history, rituals, and other aspects of their beliefs. These classes and schools instruct children, youth, and adults in preparation for religious observances or commitments. But in the very participation in religious observances, teaching and learning takes place. For example, the child in a Jewish synagogue is surrounded by artifacts, which include the ark that contains the Torahs (the scrolls on which the Old Testament is written) and that has an "eternal light" over it, located in a particular position in the sanctuary. The service follows a specific order. When, for instance, the scriptures are read, the reading is intended to be an act of teaching. The rituals are repeated regularly and constitute part of the curriculum of the synagogue—that is, a set of intended learnings. The child may be instructed directly in religious or Sunday school about the rituals, artifacts, history, and holidays of the religion, but attending services in the setting of the synagogue is also an instructional activity and a learning experience. Religious institutions educate through their functions and processes as much or more than they do in their classrooms. In fact, there are those who argue that it is only through the participation in these religious activities that such institutions educate.

Leichter has pointed out that the "family is an arena in which virtually the entire range of human experiences can take place" and that within the setting of the family, "a variety of educational encounters, ranging from conscious, systematic instruction to repetitive, moment-to-moment influences at the margins of awareness" can take place.[3] The child's first affective and cognitive instruction takes place in the family context, with some of the teaching direct and some indirect. The family is the prime setting for cultural transmission; for developing self-concepts, social and interpersonal relationships; for initial language and cognitive development. To foster these learnings, parents and siblings teach as do others in the family. (For a more complete discussion of family as educator, see chapter 5 of this volume.)

In addition to the instruction that goes on in the daily life of the family, there are many kinds and levels of cooperation between the school and the home. Parents may help their children with homework, find resources for them which they need for school work, show interest in "what happened in school today," and generally be concerned and involved in different ways and to various degrees. Such involvement and interaction between family and home and school may be either formal or informal.

Cremin has argued that the recognition that other agencies and institutions educate should cause those persons who design educational programs to be aware of other educational encounters and take them into account:

For parents, day-care workers, school teachers, youth leaders, pastors, editors of children's encyclopedias, training officers in industry, and directors of senior citizens' centers, the message is essentially the same: whatever is done, to be effective, must be done with an awareness of what has gone on earlier and what is going on elsewhere.[4]

Some Models of Nonschool Settings for Learning

Five examples follow of nonschool settings for learning—programs that function in settings other than schools and deliberately educate. In each instance, a collaborative relationship exists between school and program, but it is not one in which the school "uses" the agency or institution. In many instances, schools conduct their instruction in settings other than the school building—for example, field trips, internships, community-based experiential learning, and the like. The initiative for these activities and programs comes from the school, and it is the school that is extending its instruction beyond the classroom in order to broaden the base of learning resources. Some school districts even operate on the concept of community schools, schools that are designed to serve the entire community and not just children and youth.

In contrast to these school-based initiatives, the following examples illustrate programs that are designed and operated by nonschool agencies or institutions and function first in nonschool settings, although they may also eventually be brought into the school setting. They represent efforts to educate, deliberately and systematically, and they relate to schools and school programs as well. The settings chosen are a national park, television in the home, a city art gallery, a public library, and the home.

CHILDREN'S EXPERIMENTAL WORKSHOP

The Glen Echo Park Children's Experimental Workshop is "an innovative program in the visual and performing arts involving children with visual, physical, and learning disabilities as well as children from a variety of ethnic backgrounds."[5]

Located a few miles northwest of Washington, D.C., Glen Echo Park was originally established in 1891 as the Fifty-third Chautauqua Assembly, its founders envisioning a cultural citadel overlooking the Potomac River. It was part of the Chautauqua Movement, which flourished toward the end of the last century as a "popular cultural movement in the humanities and sciences, enlivened by concerts, vaudeville shows, and lectures."[6] By 1899, however, Glen Echo was transformed into an amusement park only to be closed in 1968. In 1971, it reopened as part of the National Park System after vigorous community efforts had blocked a plan by the owners to convert the site to high-rise apartments.

The Children's Experimental Workshop began in 1972 when a group of National Park Service employees were faced with the challenge of transforming the dilapidated facilities into a cultural and educational setting and returning the park to its cultural past. Under the leadership of Wendy Ross, the "staff decided that the Fellini-like setting would be an ideal environment for a children's day camp in the performing and visual arts . . . the program to include visually and physically handicapped children."[7] The staff decided to focus on multicultural experiences tied together by particular themes that would be applied to workshops in various performing and graphic arts areas. The park employees and outside artists were to teach collaboratively so that each would understand what the others were doing.

For the first summer (1972), schools in the District's inner city and nearby neighborhoods were given an opportunity to select students who had no summer recreation programs available to them and who could participate in one of the four two-week sessions during July and August. These students constituted half of the population; the remaining campers were accepted on a first-come, first-served basis and paid a small tuition fee if they were able. Two hundred and twelve children, ages eight to twelve, coming from a wide variety of ethnic and cultural backgrounds, attended the first Children's Experimental Workshop

Multicultural Arts Day Camp where the purpose was to stimulate and expand "the children's inherent creativity by having them focus their energies on the performing and visual arts."[8]

In 1974, Ross was concerned with keeping the program operating year round and extending the special populations involved. Grace Stephenson, who worked with the District's school for the visually handicapped, asked for help with an arts program for the school's students. With no funding and some supplies left over from the summer camp, a pottery workshop for the blind, which met three hours weekly for ten weeks, was designed. In addition, field trips were arranged where the visually handicapped could explore surroundings through their other senses. Members of the Arena Stage's Living Stage troupe worked with the children for a session. The success with blind children led to a program in pottery and puppetry for children with learning disabilities, who met twice a week for ten weeks.

A set of basic objectives for the Children's Experimental Workshop was established to guide further experimentation. These objectives included:

1. To increase use of the National Parks by ethnic minorities and other special populations: the blind, the retarded, and physically disabled;

2. To use the arts as a way of visualizing and animating a park's story;

3. To make it possible for performing and visual artists to share their talents with programs held in the parks;

4. To test out a number of art techniques as interpretive tools for environmental awareness at selected National Park sites;

5. To eliminate negative attitudes which act as a barrier to working positively with handicapped individuals;

6. To enlarge parts of the program to involve handicapped individuals as members of the staff and art instructors;

7. To offer recreation workers interested in special populations a source book for ideas based on findings of a documented program.[9]

By 1975, Ross initiated the development of a comprehensive program in the visual and performing arts that would differ from school-based programs and would extend the potential of the National Parks for these special populations. The workshop content was directly influenced by the particular disabilities of the children:

"sensory experiences were stressed when working with the blind; manual dexterity, craftmanship, and coordination were stressed with the physically handicapped; social interaction was stressed with the mentally retarded, particularly through drama and improvisational techniques."[10] In the same year, the year-round programming began. The first ten-week session involved students from the District's Sharpe Health School, which provides for physically disabled nine- to fourteen-year-olds. To familiarize participants with the program, workshops at the school were conducted for students, teachers, and administrators before the children came to Glen Echo. In addition to pottery and puppetry, the Living Stage returned to conduct a day-long workshop for the staff and teachers as well as programs involving the children.

The experiences of the Children's Experimental Workshop (CEW) demonstrate clearly that the National Parks have rich educating and educational possibilities—"rich potential for learning as well as recreation." The CEW not only directly instructs the children, but their teachers and parents as well. The CEW staff provides the school staff with in-service development involving them in orientation and teaching activities. Finally, the CEW staff—Park Service employees, artists, performers, and volunteers—are actively and constantly engaged in the processes of curriculum development.

CHILDREN'S TELEVISION WORKSHOP

The Children's Television Workshop (CTW) is the producer of "Sesame Street," "The Electric Company," and other shows that have reached tremendous viewing audiences in the United States and countries all over the world. As one evaluator put it, " 'Sesame Street' and 'The Electric Company' undertake to entertain and simultaneously to teach specific cognitive skills to large audiences . . . [and] to use the mass media for educational purposes."[11] Thus, the Children's Television Workshop is basically an educating agency. According to its original proposal, the program would be unique for several reasons: "education is its primary aim and entertainment the means; it attempts to reach a lower- as well as a middle-class audience; and expensive, popular production techniques would be used to accomplish these goals."[12]

The general aim of the first program, "Sesame Street," was very clearly stated as an educational goal: "to promote the intellectual and cultural growth of preschoolers, particularly disadvantaged preschoolers."[13] Unlike other existing children's programs that aimed primarily to entertain while presenting some educational elements, the first aim of "Sesame Street" was to teach and to enhance both the cognitive and affective development of preschoolers, especially those from disadvantaged homes. Its specific objectives were clearly educational:

1. Recognition of numbers one through ten and simple counting ability.

2. Recognition of letters of the alphabet and the sounds most commonly associated with them; in effect, the first steps in learning to read.

3. Basic language skills (the ability to handle grammatical contrasts, to differentiate among prepositions, to speak whole sentences, to express in clear language such ideas as how to get some place, or what happened today).

4. Concepts of space and time (shapes, forms, spatial perspective, the notion of time).

5. Beginning logical concepts (logical classification, concepts of relationships).

6. Beginning mathematical concepts (conservation of quantity, one-to-one correspondence, number relationships).

7. The growth of reasoning skills (cause and effect, reasoning by association and inference).

8. Beginning awareness of basic emotions (aggression, fear, anger, etc.) as a step toward mastering them.[14]

Moreover, the curriculum designers for "Sesame Street" were concerned with other kinds of development for the four- and five-year-olds who were seen as the primary viewing audience:

We would expect, also, that a child who had regularly watched the show would have grown culturally: in his appreciation of arts and crafts, his familiarity with basic music concepts, his general knowledge about the world. We would hope also that there would be other kinds of growth, more difficult to define and measure: increased imagination, greater attentiveness, a livelier curiosity.[15]

With clear educational goals in mind, the Children's Television Workshop planners had all of the problems faced by curriculum planners everywhere, plus the problems of using the medium of television effectively for instructional as well as entertainment purposes. As Lloyd Morrisett explained: "A curriculum had to be carefully constructed, translated into production ideas, and tested to make sure that the resulting show both entertained and educated."[16] More than most educational programs, "Sesame Street" was carefully evaluated in terms of its effects and goal attainment.

Though initially funded by the Office of Education, private foundations, and the Corporation for Public Broadcasting, in the early 1970s the Children's Television Workshop decided to license books and records based on "Sesame Street" and "The Electric Company" to build a sounder financial base. Subsequently, it added games, toys, and other products "to build on the educational values and popularity of both television programs." The publication and production of CTW-related materials has not only provided income for CTW but has had a significant impact on extending the programs into the home and school through other media as these are used independently. As president of CTW, Joan Ganz Cooney pointed out: "During its first ten years, CTW moved from a one-product organization into a diversified educational enterprise that now serves both children and adults in the United States and many countries of the world." Looking ahead, Cooney saw CTW "firmly committed to the exploration of other aspects of educational and informational communications, particularly those that offer possibilities for significant experiments in reaching mass audiences."[17]

The CTW outreach arm—Community Education Services (CES)—is involved in stimulating viewership among low-income children in urban and rural areas, reinforcing the lessons of the programs among target audiences, training teachers who move with migrant farm families, and engaging in activities designed to extend the impact and effectiveness of CTW programming.

In recent years, CTW has broadened its programming to include a new science and technology series for young viewers, adaptations of children's literature for commercial television, and extension of programs for family audiences. From the beginning, CTW has had a strong research department that has addressed the educational impact of its programs.

Although designed initially and primarily for home viewing,

CTW has clearly had an impact also on schools and school programs. Children coming to school with the "Sesame Street" experience, for instance, have required modifications in the school's curriculum. Publications, games, and related materials from CTW are now found in classrooms and school libraries, linking school and family to the television viewing.

MEMORIAL ART GALLERY OF THE UNIVERSITY OF ROCHESTER

The Memorial Art Gallery in Rochester, New York, is an example of a "small-city art museum [which] has dedicated itself to education and to the well-being of its community."[18] It was established in 1913 when the university accepted the gallery as a gift without endowment funds and reached out to the citizens for acquisitions and operating funds. As a result, the collection grew "unevenly, an unplanned amalgam of gifts of varying quality from local supporters" without "either a specialized collection or a collection of masterpieces."[19] Until the 1930s, university art history and art appreciation courses were all taught in the gallery, and the collection became basically a teaching collection that surveyed the world of art. When the university moved to a new campus, the gallery remained in its central-city location.

When the gallery was reopened in 1968 after being closed for the construction of a new wing, the nine staff-trained volunteer docents were overwhelmed by more than 4,000 schoolchildren who visited the museum that year. The number of children visiting the gallery increased rapidly, and a rigorous docent training program was initiated. The role of docents has grown well beyond guiding school groups and now includes art workshops, art lectures at local schools, and other community outreach activities. The volunteer docent program is seen as one of the museum's most important programs.

In addition to gallery tours, the museum provides a variety of in-school programs including: (a) loan materials—framed reproductions, slides, films, filmstrips, special exhibits, and the like; (b) lectures in high schools on art and culture correlated with social studies and other curriculum; (c) art ambassadors—volunteer docents assigned to particular schools to visit classes, change exhibits, and work with teachers; (d) visiting artists—professional artists present their own works and conduct workshops in schools. The Museum conducts in-service training sessions for teachers on request and participates in the Rochester Arts Council's semiannual in-service program that introduces participants to a dozen local cultural organizations.

Among its other educational activities, the museum conducts a Creative Workshop that provides studio experiences not just in art but in modern dance as well. Each year more than three dozen classes are available for children and adults "in weaving, enameling, jewelry, ceramics, printmaking, painting, sculpture, and drawing—ranging from beginning level to some with professional standards."[20] The outreach art classes include poor children from disadvantaged neighborhoods, physically handicapped, and retarded children. Arts-therapy classes are also included.

With a multiethnic, culturally diverse population surrounding it, the Memorial Gallery has mounted exhibitions of the arts of and by different ethnic groups both at the museum and in the communities. At three neighborhood sites, lending galleries have been set up where reproductions and even original works donated by local artists can be borrowed without charge for a month at a time. The Allofus Art Workshop is a program in which artists provide free art classes for the community in exchange for studio space. A building that had been a police station and a jail was transformed into an art workshop site.

Almost from its beginnings, the Memorial Art Gallery has viewed itself as an educational institution and has grappled with issues of balance "between utilization and conservation, education and solid curatorial work." The philosophy of the Gallery provides its response:

The guiding principle behind the educational activities of the Memorial Art Gallery is the same as for the Gallery as a whole, namely, that the inherent capability in human kind to create, contemplate, use and enjoy the visual arts needs greater development in our time. The Gallery attempts to provide the maximum number of people with the maximum number of opportunities to develop this capability.[21]

BROOKLYN PUBLIC LIBRARY

The Brooklyn Public Library is probably typical of modern community libraries that educate. The traditional educating function of the library—to store and provide access to information—is substantially unchanged, but the means for storage and access have changed over the years and the variety of information provided has increased. The library is no longer performing an archival function. Brooklyn

Public still lends books, of course, and has available a variety of published materials, periodicals, records, and so forth. It has special collections that are of particular interest or fill a special need of a special group, agency, or set of institutions—for example, ethnic, racial, and cultural groups; senior citizens; women's organizations; and so forth. The library has children's story hours and related services for young readers. It loans records, films, art reproductions.

The Library's Education and Job Information Center supplies a range of information including directories and guides to colleges and trade and technical schools, financial aid forms and directories of sources, listings of learning resources in the community, books and pamphlets on careers and job hunting, information on job training and job placement, résumé reviews, occupational guides to employment agencies, microfiche of professional job openings, and employment-related magazines. For adults who have not finished high school, the Center provides various services including diagnostic testing so that individuals can discover the areas in which they need study before taking the equivalency diploma test. It makes available study books to prepare the applicant for the test generally or for specific parts of the test, and provides videotapes for review and tutors to help small groups use the materials. The Library also offers guidance regarding various alternative methods of learning and gaining credits toward college degrees, including self-directed learning, credit through life or work experience, and independent or correspondence course study.

HOME INSTRUCTION PROGRAM FOR PRESCHOOL YOUNGSTERS (HIPPY)

The HIPPY program operates from the School of Education of the Hebrew University in Jerusalem. It is an enrichment program aimed at improving the intellectual and academic functioning of children from poor families whose mothers have had relatively little formal education. The families chosen for the program are generally large and intact, and it is not uncommon to find five or more children living in small, crowded housing. The program begins with four-year-olds and continues for three years through the first year of school. The project provides a set of structured learning materials, which are administered by the mother five times a week for a total of about fifty hours per year.

The HIPPY mother meets weekly with a paraprofessional aide

who instructs her in how to use the materials with her child. The weekly meetings alternate between visits in the home and group meetings of HIPPY mothers in the neighborhood. The paraprofessional aide is herself a local mother who is trained by the HIPPY program's professional staff and is supervised by them.

When the aide visits the HIPPY mother in her home, she brings with her a packet that includes the workbook and the materials to be used with the child that week. The aide then uses role playing to instruct the mother in how to use the materials, with the aide and the mother playing the role of mother and child. The training session lasts as long as it takes to familiarize the mother with the materials and have her feel comfortable in using them. When the mother is illiterate, the mother chooses an older sibling for the teaching role but is present when that child is trained and when the teaching sessions take place. As Lombard points out: "The mother is encouraged to participate to the limit of her abilities since she is the major focus of the program."[22] At the biweekly group meetings, in addition to reviewing the forthcoming week's materials, the mothers share and discuss problems and issues concerning their children as well as their role as mothers.

The materials deal with three basic content areas—language, mathematics, and sensory and perceptive skills—and are in the programmed instruction mode. In addition, the program "espouses a firm commitment to teaching children the 'rules of the game,' basically, how to be a good pupil. Through doing the activities, children develop habits of paying attention, concentrating, anticipating, and finding out what is expected of them."[23]

The local paraprofessional aides are trained by the central staff. In addition to training and supervising mothers, the aide is the link between the program and the schools. It is the local aide who makes the first contacts with the families and discusses the program with the mother to be sure that she understands what is involved in joining the program. The local aide is responsible for ten to twelve families in her first year and fifteen to eighteen as she becomes more experienced. In the weekly meetings with the mother, the aide goes over the child's work and maintains a record of the child's activity packet.

The biweekly group meetings are also used for a more general education activity, often related to the parenting role with the focus on such topics as "health and hygiene, children's books and games, the school system, home handicrafts, home economics, and preparation for holidays."

The local community must opt for the HIPPY program, committing itself to a minimum of three years. The community nominates a person to be local coordinator who has major responsibility for implementing and administering the program.

The basic assumption of the HIPPY program is "that consistent and relatively long-term cognitive intervention channeled through the family will affect familial interactions, and thereby assist intellectual growth. It is expected that such growth will be reflected in improved school performance."[24] An evaluation of the educational impact of HIPPY did find that the program improved the scholastic performance of its participants, particularly in preventing atypical progression of children through the educational system (that is, nonpromotion or transfer to preparatory or special education classes).

Combined/Coordinated Efforts

In the five examples described above, the nature and extent of collaboration between the nonschool and school efforts vary widely. However, there are some common guiding "principles" that are found in all five programs:

1. The program has clear educative goals that are congruent with the goals of the school. The educational objectives to be attained are clear and valid.

2. The program has a curriculum design—a plan for providing the learning engagements and experiences that will help achieve the program's goals and objectives.

3. The program has selected appropriate pedagogical/instructional strategies for implementing the curriculum. These instructional strategies use the particular resources of the agency in an effective manner.

4. The agency has the personnel and material resources needed to implement the curriculum. These resources are generally more appropriate for the program design than are the resources of the school.

5. The nonschool agency's educational goals either complement or supplement the educational goals of the school.

6. At some stage of program design, the agency and the school engage in joint planning aimed to combine or coordinate their efforts so that each is aware of what is going on in the other regarding a

particular aspect of education or mutual concern. This planning may be formal or informal, direct or indirect. The purpose of these combined/coordinated efforts is to strengthen or enrich instruction and learning.

7. Just as evaluation is or should be an integral component of instruction in the school, educational efforts of nonschool agencies should be subject to appropriate evaluation in order to guide decision making about program changes.

8. Nonschool educative agencies may provide in-service education for school personnel when such agencies have the resources needed for staff development. The aim of such staff development is to facilitate the integration of school and nonschool educational efforts.

As Cremin has argued, educators working in schools must take into account the education that occurs outside the school:

It is important for the school to engage the instruction of other educators and seek to strengthen or complement or criticize or contravene that instruction, or more generally try to develop an awareness of that instruction and an ability to deal critically and independently with it.[25]

When educators in schools and in other settings engage each others' instruction critically, analytically, and cooperatively, clearly the learners will be the ultimate winners. This is especially so when the nonschool educative agency has the resources to design educational and instructional activities that engage students in learning more efficiently and effectively than the school can. The school then needs to use these learnings to enrich the instruction it provides children and youth.

FOOTNOTES

1. Lawrence A. Cremin, "Changes in the Ecology of Education: The School and the Other Educators," in *The Future of Formal Education*, ed. Torsten Husén (Stockholm: Almqvist and Wiksell International, 1980), p. 18.

2. Ibid., p. 19.

3. Hope Jensen Leichter, "Some Perspectives on the Family as Educator," in *The Family as Educator*, ed. Hope Jensen Leichter (New York: Teachers College Press, 1974), p. 1.

4. Cremin, "Changes in the Ecology of Education," p. 23.

5. Wendy Ross and Allen Lefcowitz, eds., *Children's Experimental Workshop: Expanding the Park Experience to Children with Special Needs*, (Washington, D.C.: U.S. Government Printing Office, 1979), p. 29.

6. Ibid.

7. Ibid., p. 30.

8. Ibid., p. 33.

9. Ibid., p. 49.

10. Ibid., p. 50.

11. Robert K. Yin, *The Workshop and the World: Toward an Assessment of the Children's Television Workshop* (Santa Monica, Calif.: Rand Corp., 1973), p. v.

12. Children's Television Workshop, "Television for Preschool Children: A Proposal" (New York: Children's Television Workshop, 1968), p. 8.

13. Ibid., p. 10.

14. Ibid., p. 11.

15. Ibid., pp. 11-12.

16. Lloyd Morrisett, "Introduction," in *Children and Television: Lessons from "Sesame Street,"* ed. Gerald S. Lesser (New York: Vintage Books, 1974), p. xxiv.

17. Joan Ganz Cooney, "The 1980s: More Challenge, More Change," *1979 Corporate Review*, June 1979, p. 1.

18. Barbara Y. Newsom and Adele Z. Silver, eds., *The Art Museum as Educator* (Berkeley, Calif.: University of California Press, 1978), p. 39.

19. Ibid., p. 41.

20. Ibid.

21. Ibid., p. 54.

22. Avima Lombard, *Success Begins at Home* (Lexington, Mass.: D. C. Heath and Co., 1981), p. 11.

23. Avima Lombard, "An Overview of HIPPY," in *HIPPY International Workshop: Summary of Proceedings*, ed. Kay Weinberger (Jerusalem: School of Education, Hebrew University, 1982), p. 1.

24. Yaakov Kareev, Dan Davis, and Paula Silberstein, *An Evaluation of the Educational Impact of HIPPY* (Jerusalem: School of Education, Hebrew University, 1982), p. 1.

25. Cremin, "Changes in the Ecology of Teaching," p. 24.

Part Two
THE OTHER EDUCATIVE SETTINGS

Introduction

American schools today are caught between eras. Designed to meet the needs of an earlier and vastly different society, schools are now asked to respond to a radically new set of challenges. The result may be a good example of what George Orwell once described as "a belief bumping up against a solid reality." Surely it is a clear case of a nineteenth-century institution steadfastly trying to adapt to twentieth-century ways and means. For professional educators, the process can be endlessly frustrating; for everyone concerned, the results are too often deeply disappointing.

Since the beginning of this century, we have seen an expanding commitment to education, an increasing affirmation of the principles of popular education as the key element in the health and survival of democratic government. As Walter Lippmann once quipped, "Education has furnished the thesis of the last chapter of every optimistic book on democracy written for one hundred and fifty years." Lippmann went on to cast a skeptical eye on these last chapters: "The usual appeal to education can bring only disappointment. For the problems of the modern world appear and change faster than any set of teachers can grasp them, much faster than they can convey their substance to a population of children. If the schools attempt to teach children how to solve problems of the day, they are bound always to be in arrears." But Lippmann was, of course, talking about schooling, and indeed over the subsequent fifty years, it is to schooling that we have given our energies and hitched our hopes. And because the schools have not been able to solve the most serious problems of the society, we have become, as Lippmann predicted, "disappointed" with the potential of education.

Yet, it was not so much a matter of misplaced faith as an error of emphasis, for there are numerous institutions and agencies within our society that educate us in countless ways, most of which we have ignored in favor of the school. In fact, it has become commonplace to observe that education and schooling are not necessarily synonymous.

"My definition of education," wrote Felix Frankfurter, "is the air you breathe, what *is* in the atmosphere. That's the education that matters! What kinds of things instinctively, unconsciously enter your being." But, as one suspects Frankfurter would have been the first to admit, education entails more than leaving the individual as a mere passive recipient of atmospheric chance. Thus, the intent of this section is to pinpoint and clarify the educational potential inherent in other institutions, agencies, and settings—indeed what Justice Frankfurter would have called our "atmosphere"—and to analyze their educational advantages and shortcomings as part of the educative community.

CHAPTER V

Families as Educators

HOPE JENSEN LEICHTER

In recent years, there has been considerable interest in the family's role in education. We have come to recognize that the family is almost always the first educator of the child, and that some of the individual's most basic education takes place within the home. Children learn language—their most important social and intellectual tool—before they go to school. And families continue to be a source of education throughout life.

Despite this recognition, the concepts that we use to think about education in families and the many other institutions that educate are often drawn, either explicitly or implicitly, from our ideas about schools. This is misleading. If we are to understand adequately the rich and diversified education that takes place within families, it is vital for us to have concepts about families as educators that are formulated in family terms—concepts that focus attention on the distinctive features of families and the special ways in which they educate. We are likely to miss many of the unique educational contributions of families if we focus mainly on the extent to which they resemble what goes on in schools.

The tendency to evaluate education in families in terms of its similarity to education in schools has given a negative tone to many examinations of the family's role in education. For example, recent efforts to explore the family's contribution to the outcomes of schooling, especially school failure, have led to an emphasis on the educational deficits of families, particularly families of the poor. Debates on these issues have been heated, with charges that the causes of school failure lie in deficits in the home. And, despite countercharges that the responsibility for school failure rests with the school or the larger society, not the family, certain kinds of families have been subject to particularly negative evaluations—for example, female-headed families, where it is presumed that no male role model is present, and families where it is presumed that there are cognitive deficiencies because the mother lacks verbal fluency.

Indeed, deficits in lower-class homes have sometimes been stated in extreme terms. For example, as a solution to problems of poverty, Edward Banfield actually proposed to sell the children of the poor to qualified bidders who can offer them a "normal" family environment.[1] Evaluations of middle-class families, while strikingly different from those of lower-class families, have also been negative on many points. We hear, for example, that professional women who leave home during the early years of child-rearing are damaging their children's psychological development; at the same time, women who live on welfare in order to stay home and take care of their children are considered inadequate.

The task of understanding families is complicated by the fact that virtually everyone has experience in one family or another, and these experiences are often deeply emotional. It is hard for anyone—teacher, administrator, researcher—to avoid personal biases in thinking about families. Both the evaluations of educational practitioners and the questions posed in the literature on the family often rest on implicit pieties about desirable forms of the family. We are apt to make harsh judgments of families that do not exemplify what we cherish in our own family experience, and even harsher judgments of families that appear to repeat our traumas. Thus, personal satisfactions and regrets often provide the backdrop for presumably neutral professional evaluations and the formulation of research questions.

When educators turn to the research literature to enlarge their understanding of families, they often do not find the kinds of answers for which they are searching. What educators can draw from the literature on the family are concepts that will make it possible for them to ask more insightful questions about the families with which they are working and that can most readily be applied to educational practice.

For this reason, my aim in this chapter is to discuss a number of concepts, derived from recent research, that can offer educators

valuable guidance as they think about the particular character and
quality of familial education.

Families and Education: Urgent Questions
and Approaches to Answering Them

Given the urgent need to improve educational practice, questions
about the family's role are often raised with the expectation of
immediate answers. Yet a brief examination of the kinds of questions
that are commonly posed about families and education reveals the
difficulty of finding ready answers.

The questions of educational practitioners and policymakers take a
variety of forms. Some are phrased in terms of particular cause-effect
relationships; for example, does television viewing produce violence in
children? Some are phrased to allow for multiple factors in cause-effect
relationships; for example, what kinds of family practices are most
likely to help children learn to read? Some are action-oriented in that
they assume certain kinds of family practices have been determined to
be harmful, and ask how parents can be helped to modify these
practices; for example, how can families be helped to reduce the
amount of time spent on watching television?

Cause-effect questions also vary in the time-span implied. Some are
phrased in terms of immediate connections; for example, will more
time spent on homework improve school performance? Others imply
a long-range relationship; for example, does the rapid pace of television
have an adverse effect upon an individual's ability to devote continuous
attention to activities?

In some instances, educational questions about families are concerned with broad areas rather than particular cause-effect relationships. For example, educators working with programs for particular
ethnic or minority populations may be concerned with the relationship
of the language and culture of the school to that of families, as
illustrated in the debates over bilingual education.[2] Or educators may
be concerned about how to help families of handicapped children
achieve a realistic understanding of what their children can and cannot
achieve in school.[3]

Still broader policy questions include how parents can be helped to
cope with social and emotional problems—for example, drug and

alcohol use—that interfere with their children's education. Other
broad questions are concerned with what may be termed "virtue and
innocence," that is, how parents can best cope with aspects of the
environment that they regard as contrary to the proper development
of their children. These may involve neighborhood pressures toward
crime and delinquency, peer pressures toward drug or alcohol use,
media information that is deemed offensive, or religious and cultural
beliefs that are antithetical to those of the home. Another set of
questions relates to whether restructuring workplaces to enable parents
to be closer to and therefore have more time with their children will
improve family relationships.[4] Related to all of these are the policy
questions about how families with inadequate economic and social
means can be supported sufficiently to enable them to have time and
energy for the education of their children.

These are but a few examples of the many kinds of questions raised
about families and education. There is substantial literature on families,
from fields as varied as anthropology, psychology, economics, political
science, and sociology, as well as literature and the humanities, and it
encompasses a wide range of theoretical perspectives and methodologi-
cal approaches. Nevertheless, many of the questions and concerns of
educators have either not been specifically addressed, or are so broad-
ranging that they cannot readily be answered by particular studies.
Inevitably, however, there is pressure to make *some* decisions, to
formulate *some* policy even in the absence of conclusive knowledge.

Yet, despite a lack of evidence, specific policy recommendations are
often asserted with considerable assurance. A good example is the
recommendation in the recent report, *A Nation at Risk*, that more time
should be devoted to homework. The thesis itself raises a wide range
of questions about the conditions under which homework can most
effectively be carried out within families. But the tone of the recommendation fails to acknowledge such questions. Its certainty on the
issue is illustrated by its words to parents that "your vigilance and
your refusal to be satisfied with less than the best are the imperative
first step. . . . You should encourage more diligent study and dis-
courage satisfaction with mediocrity."[5]

Despite a host of specific and broad-ranging questions and concerns
about families and education, what we so often lack are descriptive
questions—questions about the details of the daily lives of families that

vary in circumstances, values, and living styles. Virtuous as they may seem, recommendations for greater diligence and more hard work have very different implications for different families. Given the substantial literature in the field of the family, educators can sometimes find studies that offer them a fuller picture of the way of life of families of a particular background. But given the ethnic, regional, and class diversity of the families that public education is designed to serve, not to mention the frequency of families with varying cultural mixes, educators cannot always find even descriptive studies that give them an adequate basis for understanding the families with which they are working.

The current research literature on families as educators, however, does provide certain concepts that will offer educators guidance in thinking about the many diverse families—their different strengths and weaknesses—that they encounter.

Concepts about Families as Educators

The rapidly growing literature on families as educators considers how education takes place within families, and how this education is related to that in other institutions.[6] Several studies at the Elbenwood Center for the Study of the Family as Educator represent recent efforts to develop more sophisticated understanding of families as educators. They are based on the assumption that a good deal of intensive observation is required to obtain a picture of the details of family life, and include studies of the ways in which families contribute to the development of literacy; the family's relation to television; and the ways in which individuals move through, engage in, and combine educative experiences in their social networks.[7] Certain concepts about families as educators have guided this research and they offer us valuable perspectives from which to consider families and education.

THE DISTINCTIVE FEATURES OF FAMILIES AS EDUCATORS

If we wish to understand familial education in family terms, we need to consider the role that families play in broader social and educational configurations of society, and the kinds of activities that take place within households. In an agrarian society, for example, the basic agricultural work may be carried out through household groups. In such circumstances, the world of the adult is visible to the child, and children learn to carry out adult activities by participating in them. The so-called "declining functions" of the family in industrial societies, where many forms of production have been moved to factories and places of work outside the home, mean that the activities within the household from which the child can learn adult skills, attitudes, and values are modified. As we move into the "postindustrial" or "information" era, new technologies such as computers may again alter the nature of work and bring more adult activities back into the home.[8]

Whatever the future may bring, an understanding of families in today's industrial societies requires a consideration of the kinds of activities that take place in households. One recent historical analysis argues that the industrial revolution has not reduced "housework," but rather has modified and, in some respects, even increased it.[9] While household chores may not be thought of as particularly educational (especially by those burdened with them), cooking, cleaning, shopping, sorting mail, transporting children, and the like, all require intellectual and organizational skills, as do the numerous kinds of repairs, carpentry, sewing, and "do-it-yourself" activities that go on in many homes. The recreational and religious activities of the home offer still other sources of education.

Education takes place not only in the course of everyday family activities, but also when families educate their members in values, attitudes, beliefs, and sensibilities, in a wide range of subject areas. Moreover, while not all families have members competent to teach specialized knowledge in every area—few are able to teach nuclear physics—a substantial range of content enters the home through television and through the knowledge that family members acquire in other institutions. In addition, the family has a significant role in reappraising, questioning, consolidating, and embellishing knowledge acquired through other institutions. Beyond this, the family contributes to the development of the educative styles of its members.[10] We cannot adequately understand these educational efforts or activities of families, however, if we search for an explicit curriculum or explicit time devoted to school-like activities, or even if we limit our search to activities that are commonly called "education" by family members.

Families are distinct from schools and other institutions that educate in the particular kinds of activities in which education may be inherent. They are also distinct from schools and other institutions that educate in a number of other important ways.

First, family life consists of streams of activity; one activity is embedded in another, with multiple and parallel activities going on much of the time. For example, one person watches television while another comments from a different room, another cooks, another reads the newspaper, another plays with dolls or blocks, and another bathes. The beginnings and endings of sequences of activities, although sometimes geared to external clocks, such as the beginning and ending of work or school, or the shifting of programs on television, are not necessarily formal, predictable routines. This applies even to such presumably routine matters as sleeping and eating. This is not to say that family life is chaotic and haphazard, but that the patterns of familial activity vary from one family to another, and from moment to moment within the same family, and that multiple streams of simultaneous activity are characteristic.

Second, families change significantly from one moment in the life cycle to another. Even differences between family members of different ages are modified over time. The differences between a parent and an infant, for example, are quite unlike the differences between a parent and an adolescent or a grandparent and a parent.

Third, families, whatever their stage in the life cycle, generally have a common history, a period during which shared meanings or shared "presuppositional structures"[11] arise. Indeed, one possible definition of a family is a group that has common memories.[12] The existence of such common meanings, or a common history, has a profound effect on the kinds of interactions, both educational and otherwise, that take place within families. In examining family language, for example, it has been shown that so-called "restricted" usage may be a general feature of family discourse, not merely one applying to families of particular backgrounds.[13] Of vital significance in familial discourse is a kind of family "shorthand," an array of sayings and expressions having an idiosyncratic meaning, recognized by members of the family.

Fourth, families engage in a wide range of oral communications on an ongoing basis, ranging from the serious to the jocular, from the explicit to the elliptical. Moreover, a great deal of informal oral communication characterizes the setting in which formal written communications take place. Indeed, as certain research on literacy has shown, even written communications in families may be in highly elliptical and shorthand form.[14]

Fifth, the family's control over its educational activities and aspirations has special features. All institutions are influenced by other institutions in society, but this influence varies among institutions. Families are distinct from other institutions in the areas over which they exert control. For example, while families may not be able to control or influence television programming, they do have potential control over decisions with respect to viewing.

THE NATURE OF EDUCATION

If we wish to understand the distinctive features of families as educators, an appropriate definition of education is essential. In everyday language, "education" is often equated with schooling so that family members themselves may not think of activities within the home as educational unless they resemble those in the schools. And in professional thinking, the learning and development that take place in families is sometimes considered to be socialization rather than education.[15]

One rather broad definition of education is helpful: the "deliberate, systematic, and sustained effort to transmit, evoke, or acquire knowledge, values, skills and sensibilities and any learning that results from the effort, direct or indirect, intended or unintended."[16] This definition directs attention to what is taught as well as to what is learned, to self-education as well as to education by others. It emphasizes the sometimes indirect results of education, as well as the "profound ironies" that sometimes characterize educational encounters: "what is taught is not always what is desired, and vice versa; what is taught is not always what is learned, and vice versa."[17] Yet in examining families as educators, we need a still broader definition that will encompass those events that take place on a fleeting moment-to-moment basis at the "margins of awareness."[18]

The need for a broad definition of education was illustrated in a recent ethnographic study by the Elbenwood Center of the ways in which families contribute to the development of their children's skills in literacy.[19] It became clear in this study that one missed some of the most vital literacy-related activities if one searched only for activities that were formally labeled "reading and writing," or for occasions formally devoted to "education." When, for example, we set out to gain a picture of the "literacy resources" available in the homes of the families we were studying, we found that even those families that relied to a large extent on conversation for communication, rather than on reading and writing, were inundated by print, both in the home and in the community outside the home. Noting, describing, cataloging, and tracking the forms of print within a home was a substantial task in and of itself, apart from any analysis of the ways in which print is embedded in and serves to organize family activities. Kitchens proved particularly problematic, since print is so pervasive on packaging. Print is also inescapable in medicine cabinets, in supermarkets, and on television, particularly in commercials. Wastebaskets proved a particularly useful source of literacy materials, reminding us that print does not merely reside in a household, but rather flows through it. One example of the continuous "processing" of print is the "junk mail" with which many families are barraged.

In addition to the print that comes into the home from outside, there is the writing created in the home, which ranges from neatly organized messages to scrawls found on scraps of paper, pieces of cardboard, or napkins. These can be found in places specifically designated for notes, or casually placed almost anywhere. Such communications tend to be elliptical, and often contain drawings and idiosyncratic, shorthand abbreviations, demonstrating that the line between print and other visual forms is not clear-cut.

The field notes from this ethnographic study contain some examples indicating the variety of artifacts that may be relevant when we analyze literacy within the family: books, dictionaries, atlases, maps, encyclopedias, school workbooks, reports, tests, letters to and from school, newspapers, magazines, TV guides, comic books, junk mail, notes from one family member to another, greeting cards, children's drawings, building directories, appointment books, captioned religious pictures, merit awards, personal letters, kitchen canisters, labels on food, jars, cans, medicine and bathroom products, postcards, political flyers, coupons, laundry slips, cookbooks, wall plaques, games, nameplates, shopping lists, postage stamps, coloring books, sports catalogues, diaries, Christmas cards, gift lists, record albums, sewing patterns, baseball cards, sweatshirts, photograph albums, ID cards, tickets.

In attempting to survey artifacts in the home to determine which literacy resources were available, no clear boundary could be drawn between an artifact that served such a purpose and one that did not. It was not possible to assume that certain artifacts were "educational" while others were not, or that those artifacts containing print were potential resources for learning literacy, while those without print were not. Sewing patterns, for instance, are not in the home for the purpose of advancing literacy, but they have potential as an educational resource. They not only teach sewing and the use of patterns, but help in developing spatial concepts and the ability to recognize visual forms—intellectual skills that may well be underpinnings for literacy.

It proved equally difficult to specify what kinds of familial activities were learning activities. In fact, family members and observers did not necessarily characterize an activity in the same way. Sometimes one participant would think of an activity as educational, while another did not. In an attempt to describe learning activities in which parents engage with children, another list was drawn from the field notes. Again, a wide range of activities was found in all homes: writing notes, asking questions, helping with homework, instructing a child to look something up, instructing a child to use books, doing homework with a child, giving out answers to a child, giving explanations to a child during cooking, showing a child how lists are made, allowing a child to make decisions, attempting not to criticize a child, preaching, scolding, punishing, checking to see if homework is finished, instructing a child to be independent, going over picture albums with children, teaching liturgy for Holy Communion, making up children for a school play, making a label for a mailbox, making signs, helping a child read instructions, listening to children's recitations, carrying out feminist political activities.

These illustrations indicate the range of family events and activities that may be considered educational. My point here is to *illustrate* the need for a concept broad enough to encompass the full range of educational encounters within the home—a concept that helps us to understand educational encounters in family, rather than school terms.[20]

Even if one considers education to be a deliberate effort—one that is the focus of aware attention—experiences at the margins of awareness or at the level of peripheral awareness remain part of the educational process. Much of the activity within the family is of a repetitive, moment-to-moment nature. Such interaction is different from even the most immediate recollection of it, since even short-term memory is highly selective. Yet, to understand those moments of intentionality and awareness that one might wish to regard as educational, it is essential to have a framework that sets those deliberate moments into the context of multiple levels of awareness, where the explicit shades off into the indistinct, the intentional into the incidental, and the focal into the peripheral.

For adequate understanding of education in families, we also require a definition that goes beyond the education of children by parents to include education of parents by children, the education of husbands by wives, the education of siblings by siblings, the education of children by grandparents, and of grandparents by children. In short, we need to consider the variety of educational interactions that take place within the family and its network of significant kin.

Parents are usually among the first educators of the child, but they are seldom the only educators, even within the family. Siblings are important in educating each other, as anyone with more than one child can easily observe. Children talk to each other, show each other how to do things, correct each other, tell each other about school. In addition, parents are educated by their children. In some instances, children teach their parents directly: a classic case is of immigrant parents who are taught the language and customs of the new country by their children. Parents are also taught by their children in that they relive educational experiences indirectly through them. Parents also educate each other. Any marriage brings together two people of somewhat different backgrounds—no matter how similar they may be—with different ideas and experiences and different activities in the outside world. As a result, husbands and wives become teachers of each other. Beyond this, anthropological studies indicate that grandparents play very different roles in different societies, depending on how rapidly the society is changing. But even in urban industrial societies, in which immigration and rapid social change have been significant, grandparents can and do play a vital educational role, providing a connection with experiences in other times and places.[21]

It is also important to consider education within the family as a two-way interpersonal interaction (or an interaction among many parties) rather than as influences of one individual upon another. Studies of mothering indicate, for example, that even in the care of infants, a two-way interaction between mother and child is crucial, with the style of mothering being influenced by the child's energy level, timing, and other characteristics.[22]

THE OUTCOMES OF FAMILIAL EDUCATION

We need to consider the outcomes of familial education in terms of their impact on the skills and abilities of all family members, not merely their impact on children's school achievement. Familial education may contribute to children's knowledge, values, and sensibilities—knowledge of religious points of view, for example—that may not be called upon in school.

As I have suggested elsewhere in formulating the concept of "educative style,"[23] there are a number of components of more general approaches to education that we might usefully consider as outcomes of familial education: the manner of criticizing and appraising; the mode of integrating experience over time; the level and rate of activity; the ways of combining and segregating particular tasks; the character of responses to cues from others; the ways of appraising and synthesizing knowledge, values, and attitudes of others; the mode of scanning and searching for information; the approach to embarrassment in learning situations—the list is illustrative rather than exhaustive. Moreover, in understanding the outcomes of familial education, we should be concerned with the ways in which this education contributes to the individual's approach to education over a lifetime.

THE STRUCTURE OF THE FAMILY

If we are to understand the many subtle forms of education that take place among the different members of the family, we need clear concepts about the structure of the family.

First, it is essential to have a clear picture of the composition of the domestic group and its social network. It is by now commonplace to assert that families take many different forms under different social and cultural conditions. Yet it remains essential that implicit concepts about familial structure not be ethnocentric (or egocentric). Beyond this, it is important to trace the actual network of families to understand the nature of familial and interpersonal resources. A mother living alone with a child, but in close contact and close geographic proximity to a grandmother and uncle, is in a very different situation from a mother who is isolated from ties with kin. Thus a female-headed, single-parent family may, under some circumstances, provide a male child with quite adequate role models and contact with male authority figures. The circumstances must be understood by analyzing the family's ties within its social network, not through the label "single-parent family." Similarly, families that are "reconstituted" after a divorce may vary substantially in their interpersonal climate, and these circumstances can be understood best if we attempt to trace the actual social networks.

Second, clear concepts about the boundaries of the family are essential. Generally, the boundaries of the family can most usefully be conceived of as "permeable."[24] Individuals in most families spend extensive time outside the home. In understanding the influences of families upon their members, we therefore need to have some adequate picture of the proportion of time that family members spend in different settings, and the kinds of experiences that they meet outside as well as within the home. Obvious as this may seem, assumptions about the influence of families on the education of their children often rest on an implicit picture of the family as an isolated unit with impermeable boundaries rather than on an image of the family as an open system.

Third, in understanding families as educators, we must recognize that the family undergoes continual and profound changes during the life cycle. A family's characteristics may have very different consequences at different stages of the cycle. For example, a mother whose "style of mothering" is to organize the minute details of her child's life—selecting and laying out items of clothing, selecting and organizing the child's social engagements—may have a very different impact on a young child than on a teenage one, unless the mother also changes as the child matures. An attempt to understand families as educators entails carefully considering the family's stage in the life cycle, as well as the changes that occur from one time to another.

THE PROCESSES OF FAMILIAL EDUCATION

If we wish to understand the variety of educational encounters that take place among the many diverse members of the family and its social network, we need concepts that make it possible to think about the processes of that education as it takes place on a moment-to-moment basis. This implies a shift from thinking about familial education in terms of variables—for example, income, educational level of parents, amount of reading material in the home, or proportion of familial economic resources devoted to the children's education (as these are correlated with measures of the children's school achievement)—to an understanding of the multiple activities within families as they go forward from moment to moment.

Here again, a variety of conceptual frameworks may be a useful point of departure. As I have indicated elsewhere, concepts for examining the processes of familial education may focus on areas that include language interaction, the organization of activity in time and space, memory as an interactive process, the processes of evaluation and labeling, and the processes of educational mediation.[25] Illustration of two of these areas indicates the kinds of issues to which a process-oriented approach directs our attention.

The organization of activity in space and time. Both space and time are basic dimensions of social interaction. With respect to spatial organization, cultural and situational variations have been observed in the distances that people maintain from one another, in the kinds of comfort and discomfort people experience under different spatial arrangements, and in the ways in which the organization of space itself conditions social interaction. In some recent studies of families in relation to literacy and television (conducted through the Elbenwood Center for the Study of the Family as Educator), both the spatial organization of the household and the handling of interpersonal space have proven significant.[26]

These considerations are important to educators, as we can see in the recommendations in the educational literature on how time and space should be handled in the home—that children, for instance, should be provided with a separate, specific, and quiet space for homework, and that parents should organize children's activities in space to improve their concentration and educational functioning.

We can understand the particular importance of spatial organization by considering how spatial organization conditions television viewing and how the use of space is, in turn, conditioned by the placement of television sets.[27] In examining the role of television in the family, for example, it quickly becomes evident that the placement of television sets in the household and their relation to other activities—whether a television set is in a room where many individuals commonly congregate (for example, the living room or kitchen), or in a room where individuals are separate (for example, a bedroom), or whether there are several television sets rather than just one—are all significant in terms of the ways in which families live with television, the extent of their discussion of it, and the ways in which television fits into other areas of family activity and education.

Processes of evaluating and labeling. When thinking about the moment-to-moment processes of education that take place within families, we also need to focus on the ways in which family members evaluate and label each other. It readily becomes apparent here that the cognitive and the emotional are closely intertwined (as they are in schools). Success or failure in the handling of an intellectual task can be charged with intense emotion. This is true whether the success or failure is in a formal educational setting and marked in a formal evaluation, such as a child's report card on reading achievement, or is a fleeting event that goes by almost unnoticed, but nonetheless constitutes a moment of intense emotion, such as the child's embarrassment over mispronouncing a word.

Families receive a host of formal evaluations from other institutions—schools, health care agencies, financial institutions, legal institutions. These evaluations enter the home in one way or another in terms that may vary in degree of completeness. But once they are received in the home, they are the subject of acceptance, questioning, reappraisal, embellishment, agreement, or disagreement among family members. In short, in the arena of family interaction they are reenforced or modified. Often, even the most highly educated people take professional evaluations from teachers and others with a great degree of seriousness. And even where the decision is to criticize, or, as in the case of medical evaluations, to "seek another opinion," evaluations may be "overread." In any event, how family members evaluate each other's educational skills, abilities, successes, and failures depends on the ways in which evaluations from outside the family are accepted or redefined within it.

Within the family, these evaluations may not be specifically organized or written and recorded. Yet evaluations of a family member's skills, abilities, and knowledge continue on a frequent basis, often in the context of other activities, and often with comparisons to others in the family. One child may be compared with another in terms of the ages at which they first walked or talked, in terms of their areas of greatest interest and competence in school, in terms of their energy levels and physical characteristics. Often such evaluations are in the form of stories that are told and retold by family members of characteristic events in an individual's childhood, and these stories may come to be part of an individual's self-image. This is not to say that there is a one-to-one correspondence between evaluations of others and what the individual incorporates from these evaluations. Indeed, there may often be conflicting or at least different evaluations of an individual on the part of different members within the family, to say nothing of those outside the family. Yet these evaluations, to whatever extent they "stick," are very much part of the social and emotional climate in which educational activities go forward within the family. In extreme cases, family members may be evaluated and labeled in ways that make them scapegoats of the family, or in ways that fix the evaluations so that they are difficult to modify.[28] Indeed, one goal in some forms of family therapy may be to loosen the grip of fixed evaluations and labels.

The process of evaluating and labeling is particularly significant because the present and the past come together in such evaluations. Parents commonly compare their own remembered experiences at a particular time with their observations of their children's experiences, and their approach to their children's education is tinged with the carry-over of their own experiences. If their experiences were humiliating or traumatic, they may try to create different situations for their children; if their experiences were favorable, they may seek, in one way or another, to recreate some version of them for their children. For example, the parents' own experiences with literacy in schooling may be explicitly present in their reactions to and evaluations of their children's experiences with literacy.[29]

These examples are intended to illustrate the kinds of concepts that may help to direct attention to an examination of the moment-to-moment processes of education that take place within families.

THE FAMILY'S RELATION TO OTHER
INSTITUTIONS THAT EDUCATE

An understanding of the family's relation to a host of other institutions is crucial. The experiences of children in school, of parents in places of work, are all brought home on a daily basis, and, to some extent, they enter into the educational arena of the family. Beyond these other institutions, the media, as powerful forms of education, often consume extraordinary amounts of family time.[30] Thus there is both a general problem of understanding the family's relation to a variety of other institutions that educate, and a particular problem of understanding the way in which the media, especially television, are experienced within families.

The concept of mediation illustrates possible approaches to the ways in which experiences outside the family are modified and transformed by experience within it, and how individuals move through, engage in, and combine educative experiences over a lifetime.[31] I use the concept of mediation here to refer to those processes by which the family (or any other institution) filters educational influences—the processes by which it "screens, interprets, criticizes, reinforces, complements, counteracts, refracts, and transforms."[32] While the term "mediation" is sometimes used to refer to processes of negotiation in situations of conflict (for example, mediation in labor union-employer negotiations), my use of the term here is intended to convey a broader meaning. It refers to the ways in which the family negotiates and creates meaning in the educational experiences of its members, both adults and children. The family mediates not only with respect to the school, but with respect to other institutions, particularly television.

In considering the impact television has upon children, and upon adults as well, the rationale for focusing on the mediation of the family with respect to television is important. At least some considerations of television assume implicitly that television has its impact in a direct manner—what is viewed is what is seen, or what is presented is what is learned. Yet if we approach the impact of television taking into account the "profound ironies" in education, whereby "what is taught is not always what is learned, and vice versa,"[33] we realize that there are often unintended consequences in education of all kinds, and that this applies to television as well. In short, television viewing occurs in the context of a familial setting in which discussions, criticisms, and appraisals of television take place in one way or another, both formally and informally. And, while the extent of the family's explicit supervision of television viewing, or the ways in which families make decisions with respect to viewing choices, may vary enormously from one family to another, the impact of television upon its members cannot be understood without considering the kinds of mediation that take place on a moment-to-moment basis, particularly those that are embedded in other family activities.

In one study of the mediation of television by the family, which made use of intensive, round-the-clock ethnographic observations in families, it became clear that the extent to which the family mediates television requires taking into account fleeting verbal comments and reactions. In one situation, for example, a mother, in reacting to a television ad, merely said, "Humph," but this implied a substantial criticism and a range of understandings about her view of the commercial that was shared by the family members.[34] To catch such fleeting comments and reactions, it is necessary to observe discussions of television that take place in non-television-viewing situations as well as those when the television is being actively watched. We may come to very different conclusions about parental supervision of television viewing if we do not include observations of sufficient breadth and scope so that we can consider moment-to-moment reactions to television—comments that participants themselves might not be aware they are making.

Improving Education in Families

Given the importance of families as educators, it is inevitable that school administrators, teachers, parents, and other educational practitioners should try to find ways of improving familial education. A long tradition of such efforts exists. Educators, not only in schools, but in religious institutions, health organizations, and in the media, have developed a wide range of programs to improve education in families. Such programs vary in focus, encompassing efforts to improve relationships between families and schools as well as efforts to improve educational practices and interpersonal relationships within homes. They vary, moreover, in level of sophistication and in the kinds of underlying assumptions that they make about the nature of education and child development. Detailed reviews of such efforts can be found elsewhere. Two classic reviews that analyze the features of parent education efforts are provided by Brim and by Harman and Brim.[35]

Whether efforts to improve education in families are focused on relationships between families and schools or on improving education as it takes place within the home, they necessarily require concepts for thinking about families as educators. The review of concepts in this chapter is intended to offer guidance for those who wish to enlarge their understanding of families as educators for purposes of developing a particular program, working with a particular child, or undertaking broader policy considerations.

My argument here is that education in families cannot necessarily be improved by attempting to make it more like that in schools. Policies of increased homework, greater parental supervision, and encouragement of diligence, while they may be applicable to some families, are not based on an understanding of the complex dynamics of family life. They are narrowly directed toward enhancing those areas where education in families is similar to that in schools. This may well be appropriate in many instances, but it fails to take account of the rich and varied processes by which education takes place within families.

FOOTNOTES

1. Edward C. Banfield, *The Unheavenly City* (Boston: Little, Brown, and Co., 1970), pp. 229-31. See also "Babies for Sale," *New York Times*, 13 October 1970. For a discussion of these and related issues, see Hope Jensen Leichter, "The School and Parents," in *The Teacher's Handbook*, ed. Dwight W. Allen and Eli Seifman (Glenview, Ill.: Scott, Foresman, and Co., 1971).

2. For one recent discussion of issues in bilingual education, see Richard Rodriguez, *Hunger of Memory: The Education of Richard Rodriguez* (Boston: David R. Godine, 1981).

3. See Nicholas Hobbs, *The Futures of Children* (San Francisco: Jossey-Bass, 1975). For a related discussion, see idem, "Families, Schools, and Communities: An Ecosystem for Children," in *Families and Communities as Educators*, ed. Hope Jensen Leichter (New York: Teachers College Press, 1979), pp. 192-202.

4. For a discussion of these and related issues, see Urie Bronfenbrenner, "Who Needs Parent Education?" in *Families and Communities as Educators*, ed. Leichter, pp. 203-223.

5. See National Commission on Excellence in Education, *A Nation at Risk: The Imperative for Educational Reform* (Washington, D.C.: U.S. Department of Education, 1983), p. 35.

6. This literature is reviewed in Hope Jensen Leichter, ed., *The Family as Educator* (New York: Teachers College Press, 1974), and in idem, *Families and Communities as Educators*. An agenda-setting article in each of these volumes outlines the basic research issues and the scope of the volume.

7. Studies recently completed or currently in progress in the Elbenwood Center for the Study of the Family as Educator, Teachers College, Columbia University, are illustrative of recent research on families as educators. These studies include (1) "The Family's Role in the Acquisition of Literacy for Learning"—a study of the family's role in helping children to move from the early acquisition of literacy skills to the use of literacy in other kinds of learning; (2) "An Examination of Cognitive Processes in Everyday Family Life"—a study of the intellectual processes inherent in everyday family activities; (3) "The Mediation of Television by the Family"—a study of the ways in which families mediate the television experiences of their members; (4) "Social Networks and Educative Styles"—a study of the ways in which teenagers move through, engage in, and combine educative experiences in a variety of settings from family to school to neighborhood; and (5) "The Role of Memory within the Family"—a study centered upon memory as social interaction within families.

8. John Naisbitt, *Megatrends* (New York: Warner Books, 1982).

9. Ruth Schwartz Cowan, *More Work for Mother: The Ironies of Household Technology from the Open Hearth to the Microwave* (New York: Basic Books, 1983).

10. Hope Jensen Leichter, "The Concept of Educative Style," *Teachers College Record* 75 (December 1973): 23-50.

11. I am grateful to Jerome Bruner for a useful discussion of the issues of presuppositional structures in familial discourse.

12. I am examining this point in a study of "The Role of Memory in the Family."

13. Clifford Hill and Herve Varenne, "Familial Language and Education: The Socio-Linguistic Model of Restrictive and Elaborative Codes," *Social Science Information*, No. 20 (February 1981): 187-228.

14. Hope Jensen Leichter, "Families as Environments for Literacy," in *Awakening to Literacy*, ed. Hillel Goelman, Antoinette Oberg, and Frank Smith (New York: Heinemann Educational Books, 1984).

15. Leichter, ed., *The Family as Educator*.

16. Lawrence A. Cremin, "Further Notes toward a Theory of Education," in *Notes on Education*, No. 4 (New York: Institute of Philosophy and Politics of Education, Teachers College, Columbia University, 1974), p. 1. See also, idem, "Family-Community Linkages in American Education: Some Comments on the Recent Historiography," in Leichter, ed., *Families and Communities as Educators*, p. 137.

17. Lawrence A. Cremin, "Notes toward a Theory of Education," in *Notes on Education*, No. 1 (New York: Institute of Philosophy and Politics of Education, Teachers College, Columbia University, 1973), p. 5.

18. Leichter, ed., *The Family as Educator*.

19. Some of the analysis of materials for this project has been reported in Herve Varenne, Vera Hamid-Buglione, Raymond P. McDermott, and Ann Morison, "*I Teach Him Everything He Learns in School*": *The Acquisition of Literacy for Learning in Working Class Families*, a report to the National Institute of Education (New York: Elbenwood Center for the Study of Family as Educator, Teachers College, Columbia University, 1982) and in Ann Morison, "Getting Reading and Writing: Literacy Patterns in Three Urban Families" (Doctoral dissertation, Teachers College, Columbia University, 1982.)

20. Approaches to the study of literacy in the family are discussed more fully in Leichter, "Families as Environments for Literacy." I presented a related discussion in "Family and Community Contexts of Literacy: Contrasts and Continuities" (Paper given at the Annual Meeting of the American Educational Research Association, Los Angeles, 1981).

21. Margaret Mead, "Grandparents as Educators," in *The Family as Educator*, ed. Leichter, pp. 66-75.

22. See the discussion of the education of parents by children in Leichter, ed., *The Family as Educator*, pp. 15-17.

23. Leichter, "The Concept of Educative Style."

24. See Leichter, ed., *The Family as Educator*, especially pp. 23-25. See also Hope Jensen Leichter and William E. Mitchell, *Kinship and Casework* (New York: Russell Sage Foundation, 1967), enl. ed., *Kinship and Casework: Family Networks and Social Intervention* (New York: Teachers College Press, 1978).

25. Leichter, ed., *Families and Communities as Educators*.

26. For further details, see Jennifer W. Bryce, "Families and Television: An Ethnographic Approach" (Doctoral dissertation, Teachers College, Columbia University, 1980) and Durre-Sameed Ahmed, "Television in Pakistan: An Ethnographic Study" (Doctoral dissertation, Teachers College, Columbia University, 1983). See also, Jennifer W. Bryce and Hope Jensen Leichter, "The Family and Television: Forms of Mediation," *Journal of Family Issues* 4 (June 1983): 309-328.

27. Bryce and Leichter, "The Family and Television."

28. Ezra F. Vogel and Norman W. Bell, "The Child as the Family Scapegoat," in *A Modern Introduction to the Family*, ed. Norman W. Bell and Ezra F. Vogel, rev. ed. (New York: Free Press, 1968), pp. 412-27.

29. Leichter, "Families as Environments for Literacy."

30. Bryce and Leichter, "The Family and Television."

31. Leichter, "The Concept of Educative Style."

32. For further discussion of the concept of mediation, see Hope Jensen Leichter, "Families and Communities as Educators: Some Concepts of Relationship," in *Families and Communities as Educators*, ed. Leichter, pp. 32-40.

33. Cremin, "Notes toward a Theory of Education."

34. Bryce and Leichter, "The Family and Television."

35. Orville G. Brim, Jr., *Education for Child Rearing* (New York: Russell Sage Foundation, 1959). See also David Harman and Orville G. Brim, Jr., *Learning to Be Parents: Principles, Programs, and Methods* (Beverly Hills: Sage Publications, 1980).

CHAPTER VI

The Workplace as Educator

MARVIN FELDMAN

The modern corporation does everything schools do, and more. Corporations test and corporations counsel. They instruct and they motivate. Most have placement departments. Many field athletic teams and sponsor a wide variety of interest groups. In the early days of capitalism, many provided housing and undoubtedly some still do. Most corporations of any size have medical departments for both treatment and prevention. The corporation has been described as a community—even as a culture. Japanese corporations, for example, have company songs.

The corporation certainly, and to some extent every workplace, is involved in educational activities. There are generally three types of workplace education: the largely unstructured experience of working; the more or less structured training or education in processes and products specific to the company; and training or education in more general principles or practices that are in some way necessary to the job but are also transferable to other jobs and other pursuits.

Clearly the experience of working is itself a learning experience. We see universal evidence of this in the widespread requirement of experience as a condition of employment. When Henry Ford told his recruiters not to discriminate in hiring, he was expressing his conviction that everyone was equally inexperienced in the new requirements of assembly-line production. But now, work experience is almost always desirable and often imperative.

Experience, almost by definition, cannot be taught in school. The Harvard Business School has taken great pains to simulate in the classroom some of the complexities, uncertainties, and tensions of the atmosphere in which business decisions are made. That effort has been successful to a remarkable degree. But the school increasingly requires several years of work experience for admission and is quick to acknowledge that while the case method provides a useful introduction to the real world, there is, in the end, no substitute for experience.

In terms of experience, at least, there can be no jurisdictional dispute between the workplace and the school. But in other educational activities of the workplace, there is great overlap. The activities of educators and employers are not readily distinguishable, and there are large, unsettled questions about where the responsibilities of the one leave off and the other begin.

In-plant, job-specific training is the second great area of workplace learning. It takes a thousand forms, depending on the size and nature of the business, the inclinations of the management, and the availability of resources. Some programs are formal; some are highly informal. Some are conducted in the company by the company. Others are the result of contracts with public or private educational institutions or with private vendors of educational services. Some are the result of collaboration with unions or trade associations.

A famous, if scarcely typical, example is the Xerox residential corporate education center at Leesburg, Virginia. There are courses in sales, service, and management for Xerox employees. There is a full-time faculty of 500 and a capacity of about a thousand students. Every new Xerox salesperson goes to Leesburg for an introductory course and returns from time to time for supplementary courses. There are fifty courses for service people and a wide range of management courses. These courses are, for the most part, Xerox courses. The sales courses are not simply courses in the general principles of salesmanship, although these inevitably are involved. They are courses in how to sell Xerox products. Product-specific and process-specific learning programs like Leesburg will undoubtedly continue and probably expand.

But a surprisingly large and growing part of workplace learning is in areas normally thought of as the province of the school. To the degree that teaching is costly, the corporation is always a reluctant general educator. It will not pay for what it can get free. A corporation teaches reading because it needs more literate employees than it can find or because it wishes to contribute in this way to the public good. It is in this third area of general learning that the questions of the proper division of educational responsibility loom largest. I will return to this issue presently.

The total educational effort of corporate America is astonishing in size. Marsha Levine and Denis Doyle of the American Enterprise Institute point out that industry spends almost as much for education as do *all* public postsecondary institutions.[1] The American Society for Training and Development puts the figure at $30 billion a year, not including the wages and salaries of those being trained.

Before the recent breakup, A. T. & T. was spending more than $700 million a year for education. The Company employed thousands of instructors in hundreds of training centers.

The General Motors Institute (GMI) is the only fully accredited college in the United States operated by a corporation. Three General Motors presidents have been graduates, as are four of its present top fifteen executives.

GMI, with an enrollment of 2,300, offers a five-year program, alternating work and study in twelve-week chunks. General Motors is not obligated to offer graduates jobs; similarly, graduates do not have to take them if they are offered. But most do and 60 percent of them have spent their whole working lives with the company.

Four corporations now confer bachelor's degrees: IBM, Xerox, General Electric, and A. T. & T. Arthur D. Little Co. can confer a master's degree in business administration.

More and more corporations, however, are moving toward the GMI model and forming universities. When Wang Laboratories could find only two master's programs in software engineering in the whole country, it launched a program of its own, now approved by the Massachusetts Board of Education. Arthur D. Little Co. also grants degrees that are approved by that same agency.

In New York State, the Board of Regents accredits courses offered outside the system through its external degree program. The American Council on Education has a Program on Non-Collegiate Sponsored Instruction. It has found 2,000 courses offered by 138 corporations that deserve accreditation.

One of the vital educational frontiers is the increasing, conscious, and systematic collaboration of the school and the workplace. These collaborations have led educators and employers to think through carefully which institution does which educational task best. Which are the special competencies of the school and which are the unique abilities of the employer? Which forms of collaboration best combine the distinctive qualities of both?

Apprenticeship programs are usually joint ventures of unions and employers. By the end of 1979, 320,000 people were enrolled in apprenticeship programs. Probably the best established method of collaboration between schools and employers is cooperative education. Pioneered in the 1960s by the National Commission for Cooperative Education, it has grown until 1,000 institutions and 8,500 corporations participate in cooperative programs.

Tuition-aid programs have become nearly universal among corporations of any size. Of those corporations the National Industrial Conference Board surveyed, virtually all of those with more than a thousand employees and 82 percent of the companies with 500-1000 employees have some kind of tuition-aid program.

One of the best examples of a newer form of collaboration between a corporation and a community college involves Textronix, Inc. in Beaverton, Oregon. Textronix is the largest employer in Oregon and the most important producer of oscilloscopes in the world.

In 1957, ten years after it was founded, the Company established what became one of the nation's most extensive corporate education programs. Unofficially called Tek Tech, it has served 85 percent of the company's 18,000 employees at one time or another.

Tek Tech was founded simply because the company could not find the skilled people it needed and there were then no institutions in the area to train them. When Portland Community College was opened in 1968, about half the Tek Tech enrollment was shifted to the College after careful consultations.

In this way, a careful, collaborative decision was made, presumably a course at a time. Some courses were judged to be best offered by the college and some by the corporation.

A surprising number of corporations are already offering degree programs at their plants, most often provided by a nearby educational institution. The National Institute for Work and Learning (formerly the Manpower Institute) estimates that 5 percent of the corporations with 500 or more employees have such programs, but the number is increasing rapidly. "This is the trend of the future," says Donald W. Fletcher, Associate Dean for Extended Education at California State University and College.

Burroughs Corporation has a program provided by the Detroit College of Business. Aetna Life and Casualty has a similar arrangement with the University of Hartford, as does the First Pennsylvania Bank with Temple University. There are dozens of others.

In Connecticut, Manchester Community College has worked with United Technologies' Pratt and Whitney Aircraft Group for a number of years. The program began with a three-year, thirty-unit apprenticeship program conducted by the College at the plant. But when employees sought to complete their degrees at other colleges, they encountered a discouraging thicket of problems. The company contracted with the College to provide thirty more liberal arts credits, and it is extending the whole program to three other plant sites, working with three other local community colleges.

A. T. & T. has made similar arrangements with a number of institutions in the New York-New Jersey area, including Middlesex Community College.

In a working arrangement with John Wood Community College in Illinois, the Harris Corporation contributes the technical instruction, the facilities, and the equipment. The College contributes administrative services, counseling, and remedial education.

For more than twenty years, Union College in Schenectady has accredited General Electric's courses for advanced degrees in power system engineering. Nor is the movement limited to corporations. Unions, trade groups, and government agencies are offering courses with college credit.

Smaller businesses have exceptional requirements. They need qualified people at least as urgently as larger employers, but they are less able to provide training.

The fashion industry is a clear example. It is the nation's third largest industry, but it is composed primarily of a very large number of very small units. There are a number of large firms in the field, but there are literally thousands of little ones and their ability to provide educational services internally is limited. The Fashion Institution of Technology in New York City (a public institution) was created to serve this need.

As technological change forces itself on the industry, the need for education is becoming more or less continuous. Employers, particularly the smaller ones, are turning increasingly to the schools for help in research and development, training and retraining, even in outplacement. By every indication, we are entering a new era of collaboration between the school and the corporation.

A growing segment of the corporate effort is remedial. Beverly McQuigg, a Bell System training supervisor, puts the matter plainly:

Traditionally, Americans have relied heavily on formal schools to prepare young people to enter the labor force. This reliance is fading fast. There is a growing public perception that the school system is not keeping abreast, that there is a wide chasm between the courses schools offer and the training people need for work.[2]

In 1977, the Conference Board reported that more than a third of the companies they surveyed offered remedial education of some kind, some of them for employees with college and advanced degrees. A.T. & T. spends $6 million a year for remedial education. Polaroid has run an extensive in-house remedial program for ten years.

Levine and Doyle believe that the surging growth of education by industry indicates, above all, inadequacies and inaccuracies in the product of the educational establishment. They write:

The increase in private sector investment in education is related to qualitative deficiencies in public sector education. Too many workers are poorly prepared, and too many public schools are not offering the kind and quality of education employees need. The private sector turned to its own education and training in the 1960s and 1970s not because too few people were being educated but because those who were, were not being educated well enough. The manpower skills employers needed were not for sale in the marketplace. . . . Business and industry are questioning the ability of public schools to produce a competent work force that is adequately and appropriately educated.[3]

Clearly, the educational activities of schools and workplaces are intermingled and will become more so. Sometimes this collaboration has been deliberate, but more often it has been the result of chance and accident. Unfortunately, there has been no methodical search for the best division of responsibility between school and workplace; it is now long overdue.

Moreover, there are some unresolved ethical, political, and pedagogical questions. None of them is new, but they have gained a new importance and have produced some practical stresses. A necessarily adaptable, profit-driven sector looks for manpower in a nonprofit sector which is under less immediate pressure to adopt change. But this same circumstance raises other questions. To what extent should schools shape students to the requirements of the workplace and to what extent should educators ignore the requirements of the workplace (thus, perhaps, making their graduates less employable) and insist on a more balanced and broadly liberal learning experience? What is the proper balance?

The hazard, of course, is that in collaborating the school will lose its sense of identity and become amorphous and indistinct, unable to make a clear, compelling claim on the interest and support of the community. It is becoming more and more important for schools to know who they are educating and why.

As schools form more contractual relationships with business organizations, there is a danger of excessive dependence on such contracts—a risk that the school will become simply a supplier of educational services defined by others, indistinguishable from commercial institutions.

The school, however, is the steward of a community's larger educational responsibility. The school must bring to contractual arrangements a sense of the noncommercial values that must nourish any true educational effort.

There is a story, perhaps an invented one, about a major corporation that asked a college to develop a model liberal arts course for its executives. But when the year-long course was finished, it was judged a failure—and a dangerous one—and was cancelled straightaway. Some of the participants had become so excited about history, literature, and philosophy that the intensity of their interest in business was compromised. Regardless of the story's authenticity, it raises the question of institutional integrity. Clearly educators must be more than uncritical vendors of educational services. They cannot devise or offer programs that are unworthy, that do not first of all serve the student, that are in any way unbalanced. Educators should insist that proper attention be paid to the liberal arts and the fine arts. It is not the business of education to program and reprogram automatons, but to help people become more complete, freer of disabling limitations of every kind.

Two IBM officials, Lewis M. Branscomb and Paul C. Gilmore, have explored the issue in an article in *Daedalus*.[4] In one way, it is enormously helpful when industry helps society meet "the huge costs of [its] learning requirements." But, they caution, the expansion of industry's educational involvement may make it more difficult than ever for "the committed, disciplined, and managed environment of highly structured [corporate] training to be affected by the skeptical attitude of the scholar and the innovative imagination of the research-er."[5]

That quality—that commitment to a larger educational agenda—is becoming more urgent than ever.

There is another issue: is it proper for publicly supported institutions to provide a service which, otherwise, profit-making institutions would have to provide for themselves? Why should the taxpayers pay the costs of training people for Sears or Exxon or General Motors?

The operative principle is a very simple one. The educator's responsibility is to students, and students are the primary beneficiaries of educational programs. (This ethical question often occurs in reverse. Students go to work for large companies, using them deliberately as a training ground for later business ventures of their own.) Training in techniques so particular to a single company that they have no application elsewhere should clearly be paid by that company. Otherwise, the ethical question dissolves in the larger permanent value of educational programs to the learner.

We have been hearing about the imminence of the postindustrial society for so long we have begun to wonder whether it would ever come at all. Daniel Bell began to prophesy its coming thirty or more years ago. But now it has come. The information revolution is here. We need no longer use the future tense in discussing it. Before it is finished, it will alter society more profoundly—and more beneficial-ly—than the first mechanical phase of the industrial revolution. It is not only changing the way work is done in factories and offices; it is changing the way factories and offices are organized. And it has radically altered the educational agenda and, at the same time, the means with which the demands of that new agenda can be met.

As we enter this postindustrial era, the size and shape of the educational task are changing radically and rapidly. Education, no matter how and by whom it will be provided, is confronting a greatly altered agenda.

As the children of the baby boom have passed through the schools, enrollments are declining and, according to some estimates, will continue to decline for some years. But, at the same time, the need to reeducate those who have already passed through the system is increasing enormously. *Business Week* estimates that no fewer than 45 million members of the present work force will need to be retrained in the years just ahead.

Our whole economy is converting to a new, dramatically different technological base. The particular character of technological change—electronic data processing, robotics, and all the related technologies—will sharply reduce the demand for unskilled labor while it greatly increases the demand for technicians. The problem is cruelly illustrated by the current surplus of assembly-line workers and the acute, disabling shortages of software engineers and computer programmers. The tasks unskilled people have performed in factories and offices since the beginning of the industrial era will increasingly be performed by machines. The entry-level job in the factory of the future will be as the "supervisor" of an automatic machine.

There is already evidence that technology may push everybody in the system up a notch. The so-called rank-and-file will require the skills and personal traits now required of supervisors. First-line supervisors will need the skills and human relations abilities of managers. And so on. A middle-aged Bell Laboratories researcher told a surveyor that he could remember only two or three years in his adult life when he was not taking classes of one sort or another. His experience is probably the wave of the future. Education, whether in school or at work or in some collaborative combination, will become a lifelong process.

Above all, the future will require that some of the traditional delineations of which institutions should do what for whom be revised. It is too easy to assume that industry knows the technical specifics and that schools know how to teach; the matter is far more complicated than that. Schools can learn from corporations about teaching and corporations can learn from schools about technology and even about management.

For example, the corporate world is far ahead of most schools in the use of sophisticated systems of self-instruction. Multimedia educational modules built on programmed instruction have been brought to a very high level of effectiveness. A bank official describes a typing program that brings a trainee promptly "from zero knowledge to thirty words per minute through self-instruction programs. . . . The instructors show students how to use the equipment, and students come in at their convenience."

An executive in a large chemical corporation told the Conference Board: "Colleges could utilize self-study media such as computer-assisted, or managed, instruction, for a number of 'mass courses' such as freshman math, statistics and sociology." According to the Conference Board, "Most business executives are critical of the performance of the nation's schools and colleges in preparing people for work, and deplore particularly the lacks they find in communications and mathematical skills among younger employees. Most believe, further, that these institutions would do well to emulate industry in its growing emphasis on student participation, the blending of classroom study with both programmed self-study and planned problem-solving experience, the tailoring of curricula to clearly defined goals and individual needs, and the employment of advanced instructional technologies."[6]

An overwhelming majority of the corporate executives surveyed by the Conference Board believes that some of industry's educational methods could advantageously be adopted by institutional educators: "stress on greater student involvement in education processes; tailoring of methods, course length, and curriculum to individual needs; and increased use of instructional technologies."

According to the Conference Board report, executives stress the importance of participative two-way techniques "and thus a greater role for students influencing how and at what rate they are taught." An executive in a food manufacturing company wrote, "Learning methods that stress peer support and teamwork, and that involve participation, self-instruction and self-evaluation, are missing in the schools but are essential in a business environment." Ironically, an aerospace executive wanted "more emphasis on cooperation and less on competition." A publications executive wanted a "loosening up [of the] rigidities of course-length instruction" and greater use of course modules.

* * *

This new collaborative era is making some new and unfamiliar demands on educators. For years, educators have seen business as a strange, separate world. But, if business is to be complementary to institutional education rather than competitive with it, educators must begin to form partnerships—joint educational ventures—with business. Business and industry have already initiated a number of partnerships with the schools that include providing scholarships to promising students; training programs for teachers; funding for special school programs, particularly in science and technology; and materials and resources that are not within the financial reach of most schools.

While these partnerships are currently growing, it is important for educators to remember that business—except the growing proprietary education industry—is not naturally an aggressive contender for educational responsibility. The corporation considers itself an educator of last resort. Any corporate incursion into areas where educators are willing and able to function is the result of a communications failure.

Educators must educate themselves about the educational needs of business and about the educational capacities of business. It must open its doors wide to the business community. It must solicit searching appraisals of the strengths and weaknesses of the institutional product.

And, above all, educators must learn to pool information, to trade techniques, to share experiences. Educators must participate in the meetings of business groups and invite business people to participate in theirs.

Educators, and the students they serve, have everything to gain— and almost nothing to lose—if they welcome the business educator as a partner in a common cause.

Footnotes

1. Marsha Levine and Denis P. Doyle, "Private Meets Public: An Examination of Contemporary Education," in *Meeting Human Needs: Toward a New Public Philosophy*, ed. Jack A. Meyer (Washington, D.C.: American Enterprise Institute for Public Policy Research, 1982), p. 277.

2. Beverly McQuigg, "The Role of Education in Industry," *Phi Delta Kappan* 61 (January 1980): 324.

3. Levine and Doyle, "Private Meets Public," p. 278.

4. Lewis M. Branscomb and Paul C. Gilmore, "Education in Private Industry," *Daedalus* 104 (Winter 1975): 222-33.

5. Ibid., p. 232.

6. Seymour Lusterman, *Education in Industry* (New York: The Conference Board, 1977), p. 1.

CHAPTER VII

Museums and Schools: A Meaningful Partnership

BONNIE PITMAN-GELLES

"A museum can be a powerhouse," thinks Dillon Ripley, Secretary of the Smithsonian Institution, though only if "museum people and the public get away from the 'attic' mentality."[1] While it is universally recognized that the objects in the collections and exhibitions are the heart of a museum, there is still considerable discussion among educators and museum professionals about the role museums can and do play in helping people learn. One problem is that museums are not easily defined as formal educational institutions with a curriculum, students, and a faculty. Museums have a different mission and carry out their responsibilities for collecting, preserving, and interpreting their collections in hundreds of different ways.

The "power" that a museum has is contained in the learning it fosters through the objects it displays. The impact of these objects on a child or adult—whether in a school group, family outing, or on a visit with a friend—is real and immediate. Learners can engage in an experience that involves all of their senses or they may be provoked to use their imagination as they view a skeleton of a whale, walk around a brontosaurus examining the feet, or pause for a moment in front of a tomb figure from ancient Egypt. Such images can be imprinted in a visitor's mind for a lifetime. The physical reality of objects in an exhibit, previously known to the viewer only through books, slides, or television, can lead to a new level of understanding. When confronted with an object's actual size, color, weight, and mass, the viewer is led to a type of learning that is both demanding and exciting. Many visitors walk away when they do not recognize an object, saying that they cannot look at it. It takes time and practice to "read" an object visually, as well as verbally (labels or catalogs). But truly to see and learn more—this is in large measure the mission of museum education.

Though museums have always presented exhibitions to the public, it is only in the last one hundred years that museums have taken seriously the responsibility of the "education" of visitors. Like universities, museums are responsible for research and publications, but museums also have to communicate information about their collections to the public through exhibitions and programs.

The development of museums in America began slowly. The Charleston Museum, established in 1773 as a museum of natural history, was America's first museum. The Smithsonian Institution, created by Congress in 1846 for the "increase and diffusion of knowledge," was chiefly devoted to research until George Brown Goode joined as the Assistant Secretary in 1873 and developed the Smithsonian as a center for science, arts, and the humanities. In the 1870s, three other great American museums were founded: in New York, the American Museum of Natural History and the Metropolitan Museum of Art, and in Boston, the Museum of Fine Arts. The founders of these museums believed in their educational values, which were embodied in their charters. At the turn of the century, with the introduction of the automobile and increased mobility for Americans, less traditional kinds of museums were established—museums in national parks, and museums of preservation projects, and outdoor museums (for example, Colonial Williamsburg in 1926). These museums drew millions of visitors who traveled in the family car.

The turn of the century, in fact, saw American museums becoming centers of education and public enlightenment. The first gallery teachers, or docents, were introduced by the Museum of Fine Arts in Boston in 1907 to help visitors see and learn more about the beauty of the collections. The turn of the century also brought about the establishment of children's museums, first in Brooklyn in 1899 and later in Boston in 1913. These first children's museums and the hundreds of others that have followed were founded by teachers and parents interested in supplementing school programs with real specimens and artifacts. Initially concerned with natural science, the subject matter has been broadened to include all aspects of daily life, aesthetics, history, cultures, science, and computers.

By the end of the 1930s, Frederick E. Keppel, president of the

Carnegie Corporation, observed that the shift in emphasis from the "custodial function" of the American museum to its "opportunities for educational and other services" had become an accomplished fact. During these years, interest also increased in science and technology and how they were shaping our future. A new type of museum that was able to communicate to the public all of the contributions, dangers, and potential of science and technology in society opened in Chicago in 1933 as the Museum of Science and Industry. Such museums are more concerned with transmitting information and involving the visitor in learning and discovery through new exhibits and programs than they are with collecting and preserving objects from the past.

Museums took another leap forward during the 1960s when funds for education and cultural activities were plentiful. In addition, the Tax Reform Act of 1969 defined gift benefits to "educational and charitable organizations" in such a way that museums wanted to be considered as educational institutions under the law. Because the definition of an educational institution is broadly conceived, it allows museums to present themselves as centers of a learning process that occurs primarily through objects.

Museums are no longer "cabinets of curiosities," but places where unique educational resources and opportunities are available to children, their parents, and their teachers. Today's museums include public spaces such as exhibition galleries, bookstores, restaurants, planetariums, auditoriums, classrooms and libraries, nature trails, art studios, insect zoos, and media production facilities. People browse, ask questions, explore, investigate, study. They may borrow paintings and fossils to take to their homes or classrooms.

The international community has recognized the educational work of American museums for some time; in the opinion of Germain Bazin, a chief curator of the Louvre:

Perhaps the most significant contribution America has made to the concept of the museum is in the field of education. It is common practice for a museum to offer lectures and concerts, show films, circulate exhibitions, publish important works of art. The museum has metamorphosed into a university for the general public—an institution of learning and enjoyment for all men. The concept has come full circle. The museum of the future will more and more resemble the academy of learning the *mousseion* connoted for the Greeks.[2]

Learning in the Museum Environment

Today, we commonly acknowledge that people must continue to learn throughout their lives. The rapid social, economic, and technological changes in our world cause information to become quickly outdated and require people to view education as a lifetime process. For schools, this means that the focus is not on just the subject matter that must be taught, but on the skills to learn—to learn how to learn, to be motivated to learn, and to experience the joy of learning through accomplishments. Museums are in many ways ideal components for lifelong learning experiences. They provide endless sources of ideas and amazement and can almost be seen as encyclopedias of objects, a resource waiting to be discovered and used.

Malcolm S. Knowles has recommended a set of learning skills that should be taught in schools. This list of skills also applies to learning in museums. Knowles's skills for learning include:

1. The ability to develop and to be in touch with curiosities. Another way to describe this skill would be the ability to engage in divergent thinking.

2. The ability to formulate questions, based on one's curiosities, that are answerable through inquiry (in contrast to questions that are answerable by authority or faith). This skill is the beginning of the ability to engage in convergent thinking or inductive-deductive reasoning.

3. The ability to identify the data required to answer the various kinds of questions.

4. The ability to locate the most relevant and reliable sources of the required data (including experts, teachers, colleagues, one's own experience, printed material, computers, the various audio-visual media, and the community).

5. The ability to select and use the most efficient means for collecting the required data from the appropriate sources.

6. The ability to organize, analyze, and evaluate the data so as to get valid answers to questions.

7. The ability to generalize, apply, and communicate the answers to the questions raised.[3]

Theodore Lownik Library
Illinois Benedictine College
Lisle, Illinois 60532

Children and adults who come to museums have a variety of learning skills, and, under the proper conditions, they can use these skills to acquire knowledge and develop perceptual awareness. Unfortunately, many museums present barriers to visitors learning as much as they might by failing to provide sufficient information on the purpose, content, and organization of the exhibit or program. Museums that take seriously the responsibility of providing a learning environment are concerned with the *visitor's* ability to have better access to information and ideas. This access might consist of labels, a discovery room, tour, audio-visual orientation center, or interpretive programs, to name a few. The museums that succeed in developing learning environments design programs and exhibits that provoke visitors to think or read more, to visit new places, seek new experiences, or increase their curiosity about something they have seen in the museum.

Each time a visitor enters a museum, the potential for seeing objects in new ways increases. As the visitor matures, gains experiences, or feels new emotions, he or she sees things in quite different ways. This personal response to objects is an important and inherent part of teaching and learning in museums. The individual response by the viewer must be nurtured, for it is part of creative thought and expression. The study of perception has long attracted the attention of the philosopher, the psychologist, aesthetician, historian, and art historian. Indeed, questions relating to visual awareness, visual thinking, and perception concern both laymen and specialists. In his book, *Visual Thinking*, Rudolf Arnheim points out that currently the school's educational activities are too biased toward verbal abstractions and that visual form is not recognized as a medium of productive thinking.[4]

Schools and museums vary in significant ways. Schools are based on the study of different subjects and are organized into curricula that require different levels of measured performance and achievement to move forward academically. In schools, schedules are set, time and content are regulated, objectives are established and measured. Frequently, children in a class are closely related in age but vary in social, economic, and educational backgrounds. Another distinction is that the school learning environment is primarily verbal, while the museum environment is visual, using objects in collections and exhibits.

Today, there is considerable discussion about how people learn in museums, and part of this debate centers on formal and informal learning. In truth, the museum experience includes both types of learning. Museum visits are generally perceived as "recreational" with some educational opportunities, but the main reason for going is not seen by visitors as "education."

Informal Learning

Museum exhibits, the primary educational resource that museums present to the public, are carefully planned and frequently have specific sequences in the presentation of the objects. These sequences form a determined pattern of movement through the exhibit. Also, various types of information are available for different learners. Nevertheless, the visitor may choose to follow the sequence and learn from the exhibit or walk past the cases without stopping to view the objects. This random access to information often is used to characterize the informal learning experience of a museum. Museums are not schools in the conventional sense; there is no set curriculum to be studied, but the open doors and numerous crannies offer a host of experiences and knowledge.

Other characteristics that are used to identify the museum as an informal learning environment are:

1. Attendance of visitors is voluntary.

2. Learners are self-directed, choosing what they will learn and how they will learn it.

3. There are no prerequisites for learning; no credentials or certificates of learning are needed to qualify the visitor for entrance.

4. The museum continuously serves a heterogeneous audience with diverse ages, interests, social and economic backgrounds, and life experiences.

5. Social interaction is encouraged, especially among friends and family.

6. There is no prescribed amount of time to be spent in the museum; visitors may come and go as they choose. They may come to the museum as many times as they wish and choose to look at exhibits or seek items for purchase in the gift shop.

Formal Learning in the Museum

Museums also provide more formal learning experiences through lectures, symposia, seminars and classes, and teacher training programs.

120MUSEUMS AND SCHOOLS

These programs have stated objectives. They require the learner to participate in a sequenced and structured event, and in some cases, they result in academic credit. Learners usually participate because they are personally motivated and interested in learning more about the subject matter. They may pay a fee for the program, but there may be few requirements for completing the course other than their own satisfaction. To learn about a specific topic, participants in the "formal" education programs of a museum are frequently grouped by age, interest, or experience. Often these programs are presented as an expressed curriculum and are organized in a series format with sequenced events.

Schools and universities have long recognized the valuable resources in a museum staff and in the collections. These institutions have established formal programs that give academic credit to teachers and students who successfully complete an officially adopted program that can range in length from one week to a year.

The discussion of the museum as a formal or informal learning environment is complex. There is an agenda, hidden or overt, articulated or unarticulated, that affects the informal learning in a museum exhibit, and it is often just as important as the pedagogical agenda of more formal educational learning. In fact, museums are not totally unconstrained learning environments. In developing exhibits, curators, though now always learner oriented, present images and ideas that are intended to have some desirable effect on the learner. Indeed, there is much that museum people have to know about their audiences, about the way to develop exhibits and programs to serve the audience, and about the ways to change the existing patterns for display and interpretation to the public.

Exhibitions as Learning Environments

As vibrant and lively institutions, museums large and small, specialized or varied, house and conserve the natural and man-made wonders of the world, the creativity of artists, scientists, writers, craftsmen, farmers, and others who have recorded their experiences. First and foremost, museums are collections of objects and specimens—dinosaur bones, Renaissance paintings, jade pendants. These objects allow people to inspect the old, and they promote new ideas and discoveries by the manner in which the staff and the visitors arrange and order the objects. The unique quality of museums as places of learning is that they present these concrete expressions of natural and human history to the public.

People come to museums individually and collectively in families or school groups to see the exhibitions and collections. They come to look, to learn, and often to participate. The museum experience can act as a catalyst, introducing people to new ideas and interests and motivating people to seek further knowledge through closer examination, return visits, or self study. Today museums offer interpretive programs and exhibits to help visitors acquire knowledge, concepts, and perceptual skills so that they can look and discover on their own. Exhibitions are at the center of a museum experience, for it is in the exhibit that the visitor is engaged either actively or passively in looking at the resources of a museum. But the types of exhibits are as varied as the individual museums themselves.

The written word is the most traditional supplement to objects on display. Labels, gallery guides, and catalogues are all used to help the learner identify the objects in the exhibition, to give background information, and to emphasize the main ideas or pose problems that the visitor can solve. Written materials and audio-visual materials such as slide tapes, video tapes, films and sound tapes, and video discs often accompany exhibits. They direct the visitor's learning by asking questions, giving information, and provoking the learner to continue to look. They also provide basic background information. With all of these resources, it is still the option of the learners to use them, for they can also walk past the label or tape and move on to the next interest.

Museums have been increasing the opportunities visitors have for learning from staff or volunteers who give tours, do demonstrations, or role play characters in the galleries. These learning experiences provide children with opportunities to ask questions, to see a process not easily described in a label, or to touch a live animal. It might be argued that the student who visits a gallery with a member of the museum's staff or a docent is the most privileged of all visitors. If the teacher is good, the student has the benefit of the most effective mediation between the museum's collections and his own mind: a responsive human presence. The teacher can and should be sensitive to the student's excitement and confusion. A good museum teacher can use interpretive skills on the spot to "design" an exhibit so that it is effective for the audience. The problem of this approach is the tremendous cost of an increased staff.

Designing an exhibition or learning environment for a museum requires the skill and knowledge of many different people. The curator is traditionally the lead member of the exhibition team. The curator brings together the objects to be presented to the public in the exhibition and also writes the catalogue. The curator's concern is primarily with the selection of objects to illustrate the ideas of the exhibit, the accuracy of the information, the preparation of written materials, and the presentation of the key concepts in the exhibit. The exhibition designer assists with the specific installation of the works, deciding the lighting, selecting the colors and type style, and laying out a pattern of movement through the gallery. The educator assists with the interpretation of the objects for the visitor. The educator trains the docents or staff members who will lead the public on tours and organizes the programs and events that accompany the exhibition. The educator also organizes and prepares materials for the appropriate audience. The primary concern of the educator is what and how the visitor can learn from objects.

These three main players—the curator, the exhibition designer, and the educator—create the museum's learning environment. Problems arise when the three do not collaborate to develop clear objectives for the exhibit or to assess the effectiveness of their work formally and informally. In fact, these three players often work in a hierarchical fashion, sometimes passing on defined responsibilities. The learning experience of the visitor may not have the same importance as the aesthetic or historical organization of the exhibition concepts. The supplementary written and audio-visual resources may be written in a fashion too erudite; they address the need of the museum staff to appear scholarly rather than the visitor's need to know and be stimulated to learn. The conflict over the visitor's experience and whether it should be directed by the "object-oriented" or the "learner-oriented" staff is an issue of debate in museum professions. Exhibits represent the main ideas of an institution, and, properly presented, they are the most tangible contact museums have with the public.

Learning through School Programs

Schools and museums have worked together for many years. Museum services to school children and teachers can be divided into three types of programs: (a) programs that occur when students visit the museum; (b) programs and services that are taken into the classroom; and (c) museum programs for training teachers. There are hundreds of ways that these services are organized depending on the types of collections that are used; the mandate of the museum to provide the service on a local, state, or national level; the geographic, ethnic, and economic resources. Though this chapter does not provide an opportunity to enumerate these programs, they are well documented in museum literature.[5]

SCHOOLS VISIT MUSEUMS

Tours by students of the collections within a museum are the most popular type of programs. They have changed a great deal in recent years. No longer are students led through the endless galleries by a harried docent who talks continuously while the students strain to understand what is being said, and while they attempt to catch a glimpse of the object. "Sightseeing" tours of the museum's treasures— the mummy, dinosaur, and diamonds—are an outdated format of education departments in most museums. They are being replaced by programs that involve and stimulate the learners' interest in acquiring new information. The activities used in the tours relate the objects in the collection to the learners' understanding of the world and help to develop their skills of observing, classifying, and generalizing information.

School classes that come to museums may be guided by the teacher or by a museum staff member or volunteer. Self-guided materials have been developed by museums in the form of teacher guides, training sessions, and workbooks. For example, the Museum of Science and Industry in Chicago has a Teacher's Guide that helps teachers to select the tours, demonstrations, and exhibits that relate most effectively to their curriculum. Moreover, it provides information on how to organize and book the tour, as well as suggestions for previsit activities.

Children frequently receive their first introduction to museums when they come with their school for a tour. Tour programs range in length from a single one-hour or half-day visit to a series of visits organized in a sequence and spaced over a year. With some programs, teachers are sent study guides, slides, or films to help prepare the students for their tour. Single-visit programs exist in some format in nearly every museum, and, like those at the Peabody Museum of Salem, they allow children to learn, in one hour, about the whale, its physical characteristics, its struggle for survival, and its death. The program includes a slide presentation that introduces the museum's collection of whaling materials and the natural history of the whale. The similarities and differences between whales and people are discussed as children are asked to breathe like whales, handle a whale vertebra, and then discuss other shared mammalian characteristics. The children enact scenes from a fifty-foot panoramic painting of a whaling voyage including life at sea, storms, and the killing of a whale. The tour continues with an examination of the whaler's life through the reading of prints, paintings, diaries, and other artifacts. The experiences of a single visit tour are intense, and provide a powerful introduction to children who may still struggle with the idea of what a museum is.

Because museums and schools recognize the limitations of a single visit, they emphasize programs that provide opportunities for preparing the students to return to the museum, or they offer follow-up activities in the classroom. Such sessions may last for half a day, overnight, or an entire year. Many of these programs also include teacher training sessions and resource materials.

A series of visits provides opportunities for a more focused and in-depth look at the museum's collections. Teachers have a greater role in the program and help students to learn while they gain experience in working with the objects. The advantages of series or in-depth programs include increased time in the galleries, opportunities for a variety of learning experiences such as workshops, demonstrations, and handling objects. The National Zoological Park in Washington, D. C., offers a good example of this type of programming in "Zoo Animals—A Closer Look." This program is available to fourth graders and includes seven sessions, one in the classroom and six at the zoo. Also included is a teacher workshop that is required for participation in the program.

Programs for credit, like series programs, are often the result of joint planning between the museum staff and the classroom teacher. Courses for credit, offered by museums in association with school districts, have increased in number as public education has begun to make expanded use of community organizations and out-of-school learning environments. In offering courses for credit to students at the elementary or secondary levels, museums must pay close attention to curriculum requirements and be prepared to meet all of the specifications set forth by the board of education, which often requires that the museum adapt its objectives for a program. Students enrolled in these programs work at the museum just as they would in the classroom.

One of the nationally recognized programs for credit is offered by the Exploratorium in San Francisco. Since it began eight years ago, the School in the Exploratorium has been experimenting with projects to improve science instruction in the public schools and to discover ways in which teachers, students, and curriculum developers can rely on the museum as an adjunct resource for learning and teaching. Through the School in the Exploratorium program (SITE), a school class can pursue a curriculum based on exhibits under the guidance of a SITE instructor. Public school classes spend one full school day each week for three to five weeks in the museum. The curriculum, developed by SITE staff, is based on the study of light, sound, and perception and includes such topics as reflection, refraction, color, eye physiology, visual perception, strobe and motion makers, the physics of sound, and music makers. Before the first session, the class visits the Exploratorium on a field trip, and participating teachers attend a teachers' workshop. Each session combines discussion, experimentation, and small-group exploration of exhibits. Students and teachers design projects associated with the session's ideas to take back to school. While at the Exploratorium, the students study related exhibits, conduct experiments, and learn about their five senses. At the end of each museum session, the class is given lending library kits that contain small exhibit-type props, books, equipment (such as light sources, tuning forks, color filters), and suggested activities for experimenting.

MUSEUMS VISIT SCHOOLS

For nearly one hundred years, museums have offered outreach

programs to people who cannot come to the museum. The first teaching sets were sent to New York schools in the 1890s by the American Museum of Natural History, and the Children's Museum in Boston has circulated resource units to schools since it was founded in 1913. Museums have programs that send lecturers, volunteers, objects, slide sets, reproductions, scientific equipment, video tapes, and original artifacts to classrooms throughout the country. These services are offered on local, state, and national levels in an effort to further the children's understanding of the museum in distant places.

The relationship between the museum and the users of outreach materials, whether they are schools or community groups, determines in large measure the success of this type of program. A motivated teacher is an essential component, since these programs are scheduled at their request or the materials are picked up on their own time at the museum.

Developing and operating programs and resources that go into the classroom cost the museum money. Staff, storage space, transportation, and repairs, as well as developing new products or programs, must all be considered as items that require money, time, staff, and other resources. Careful attention must also be given to the scheduling of loan materials or a resource specialist. The involvement of teachers, curriculum supervisors, and others can improve the "usability" of these programs.

Museums provide services to the classroom teacher through resource specialists, audio-visual and written resources, traveling exhibits, and loan kits. Resource specialists, whether staff members or volunteers, visit classrooms taking live animals, artworks, reproductions, or audio-visual programs. The presentations are tailored to meet the needs either in a classroom or an auditorium and can range in length from twenty minutes to two hours. These programs are very effective in reaching handicapped and hospitalized audiences.

Audio-visual resource materials bring collections and special exhibitions to students in the form of slides, films, and video tapes. The extension services, such as one operation by the National Gallery of Art in Washington, D. C., circulated audio-visual resources to over four thousand community groups. In general, extension services can also include portable loan kits that come in two formats: those with artifacts in sealed cases and those with objects that may be handled.

These kits can include a range of written and audio-visual materials, artifacts, and specimens. Some of these kits are packaged in brown boxes while others are in steamer trunks. These resource units can involve children in activities such as weaving, grinding corn, drilling soapstone, or learning how to "read" an object.

Museums also circulate exhibits to be installed at sites as varied as a classroom, a shopping center, a library, or a town common. Other exhibitions travel in mobile vans. Many of these exhibits are specifically designed for children, though it is recognized that they can serve a more general audience. Some exhibits are participatory and involve children with games, puzzles, and other activities that let them practice their mathematical thinking, while a mobile exhibit or gallery-on-wheels can bring Pueblo life or Renaissance art to isolated communities.

Printed resource materials, such as newspapers, journals, and newsletters, are another way museums extend their programs and resources into the classroom. Some are collections of poems, stories, and research papers written by children. These honor and recognize the contributions that children make. They serve as documentation of their accomplishments. Newspapers like *Boing* and magazines like *Art and Man* are available to teachers, published by museums on a local, state, and national level for various audiences.

Museums continue to provide services to children in schools, hospitals, and communities. Video discs, satellite television, and expanded use of computers will result in new programs that will reach even larger numbers of children. Nevertheless, museums will encourage and promote actual visits to the exhibitions to see the original "evidence" that was seen previously on a slide or in a reproduction. This visit remains the museum's primary objective.

MUSEUMS TRAIN CLASSROOM TEACHERS

Museum educators have increasingly recognized the important role that the classroom teacher plays in effectively carrying out their programs. The classroom teacher is with the students for an entire year, while the museum shares only a small amount of the student's time. As a result, there is great value in having a teacher who understands the role of the museum and how to use its collections and resources. Such a teacher can prepare the students and follow up with them. Teachers who are actively involved with a museum provide constructive and friendly criticism about the programs and materials.

Teacher training programs require clearly established objectives, defined content, and evaluation methods. Communicating and interpreting through objects in an exhibit is a type of teaching that usually occurs only in museums. Few teachers have the skills to teach by using paintings or the resources in a historic house. Teacher training programs should be developed with people from the school system as well as with the teachers. These programs range from single in-service credit or noncredit programs that provide specific expertise to in-depth summer institutes or graduate credit programs or sabbaticals. At their best, these programs do much more than impart basic information to teachers. They develop the skills teachers need to work with the museum's collections, learn how to teach from objects, help develop curriculum, and design resources for their students' use.

Museums frequently provide orientations and workshops for teachers to introduce them to the museum resources, provide information on planning museum visits, and publicize their activities. Museums also actively participate in in-service credit programs, which are required by the state department of education to maintain certification or obtain salary increases. Museums offering programs for credit must meet all the requirements and frequently seek the cosponsorship or the support of a college or university. These programs range from a half-day in-service workshop for art, humanities, and science teachers to a fifteen-week course that covers the art and history of China. Some programs train the teachers to do research and design primary and supplementary source materials for classroom use, while others help teams of teachers from participating schools to develop programs for use during an entire academic year.

Among museums that lead the field in teacher training and the development of resource materials for classroom use is Old Sturbridge Village. The Teacher Center at Old Sturbridge Village trains teachers from all over New England to develop curricula that make full use of the village's exhibits, artifacts, and other materials on nineteenth-century New England. The two-week program suggests different approaches to studying modern communities and is available for three graduate credits from the state colleges. While exploring significant social issues, teachers work with primary sources such as pictures, objects, and buildings. They also learn effective methods of combining field experiences, museum objects, and classroom activities and begin to design curriculum studies that use their own community resources. Each month during the school year, they return to Old Sturbridge Village to discuss teaching problems they might be experiencing. Because of the emphasis on curriculum development, the State Department of Education in Massachusetts accepted this program in certifying elementary and secondary teachers.

In many communities, museums have resource centers that offer materials ranging from slides to models, mounted animals, or reproductions that can be borrowed. These resource centers can operate like libraries, loaning and maintaining the materials, or they can also be a training center offering classes. One of the best examples of a comprehensive resource center exists at the Children's Museum in Boston, which serves teachers, parents, community workers, and other adults who work with children. The center maintains a library of books, pamphlets, and information on subjects that are in its collection. It also maintains resources on child development, workshop rooms, a "recycle" center, and a kit rental department. The staff of the center is involved with training, the development of new kits, writing books, film and television production, and consulting with universities, neighborhood groups, and schools.

Not every museum has the ability or the mandate to operate full-scale resource centers or to develop materials for circulation in the schools. However, as in the training of teachers, these programs help to form important ties with the classroom teacher.

Museums that offer workshops, develop materials, or maintain a resource center must have a very clear rationale for their work. These programs require a commitment of time, money, staff, space, and resources. The revenue they bring in rarely covers expenses. The importance of supporting this type of work has been clearly stated by Newsom and Silver:

Museums hold in trust an endless supply of ideas, visions, human mysteries to be unlocked for audiences of all kinds. It may be true that none of the museum's several audiences is more frustrating or more difficult, but it is clear that none is more important than teachers, none more worthy of all the energy, imagination, and intelligence the museum can command. It is not too much to urge that museums put the best people they can find to work on that job.[6]

School and Museum Collaboration

Museums and schools need to increase their commitment to work together and diversify their vision of each other and their respective capabilities. Together they have the potential to cause change as they combine the strengths of each learning environment to affect the student's ability to explore, compare and contrast, and generalize the information they acquire.

When museums and schools develop programs together, they must recognize that there are two major points of view in operation. The school teacher is concerned with the demands of the curriculum and wants the museum to assist students in meeting these demands. The museum educator is concerned with the interpretation and use of the collections and ways to involve the student in exploring and discovering new knowledge from them. School teachers regard museum staff members as content specialists trained in art, history, natural history, or science, with little understanding of how children learn and often no experience or understanding of life in the classroom. School teachers are often uncomfortable in museums, as the learning environment appears unstructured; they dislike the loss of control over their students. Because teachers have been trained to use words and primarily two-dimensional resources, they lack the background to work with the objects in a museum.

In contrast, museum educators perceive the classroom teacher as being unwilling to use the museum to its full potential, teaching students how to learn from objects rather than focusing solely on the content demands placed by the teacher. The museum educator often feels that the teachers are unable to use their resources and unwilling to recognize when they need assistance in doing so. As a result, museums frequently strive to develop "teacher proof" resources and programs. Museum educators are frustrated by teachers who send students with multiple choice questions to answer while on the tour, disrupting the students' ability to look and learn from the objects.

To bring together the museum educator and the classroom teacher to learn from each other and to build bridges is an important part of collaborative programming. Increasingly, museums and schools are discovering ways to collaborate, recognizing the strength of their bonds. Organizations like the Cultural Education Collaborative in

Boston and the Museums Collaborative in New York have undertaken projects that document the meaningful changes that can occur.[7]

Collaborations that result in teacher training or the development of resources should involve teachers as soon as they are able to do so. Also important is the support and endorsement of key officials both in the school system and in the museum. When informed and supportive of a project, curriculum specialists and principals, as well as directors and curators, can make the time and resources available to implement a program. Curriculum supervisors are often able to assist with training sessions or arrange in-service credits for teachers.

Building a successful collaborative relationship is a long-term enterprise requiring that the museum staff and the school, from the start, are willing to change as they share in the "ownership" of the final product. The expectations, past experiences, schedules, as well as knowledge of the abilities of the staff and budget, must be communicated if the two organizations are to work together in the development of a successful resource or service. Both organizations must be motivated and able to share in the planning, development and implementation, and continuance of the program. To work together effectively, the collaborating organizations must share information and make the following commitments:

1. Learn as much as possible about the other agency, its goals, audience, resources, and schedules, in an effort to dispel myths and develop appreciation for its work.

2. Respect each other and have realistic expectations about the project. This includes setting clear and realistic schedules and products.

3. Define the roles, responsibilities and timelines, plans for evaluation, and the maintenance of the program, together.

4. Be flexible. The administrators in both institutions are responsible for allocating time, people, and funds to help the project succeed. But the schedules, commitments, and availability of resources will require many alterations throughout the project.

5. Give praise honestly and frequently to the contributors.

6. Continually communicate. From the beginning of a project and long after its completion, it is important to share information, ideas, frustrations, and successes. Communication between everyone—administrators, curators, principals, teachers, and museum educators—is

critical if each is to understand where the project is going and if each is to know what is expected if it is to succeed.

Collaborations that work effectively can permanently enrich both the museum and the school. These partnerships foster ongoing, uninterrupted dialogue between the community and the museum. Successful collaborations are a result of the commitments made by people. The new insights, understanding, and involvement by the school and museum can change the way in which museums are perceived and operate.

The Key Components for Learning in Museum/School Programs

Museums provide almost endless opportunities for teaching and learning in science, art, history, and natural history to students, teachers, and parents. Yet, care must be taken to develop links between the experiences these visitors have in the museum and their daily lives if the event is to have significance and encourage application. The idea of continuing the museum experience is important because as learners mature they can see with greater sophistication the links among objects, learning, and culture.

Some of the formats that museums use for teaching with objects have already been discussed. However, the manner in which a program or exhibition is organized to develop a relationship with learners will help them continue the experience after leaving the museum. It will also help them to learn more while they are in the museum. The three levels at which a relationship should be established are: the child's daily experience; the interaction between the child and the object or exhibit; a connection between the museum experience and their everyday world. Together these three steps have the potential for helping the students to see, learn, and experience the objects continually over time.

Begin with the child's experience. Use experiences that learners have had to introduce them to the concepts and techniques that will be used in the museum. Children have made collections of butterflies, kept diaries, taken photographs, and considered the role of their family members. Use concrete examples to draw out ideas about collecting, family roles, transportation, or changes in a community. Such activities can be done in classrooms by teachers or at the beginning of a tour and are a great deal of fun. Ideally they result in shared knowledge, new insights, and open minds.

Establish a link between the museum experience and the child's classroom experience. Arriving at the museum is often an exciting but forbidding event unless the group has been to the museum before. The first visit is the time to link ideas and experiences or apply the skills learned in the classroom to the museum setting. Building such a bridge between the museum environment and its objects and concepts helps children look at the exhibits in a way that focuses and personalizes their experience. For example, children can compare the nineteenth-century kitchen to their own, examining similarities and differences.

Link the museum experience to the child's everyday world. To make the museum experience meaningful *after* the visit is even more important than at the beginning when an opportunity still exists to engage the learners. How can the children use their new information or skills when they go back to the classroom or home? What will they remember us for? They might, for example, be able to examine and compare lighting technologies from different periods of history or examine a bird outside their window, considering how it has adapted to its environment and become camouflaged.

How we look, what we see, and how we react to the same object is intensely personal and varied. We readily accept factual information about an object such as height, width, names, and dates. However, responses to the subjective elements in ideas, colors, shape, and history are personal and influenced by previous associations and experiences. This personal response is inherent in visual awareness, and it has to be recognized, nurtured, and attended to by anyone teaching in museums.

At one time, museums centered their educational efforts on giving information through lectures. Such lectures, even by well-informed teachers, created barriers that hindered children from seeing the object for themselves and from forming their own impressions. Today we recognize that part of the task of museum educators is to make known what others have thought and created at different times, and to promote a historical, objective framework. A child's confidence in his barely formulated visual image can all too easily be shattered if subjected to a battery of unknown facts. To become meaningful, these facts must relate to the child's experience and to what one object conveys to the eye.

The learning in a museum requires an inventive blend of content, sensory experience, and hands-on activities. Too much emphasis on any one of these elements can decrease a program's effectiveness. The content must be appropriate to the age level and be well presented in the museum's collections. Sensory experiences help children to remember and become active thinkers and doers. Museums can use their full potential for promoting learning when the learner can see, hear, smell, taste and manipulate the objects and concepts being presented.

In his book, *The Senses Considered as Perceptual Systems*, James Gibson wrote: "perceiving helps talking, and talking fixes the gains of perceiving."[8] A child familiar with this visual process of looking, discussing, and comparing an object of today with an object perhaps from Greece or China can learn to comprehend the similarities and differences despite differences in medium and use. If a teacher is alert to the advantages of studying particular themes, such as "horses" and other animals in other civilizations, the child has a guideline to make discoveries that can then be shared with classmates. The process of sharing verbally is indeed a part of visual learning and helps to record and document the image by describing in detail.

It is constructive for children to compare their observations and choices with those of their peers. A child, seeing through another child's eyes and learning about differing reactions, gains fresh insights. Such discussions, if begun in the museum, can be continued in the classroom where visual memory can be developed.

Learning in musuems does not occur solely through visual response, but the aim is to develop a learning situation that fully uses the visual potential. Sir Kenneth Clark, in his writings on looking at paintings, gives an enlightened description of the interplay between visual and verbal experience. Noting that looking requires active participation and a certain amount of discipline, he comments that after his senses tire from the initial impact of looking, he must use knowledge about the artist and his life and times to continue to pursue the work and to discover new sights and continue to be engaged. To succeed, museums must continually seek the balance of perceptual, tactual, and cognitive learning.

Recommendations

The future work for museums and schools as environments for

learning is particularly complex today. Changing social values, shifts in the age of the population and where they live, the disappearance of traditional family structure, a birth rate that has fallen below natural replacement rates, mid-career training programs with over 50 percent of all jobs related to the handling of information, and the possibility of thirty million homes having computers by 1990—these are only a very few of the events that are causing our country and the world to change. Museums and schools need to find ways to work together more effectively to foster learning in this contemporary society.

The following recommendations support the work museums and schools must do together to bring about change. They result from my work, observations, and writings, as well as from discussions with colleagues in the field. These recommendations should not be considered as a definitive list, but a preliminary record of the key issues that need to be addressed by both organizations.

RECOMMENDATIONS FOR MUSEUMS

The following are recommendations for museums as they work for schools:

1. *There must be a supportive administration in the museum.* Such support is a key element if the museum is to be a successful learning environment. Without the support and involvement of the director, staff members, and trustees, the necessary funds, personnel, and resources will not be available to develop or carry out the educational mandate. Without administrative support, the museum's role as an educational institution is the isolated responsibility of a few, who have little authority to bring about change.

2. *The museum's staff must understand the ways people learn.* They should expand their commitment to use this knowledge to communicate with visitors. Curators, educators, and others involved in developing programs and exhibitions should try to merge the formal and informal learning experiences offered in a museum so that they can become a series of opportunities that are available to visitors over time.

3. *Museums must evaluate their exhibitions and programs to assess the effectiveness of their work and to determine the quality of the visitor's experience.* Evaluation—quantitative and qualitative—that offers knowledge about mistakes and progress is an essential ingredient in planning for future exhibits. While rigorous evaluation studies are not always

appropriate or feasible, a commitment to review and record in a responsible manner is essential.

4. *Museums must develop their understanding and use of new technologies.* Cable television, video tape, video discs, satellite transmissions, and computers are all used in schools, homes, and places of work. These technologies will help museums to access the collections they have in storage, making them more available to scholars and students. Computers and television can link schools and museums together for programs, resources, and special classes or presentations. Working together, museums and schools need to develop new approaches for teaching, using these technologies. Yet, despite the increased access to information that new technologies will provide, schools will need to continue to include visits to museums so that students can look at the real objects in the collection.

RECOMMENDATIONS FOR SCHOOLS

The following are recommendations for schools as they work with museums:

1. *The support of parents, teachers, and school administrators is necessary, if time and funds are to be found for visits to museums and other cultural resources within their community.* It is not enough for museums to offer exhibits and programs; school children must be able to attend. At a time of financial curtailments and increased demands on teachers' time, museums need the support of the school community if visits and programs are to continue.

2. *Schools need to increase the value placed on visual learning.* Visual perception is recognized as a key component of creative thought. Learning in a museum often begins as a visual experience; it then branches out into a range of learning experiences that can include comparing and contrasting, problem solving, and the like. Visual learning is a responsive learning mode as students write, draw, photograph, or research the image further.

3. *Schools should support and participate in quality programs that will help teachers learn how to use the resources in museums for teaching.* Moreover, teachers should receive support or acknowledgement of their participation by school administrators. Teachers will gain from participation in such programs as they develop new skills, develop new materials, and see their students learn.

RECOMMENDATIONS FOR MUSEUMS AND SCHOOLS
TO WORK TOGETHER

When collaborating, schools and museums should consider the following recommendations:

1. *Museums and schools should select appropriate partners, secure needed funds, identify staff, and use teaching techniques that will engage the learners.* Museums are not responsible for the development of school curriculum or resources, nor are they usually equipped to do so without the support of the schools. Museums should provide the resources for strategies for learning from objects—strategies that can be used for a lifetime by teachers and students. Schools must recognize the unique learning experiences students can have in museums and understand and appreciate the cultural and historic and scientific knowledge gained from an examination of objects.

2. *Museums and schools should work together to develop centers where teachers in schools and universities can come to use resources and to be trained.* Together in these learning centers the museum educator and the classroom teacher can work on programs that capitalize on the skills each one brings to the program.

3. *Museums and schools should put forth their best resources to increase the opportunities for a successful collaboration.* A commitment to excellence in all phases of a program will allow the best ideas, staff, funding, and other components to be available. Collaborative programs are based on trust and on an ability to share. These two ingredients, combined with a supportive administrative environment and a good staff, are critical factors in a collaboration.

4. *Museum and school partnerships should develop, evaluate, and document their efforts.* Programs involving teacher training, curriculum and resource materials, exhibits and programs for students are among those that are currently undertaken in partnership programs. Schools and museums must document both the products and the process of their work in order to provide others with opportunities to expand.

5. *Museums, schools, and community leaders must actively support and acknowledge the role museums and other cultural organizations have in providing excellent opportunities for learning.* Because our society under-values perceptual learning, especially sight, museum experiences are often undervalued. First a child learns through sight; language and

numbers are then employed to help in exploring what has been perceived.

The educational functions of museums have many implications. A museum that is highly committed to its educational responsibilities will change the way it is perceived and used by its community. A combined use of the collections, exhibitions, and research facilities enhances the learning experience and can make museums "powerhouses" in the education field. Museums that have organized themselves this way are succeeding, and they are becoming increasingly acclaimed for their success. In 1909, John Cotton Dana, founder of the Newark (New Jersey) Museum, wrote:

A *good* museum attracts, entertains, arouses curiosity, leads to questioning and thus promotes learning. It is an educational institution that is set up and kept in motion—that it may help the members of the community to become happier, wiser, and more effective human beings. Much can be done toward a realization of these objectives—with simple things—objects of nature and daily life—as well as with objects of great beauty. The museum can help people only if they use it; they will use it only if they know about it and only if attention is given to the interpretation of its possessions in terms they, the people, will understand.[9]

Schools and museums share the responsibility for changing the way they work together to teach children. Reduced economic, physical, or psychological support will affect their ability to succeed. Productive partnerships between institutions take time and occur only as each success is noted. The path ahead is not restricted; the opportunities for programs are as numerous as the resources and creativity of the institutions. The commitment of individuals in museums and schools will help teaching and training programs to gain stature with the professions. But the primary beneficiaries of museum-school partnerships are the children. When children see, think, and experience life in a way that increases learning, the work of both organizations has succeeded. And so, it is for the children that these efforts to build meaningful partnerships must continue.

FOOTNOTES

1. Daniel S. Greenburg, "There's a Windmill in the Attic: S. Dillon Ripley Is Blowing Dust Off the Smithsonian," *Saturday Review* 5 June 1965, p. 48.

2. Germain Bazin, *The Museum Age* (New York: Universe Books, 1967), pp. 26-61.

3. Malcolm S. Knowles, "Lifelong Learning in the Museum," in *Museums, Adults, and the Humanities: A Guide for Educational Programmers* (Washington, D.C.: American Association of Museums, 1981), pp. 134-35.

4. Rudolph Arnheim, *Visual Thinking* (Berkeley and Los Angeles, Calif.: University of California Press, 1969), p. 295.

5. For specific examples of museum/school programs, see Barbara Newsom and Adele Silver, eds., *The Art Museums as Educator* (Berkeley: University of California Press, 1977) and Bonnie Pitman-Gelles, *Museums, Magic, and Children* (Washington, D.C.: Association of Science-Technology Centers, 1981). *Museums, Magic, and Children* describes programs in children's museums centering on art, history, science, natural history, zoos, and botanical gardens. It is available through the Association of Science-Technology Centers, 1413 K Street, N.W., Washington, D.C. 20036.

6. Newsom and Silver, *The Art Museum as Educator*, p. 470.

7. For further information on collaborative school programs, contact: Polly Price, Cultural Education Collaborative, 59 Temple Street, Boston, Mass. 02116; Susan Bertram, Museums Collaborative, 15 Gramercy Park South, New York, N.Y. 10003; Peter O'Connell, Old Sturbridge Village, Sturbridge, Mass. 01566.

8. James Gibson, *The Senses Considered as Perceptual Systems* (Boston: Houghton Mifflin, 1966), p. 282.

9. Newark Museum, *A Survey: 50 Years* (Newark, N.J.: Newark Museum, 1959), p. 9.

CHAPTER VIII

Religious Institutions as Educators

BURTON COHEN AND JOSEPH LUKINSKY

To understand a religious institution from an educational perspective, we think that it is useful to view it from the following standpoints:

1. *Direct explicit religious education* is the obvious vehicle of religious institutions. Their activities take place in classes, in schoolrooms, for children and adults, through preaching, study groups, discussions, Bible study, lectures, and in informal groups where learning is the goal.[1] The methods used in the last category include "informal" methods such as those derived from encounter and group dynamics theory.[2] Formal classes or informal study groups under religious auspices provide also for sociability, interpersonal relationships, and recreation. This was especially true in earlier times when opportunities for entertainment and sociability were much more limited.[3]

2. *The setting as a whole educates.* It is not only the planned "educational activities" that educate. The Board of Trustees meeting that considers how much to pay the janitor or whether church investments are ethically placed educates.[4] Religious celebrations, liturgical experiences, worship services, holidays, meetings of women's and men's groups, retreats, work in the kitchen, pastoral visits and counseling, committees for social action, community involvement in political issues—all these are resources for religious education, for manifesting the overall institutional mission. Historically, churches and synagogues have often served as meeting houses for secular public purposes. Since the days of mass immigration to the United States and down to the present day, churches have served as centers for Ameri-

canization, as general meeting houses and community centers. These functions were (and are) not perceived as "extra" in that they broaden the purview of church teaching.

The diversity of "religious institutions" makes it difficult to talk about them in general and also limits the value of extrapolating from specific examples of them. In seeking the educational possibilities of religious settings, therefore, we are looking for those general factors to which schools can relate. We will try to identify the characteristic *kinds* of learning that are available in these settings without reference to the quality of the actual learning, which may vary greatly from place to place.

A helpful statement that can be fruitfully unpacked, we suggest, is the following:

Religious institutions initiate people into a world-view, a way of constructing the world that has implications for living. This initiation involves both cognitive and affective experiences, especially those that heighten the feeling of roots and community and the commitment to ethical behavior. Most of the activities of such institutions contribute in one way or another to this initiation.

In the following section, we will expand on this statement as a basis for proposing connections with schools of different sorts and for understanding the issues that may arise from them.

Teaching a World-View

Invariably people make choices concerning their lives. But choices are made on the basis of experience and derive from one's point of view or "world-view."

What is a world-view? It is philosophy in action, expressed in a way of life and related to all things. It is a way of constructing and understanding the universe, a source of values, meaning, interpretation, and decision making.

In our time, we have become more sophisticated about world-views and where they come from. We have learned that everyone has a world-view. Religious institutions in partnership with the family are a major source for communicating integrated world-views. These may overlap or conflict with the prevailing world-view of the culture as a whole, which is communicated in part by the schools.

A religion has its own way of ordering reality and deriving implications for life from that construction. Religions are characterized by a fund of controlling myths and metaphors, revered stories, traditions, celebrations, liturgies, and observances that dramatize and enact the belief structure as a whole. The world-view of a religion deals, explicitly or implicitly, with the reality of God, the nature of man, the value of life, the meaning of suffering, the responsibilities of the individual and the community to one another, the significance of history, and the nature of man's hope and destiny. This involves not only a set of beliefs but a way of living according to them.[5]

If, as we have suggested, the entire religious setting has implications for how participants in it are to live their lives, it is understandable why it is crucial for believers who hold particular religious world-views to be able to initiate their young into those views in the most effective manner. In a democratic society such as ours, people have a right to do this as long as they do not interfere with the free exercise of that same right by others. This right belongs to everyone, and, whether or not they are aware of it, it is exercised by each generation as it tries to socialize the next one to its values.

There are two chief modes by which the young are socialized. There are those groups that use what some might call "brainwashing" methods of indoctrination; they try to shut out all influences other than their own. While this is almost impossible in an open society in the long run, we cannot rule out the right of people to try to do it. In this mode, initiation into a world-view involves *transmission* of a total outlook from one generation to the next.[6]

Nevertheless, many who consider themselves "enlightened" religionists accept the developmental and ideological necessity and right to initiate the young into an alternative belief system; at the same time, they also recognize that at an appropriate time it is desirable to give them the intellectual and emotional tools to enable them to choose their own commitments eventually. They do this, of course, with the hope that the young will choose within the bounds of that way of life previously chosen *for* them. In contrast to the transmission mode described above, this mode can be characterized as the "nurturing" or "initiation" mode. In this mode, deep emotional commitments are accompanied by the development of critical tools that give students the resources to compare their own beliefs with those of others, to deepen their understanding, to modify and finally develop their own freely chosen ways of understanding the world and their role in it.[7] Proponents of the transmission model see the development of such critical tools as an unwarranted and undesirable threat and intrusion. The relationship between the modes is more likely represented by a continuum than by a dichotomy.

A world-view has real valence and is a dimension of all live cultures and civilizations. It is not just a verbalized set of doctrines. In looking at religious settings, we need to be able to distinguish between verbalized affirmations and the actual beliefs and values that are at the roots of behavior and sensibility. If schools are to relate to what is learned in religious settings, they must develop the means for making this distinction.

In democracies people live in two civilizations: their own primary one, which is derived from family values and religion; and their public one, which is formed by communal resources including schools. Each of these civilizations has its world-view, and there are many possible relationships between the two. One may be overwhelmed by the other, in which case the "loser" survives only as a residue or veneer, largely irrelevant to life.[8] In our society, the religious view has sometimes become superficial. Yet, in some instances (such as in certain fundamentalist homogeneous communities), it has tended to overwhelm the public view.

We need not rule out such "irrelevant" world-views as being altogether valueless. At least potentially, they may provide alternatives to the prevailing majority views. There is always the possibility that this potential will be energized in different circumstances. Preserved even superficially, it may come to life as people mature, even after generations have passed. Even at a low level of meaning, its very existence may provide for enrichment of understanding, an added dimension, or, to use Berger's term, "a hint of transcendence."[9] It offers the possibility of seeing the world differently from the pressuring majority.[10]

The Affective Side of World-Views: Celebration, Roots, Community

Religious settings do not teach "about" a world-view; they *teach* a world-view. They are therefore involved in affective experiences and in the issues of affective education.

All education is necessarily affective; it affects, and is affected by, the emotions. The absence of conscious concern for the emotional side of students or the conscious neglect of it is in itself an affective statement. Humans thirst for the experience of awe, wonder, mystery, and poetry, of unity with nature, for a sense of belonging in the universe, of a link to others and to a higher purpose. There are many ways in which this need is satisfied.[11]

Affective experiences and the experience of community can be seen as intrinsic goods even apart from their substantive content. For example, fellowship is a value in its own right, though we would need to consider the substantive form such fellowship takes and would oppose a fellowship of fascists or racists.

Religious settings provide for affective experience by definition. The initiation into a world-view is at the same time socialization into a fellowship of believers in that world-view, allowing for differences within given frames of reference.

In recent years, we have become ever more aware of how identity is related to this process of initiation.[12] Religious settings provide for affective experiences related to the human life cycle, to the reinforcement of family and communal ties, and the reenactment and celebration of significant paradigm events in the history of the religious community. Communal experiences in religious settings relate to both the horizontal and vertical dimensions: we carry on the community of the past as we identify with its values, and we preserve it through our actions in the present so that we can pass those values on to our descendants in the future. Psychological identity grows through roots in a historic way of viewing the world, through relationships to peers who view it in a like manner, and in links to adults who model a tested way of life for their children even as they meet the challenges of change and modernity.[13]

Even the teaching of "subject matter" or doctrine in a formal religious school setting has an affective load to the extent that such teaching has to be more than "for your information." We are not talking here about success in teaching; obviously there is plenty of failure. It is just that the intent in religious settings is always to affect individuals, to confront them and force them to relate seriously to the material studied, to be present to it, and to make it their own.[14]

If the affective domain is one in which people need to develop, it is thus possible to claim that religious settings provide important and appropriate nuances, some of which are not as likely to be found, at least to the same extent, in public schools.

World-Views and Moral Education

Both schools and religious institutions have become increasingly aware that moral education, in the words of Purpel and Ryan, "comes with the territory."[15] This has led both to the adoption of specific direct moral education programs and a concern for the overall moral atmosphere of their respective settings.[16]

While it has always been assumed that religious settings "do" moral education, what is new is that religious settings have adopted the approaches characteristic of their secular counterparts to the widespread neglect of many of their own traditional approaches. Many people no longer see religion as automatically relevant to morality. The fundamentalist claim that there can be no morality without religion is often hard to take seriously when that claim is associated, as it often is, with social and political views that are regarded by many as reactionary. But religion has always treaded the fine line between duties to God and duties to fellowman; it is always in danger of falling over one side or the other. The worship of God without a corresponding concern for fellow creatures was criticized by the ancient Prophets; it is not a new phenomenon. Neither is the relatively recent insistence by some people that the *only* purpose of religion is to promote moral behavior. In both cases, the response has been to overlook those traditional resources that no longer seem directly relevant to the task.

Without denying that in recent years religious settings have learned from the research and curriculum development in the moral education field—and could well learn even more—our task here is to reflect upon those aspects of religious settings that lend themselves to moral education in a way that is distinctive to them, that would be hard to replicate in schools, and that could well be considered by them. Regardless of whether their impact upon morality is clearly discernible or not, it still behooves religious educators to be clearer about what they can claim to add to moral education. Our own thoughts on this topic attempt to focus what we have said earlier about world-views, the affective, and the communal.[17]

Morality (used here broadly as a "commitment" orientation within the general framework of "ethics") may be approached directly by considering what is right or wrong or what "ought" to be done in specific cases. The discussion of moral dilemmas in the Kohlberg-influenced moral education programs and the clarification of value priorities in the values clarification activities created by Raths, Simon, and their followers[18] are examples of *direct* moral education. These programs have also been adapted by religious settings. But with respect to these direct approaches, the traditional materials in religious settings are potentially richer, coming as they do out of literary traditions stemming from the Bible and other sacred texts. The traditional materials have a moral dimension, but they are more complex and sophisticated, rich in literary allusions, and of compelling interest in ways that speak to many developmental levels. The moral issue may, in fact, be best brought to light when the story or other material has struck deep personal roots for other reasons. In contrast, the "moral monomania" of direct "moral education" materials tends to come across as one-dimensional. As a steady diet, they are boring and tendentious.

Religious settings are life-contexts where real community values are manifested and created—values relating to historical communities and events, heroes of the past, and a thick, many-layered religious language that is imbedded in concrete human situations of interpersonal stress, regret, struggle, conflict, hope, and aspiration. The community faces real value decisions that emerge out of its heritage and exemplifies a mode of deliberation as it works with the tension between the past and issues of the present. Occasions for celebration, participation in liturgy, and opportunities for service initiate members of a religious community into a system of values and reinforce them through the strengthening bonds of fellowship. The moral is interwoven in this complex religious tapestry, and it is separated only with great difficulty. The individual's motivation to be moral is supported by the community's struggle; the individual is not alone, an orphan in history. This process goes beyond "knowing" what is moral or "searching" for the solution to hypothetical, abstract dilemmas.[19] It is a process of socialization, belonging to a community whose thrust is moral because of its overall orientation.

Religious settings have their failings, their hypocrisies. The above statements are not an attempt on our part to paint a rosy picture of reality. It is just that such settings have the potential opportunity to bring about a primary developmental attachment to values, including moral ones, and these may arguably provide a firm base for whatever happens later and in other contexts including schools.

The religious setting, moreover, has a point of view and is, paradoxically, in many respects *freer* to deal with controversial issues, even if it has an ax to grind, than public settings which tend to be cautious and avoid controversy. Values are the "bread and butter" of religious settings, and the religious educator need not tread gingerly. Moral deliberation in religious settings thus has potentially an *affective*, commitmental thrust that distinguishes it from similar deliberation carried on in other settings. People who have had the experience of moral deliberation in such an environment are primed and ready for something analogous and possibly broader in schools.

Curricular Implications

Our purpose has been to suggest in general terms what religious institutions do and what people learn in them. We have suggested that the vast diversity that characterizes religious settings makes it especially difficult to determine the public school's relationship to this learning. Historically, this complex question has been approached in different ways.

The first and classic approach has been to avoid it. The fear of trespassing upon constitutional principles, of infringing upon people's personal views and rights, and the desire not to offend often have led us to ignore the learning that takes place in religious institutions. But ignoring it leads inevitably to conflict or to compartmentalization or both. Worst of all, it leads to the loss of a potentially fruitful relationship between these two centers of learning, the waste of a great potential for significant mutual reinforcement, and the opportunity for learning how to deal with conflict in a democratic society. We contend that avoidance is no solution.

A second and newer approach is to teach "about" religion in the schools.[20] Inspired by the decision of the U.S. Supreme Court in *Schempp* (1963),[21] serious scholarly and practical efforts have been made to carry out this approach. While it still holds much promise, and should be encouraged, the practical difficulties of carrying it out seem to be enormous. Moreover, very little widespread application has been achieved so far. The approach is based upon the assertion of the *Schempp* decision that although religion itself is forbidden in schools (prayer, Bible reading, and so forth), religion has been so fundamental a force in human society that no worthy education can omit teaching "about" it without leaving a fundamental gap in students' understanding of the world, past and present. Much of this literature is relevant to our own approach, and we mention it here for this reason.

A third and, to our thinking, more useful approach would encourage schools to take account of and relate to what is learned in religious institutions. This approach is in the spirit of Lawrence Cremin's suggestion that we think about education "relationally,"[22] and in the spirit of all serious curriculum theory that stresses the curriculum developer's need to consider the nature of the learners, the milieu from which they come, and the society for which they are being educated. While this would apply also to the curriculum of a religious setting (that is, *its* need to know what goes on in the schools in order to create its own curriculum), our stress is on the need of schools to relate to what is done in religious settings, to capitalize upon the resources that are therein produced and that can be exploited by the school with good effect.

In our previous discussion, we suggested that public school educators ought to consider seriously three aspects of religious education: the integrated world-view that religious education aspires to give the child; the affective, communal, and identity-enhancing experiences that manifest this world-view in the religious setting; and the ways in which moral education is mediated under religious auspices. It seems obvious to us that in order to relate to their students as individuals and to create their curricula accordingly, schools need to relate to these three aspects in general and as much as possible to their specific manifestations in each local community. Relating to this diversity cannot be escaped; it is a necessary part of knowing one's students.

Schools bring together people from many contexts, each of which makes truth claims of various sorts. (It should be clear that children who come from a nonreligious context are also bringing with them some sort of truth claims.) The consciousness of individuals is formed through the interaction of these claims with those of other students and of the culture in general. A student's primary commitments (for example, those which originate in the family and its church) play a determining role, and the schools ignore them at their peril. Surely, the school can relate to them with a greater degree of sensitivity than it does now.

A strong particularistic religious background steeped in a world-view may have many implications for learning in school. It may be the source of attitudes toward the value of learning, desirable behavior, and respect for authority and tradition that can be transferred to school contexts. Family values, often so characteristic of the religious outlook, can be transmuted into group awareness and loyalty.

Beyond attitudes gained in a religious setting, even cognitive skills can be reinforced and exploited in the school setting. A literature course in school could well be raised to a higher level if it could be assumed that the students, as a result of their religious education, have learned to analyze, with analytical and poetic sophistication, a literary text equivalent in difficulty to a chapter of the Prophets.

The aesthetic is not the primary concern of the religious setting, but it is a dimension that is hard to separate from it. The result of the affective stress in religious settings may well be to enhance students' sensitivity to the poetic, the arts in general, and the aesthetic aspects of the disciplines.

Since public schools are also concerned with the affective domain, they can define their own role best if they are aware of the kinds of affective sensibilities being developed elsewhere. Even when it is relatively ineffective, the religious institution is one of the prime settings for this. Schools can more effectively plan their overall curricula, including areas like citizenship and moral education where the affective domain is crucial, if they know what sensibilities the students bring to the school.

It is often claimed that schools could focus greater attention on the cognitive domain if they were able to be assured that necessary affective developmental experiences were taking place in family or church settings. We think that this view is mistaken; it is a "cop-out." The affective and the cognitive can be separated from one another only for purposes of convenient discourse, not in actuality.[23] In view of the interdependence of the cognitive and affective domains, we suggest that any such division of labor between school and religious settings be rejected. All the more important, we feel, is the attempt of schools, concerned as they necessarily must be with the affective, to relate to what students experience elsewhere—in this case in religious settings.

Both schools and religious settings have a concern for moral education, and both do it directly and indirectly. They both do it directly by employing programs aimed at achieving moral education objectives. Religious moral education is embodied in teaching about what is right and wrong as a dimension of religious traditions (such as Bible stories) and norms (such as the Ten Commandments and the Golden Rule in its different formulations) and as a dimension of a morally concerned religious community.

Schools have always taught material aimed at affecting moral behavior. This material has ranged from the type of moralizing texts represented by the McGuffey Readers to the sophisticated Kohlberg-type programs and the values clarification exercises already mentioned. The cross-reinforcement possibilities here are manifold; at least it would be useful to know what is done in religious settings and how it is done.

Indirectly moral and affective education takes place both in schools and religious settings in all subject matters, and often unintentionally. In the religious setting, empathy, awe, wonder, community loyalty, and the like are gained through study, liturgical experiences, community celebrations, and group experiences, all of which embody interpersonal relations. But we often overlook the fact that the affective and moral are part of ongoing school activities, too. Awe and wonder may be associated with the teaching of astronomy without smuggling in doctrinal religious ideas. (The mechanistic approach, it should be realized, is also a "theological" stance.)[24] Communal celebrations of American holidays, each with its secular liturgies, are legitimate and nonsectarian.[25] Empathy, that capacity for seeing the world from another's shoes and so essential to all ethical deliberation, is a legitimate and desirable element in the interpersonal nature of most learning situations.[26]

The idea of the Judeo-Christian tradition that man is created "in the image of God" is the basis for Western man's affirmation of the worth and dignity of human life, basic to all ethical deliberation. If, for example, a student has derived this affirmation from a religious education, that would be a useful fact to be taken into account in curriculum development for moral education in the schools. Ethics may be shared and universal, but they are motivated differently by different religious groups. The main point for the schools is that the motivation is present and not necessarily the specifics of how the motivation may have been achieved.

In short, schools cannot properly create curriculum unless they are aware of who the learners are and where they are coming from. What is learned in schools and in religious settings may be mutually reinforcing or contradictory, or both. Each side can benefit only if it knows what is done by the other. Without getting *directly* involved with one another, an indirect dialogical relationship may emerge.

DEALING WITH CONFLICT

The fact that public schools and religious settings are components of educational configurations does not mean that the relationship is likely to be free from conflict. Given that the very diversity of the religious settings that we have described is a source of intrareligious conflict, consider how much more so is the relationship between them and the schools. Religious settings may provide students with integrated world-views, but this is not an unmixed blessing for the public educator. These world-views may be authoritarian and those who hold them dogmatic and closed-minded, making it impossible for them to tolerate, respect, or even consider another point of view. Parents or religious leaders may apply pressure that the school curriculum not present material perceived as inimicable to their religion. This has historically compelled educators to construct curricula so as to avoid controversy, thereby encouraging a blandness in school curriculum and learning materials. Moreover, with the diversity of religious viewpoints represented in a school, it may be well-nigh impossible to take every potential "offense" into account.

Yet, knowing about the divergent views that exist is only the beginning. Dialogue is only possible when the two sides recognize the existence of each other even when they disagree on basics. It is only possible, for example, to understand a student's difficulties in learning when one knows where that student is coming from.

A case in point:

"Secular" learning, including much of modern science, is rooted in metaphysical assumptions that derive from the prescientific presuppositions characteristic of religious faith. Recent work in epistemology and in the philosophy and history of science has stressed the idea that knowing is not just the objective observing of something outside the self. What the knower brings to the experience is itself part of the knowing.[27] Therefore, people who possess a religious world-view bring that to their experience of the world. Even those whose religious world-view has been transmitted in the most authoritarian manner bring a perspective to school that could well be viewed, in its possibilities for contributing to learning, in a positive light.

The Biblical account of creation, for example, has implications for the understanding of science *even* when the details of the fundamentalist position on creation clash with the schools' presentation of scientific truth as they see it. Even such conflicts as the creationist/evolutionist controversy of recent years have significant curricular potential for the schools. Thoughtful scholars and philosophers have, for a long time, seen the Genesis theory as a mythic structure for seeing the world as a place where the laws of nature have been implanted and which is, therefore, harmonious and meaningful. The Biblical view of creation, which implies the unity and the harmony of nature, therefore, may be understood as one of the historical sources of modern scientific thought and inquiry, and of the motivation to engage in them.[28]

Thus, on one level, there is obvious controversy, and the schools ought not get into the discussion over the doctrinal issues in a church's concept of creation. On the other hand, the very fact that such a concept is "there" could well be taken into account. Knowledge of this sort about the ideas and experiences that students bring with them to school, which derive from their religious backgrounds, represents a curricular challenge to the schools. Thus, there may be a way to relate positively and usefully even to the fundamentalist position.

This does not mean that conflict would be totally eliminated. Why should it be? There can be a creative tension between conflicting views. For most people the right to pass their cherished beliefs from generation to generation comes along with the understanding and acceptance of the fact that those beliefs will be challenged. If a belief is valued and valuable, those who hold it are not afraid of such challenges. Living in the creative tension between two respected frameworks may lead to a more acceptable synthesis, but that cannot be forced.

The Schools and Democracy

Schools are settings that mediate the diversity of a pluralistic society. Schools indeed have been the classic center for bringing together people of different backgrounds; they have been the place that helps develop the skills of community, of learning to live with others who have different interests. Schools have been the classic American "place."

In "melting pot" theory, this task involved consciously ignoring what keeps people apart and striving directly to find common ground. In light of the increased commitment to religious and cultural pluralism in recent times, we propose that the "public," community-building tasks of schools can best be achieved if they *build upon* diversity rather than try to ignore it. America needs a place where public issues can be deliberated and where people can be influenced to care about them. The schools for all intents and purposes are the best choice for that role. This is what we mean by "civic consciousness and public duty," the producing of which ought to be primarily the task of the schools. Those who leave the public schools for private schools, religious or otherwise, have the right to do so, but they also have the responsibility to find another vehicle to honor these purposes. If they do not do so, then the education they provide is in danger of being egocentric and chauvinistic; it will not respond sufficiently to the needs of the students, the community, or society at large.

The history of the United States has demonstrated that people can be loyal to more than one framework, especially when their loyalties overlap in many respects. Where there is potential conflict, people have to learn to deal with that conflict or live with it. If they live in two communities of belief at the same time, they have to learn to deal with issues that arise when the demands of differing primary loyalties are in conflict. Learning how to make such choices is part of the human dilemma in democratic societies, and schools are places where such learning can be accomplished. Schools cannot shrink from the task, for it will not take place automatically; they have to "make it happen." If students already have religious experiences that are pertinent, then they have an advantage, a head start. We have tried to show that among those life experiences that provide such a resource are the experiences that people have in religious settings.

If people already have the experience of participating in their religious community, then perhaps *that* basic attachment can be expanded to the larger community as a whole. Again: *perhaps* it can be expanded. But perhaps not. This is the challenge to the school; it will not happen automatically.

Dewey saw the school as an embryonic community in microcosm, a model of how the society cares about the individual who, in turn, grows in his or her dedication to the society. He saw the school as a simplified version of the community at large with all its stresses and strains, yet complex enough to provide a laboratory for learning how to live with others.[29] In a religious setting, people learn to submerge their personal differences or to deal with them in the overall framework of the mission of their religion. In doing so, some of the differences get smoothed over, some get sharpened, some remain, but individuals eventually come to share the basic religious perspective and way of life that characterize the setting.

This experience is brought to school where the proponents of one religious way then interact with the proponents of others. Here, too, the search is for something in common—our *American identity*, that public dimension that we come to share with others who may be in other respects very different from us. It is *more than* "Civil Religion"; it is the measured intentional growth of interpersonal caring and communal competency.

Schools create American community by discovering the areas of common interest, which people share regardless of their differences. A starting point could be that *deliberative* background from previous religious experience which people bring to the new encounter. To know the nature of this extra-school experience can only be a plus, and it should not be ignored. Such loyalties have generally been seen as a *barrier* to intergroup communications, and they have been thought to have "no place in school." Schools cannot deal with particularistic elements, with specific religious beliefs. However, the fact that such a backdrop of experience exists makes the development of other loyalties more likely and feasible.

Schools adopting the approach that we have suggested would indeed provide a challenge to religious commitment; the very exposure to other perspectives has the potential of undermining primary loyalties. People do make their ultimate life choices on the basis of their awareness of options, but that does not mean that the school experience will lead inevitably to students rejecting the views of the family and church. The very fact that the school deals with these sensitively, with an understanding that there *can be* overlapping loyalties, and that one does not necessarily exclude the other, provides simultaneously the opportunity for choice and the possibility of commitment to both the religious community and the community at large. A firm grounding in a religious point of view may ensure that that view will not be rejected peremptorily when it clashes with others. Under the right conditions, a new synthesis may arise that produces a more sophisticated faith, and this is another curricular challenge which will affect indirectly what happens in schools. Religionists who cannot chance this tension, however, would most likely be those who cannot take a chance on public education either.

In sum: schools deal with what it means to be a member of the American community. They can best do this if they help people draw upon their knowledge and values, derived from family and religious settings, to create this additional meaning together with others who do the same. Admittedly, we live in a time when religious world-views are no longer meaningful to many people. For these people, perhaps, primary meaning structures might derive to a greater extent from the school experience alone. For others who have had the advantage of family and religious education in their development, the school may add an enriching dimension to what they already know, and both sides may be changed in the process.

Children can learn to work with others of different persuasions if they have a firm sense of themselves. Schools must, therefore, realize that they are not only the victims but also the beneficiaries of the religious backgrounds that students bring with them to school.

FOOTNOTES

1. Formal learning in religious settings other than universities may be on an advanced level. See Samuel Heilman, *People of the Book* (Chicago: University of Chicago Press, 1983), for a description of informal adult groups organized for the relatively advanced study of Talmud in synagogues and private homes.

2. Philip E. Slater, "Religious Processes in the Training Group," in *The Religious Situation—1968*, ed. Donald R. Cutler (Boston, Mass.: Beacon Press, 1968), pp. 765 ff.

3. Lawrence A. Cremin, *American Education: The National Experience—1783-1876* (New York: Harper and Row, 1980), pp. 378 ff.

4. C. Ellis Nelson, "Conscience, Values in Religious Education," in *Foundations of Christian Education in an Era of Change*, ed. Marvin J. Taylor (Nashville, Tenn.: Abingdon Press, 1976), pp. 68-79.

5. Peter L. Berger and Thomas Luckmann, *The Social Construction of Reality* (New York: Anchor Books, 1967); Peter L. Berger, *The Sacred Canopy: Elements of a Sociological Theory of Religion* (Garden City, N.Y.: Anchor Books, 1969). See also, Clifford Geertz, "Religion as a Cultural System," in *The Religious Situation—1968*, ed. Cutler, p. 639.

6. It should be noted that it is only in the modern period, when religion becomes compartmentalized and split off from the rest of life, that the question of "religious education" as a separate enterprise arises. As schools have taken on the teaching of the matters of everyday life, formalized as the sciences and the humanities, religious education gets limited to those areas which are "religious" in the narrow conventional sense. Until the modern period, religion was viewed as coextensive with all of life and there was no such thing as "religious education" per se.

7. The classic paper on this issue is by R. S. Peters, "Reason and Habit: The Paradox of Moral Education," in *Philosophy and Education*, ed. Israel Scheffler, 2d ed. (Boston: Allyn and Bacon, 1966), p. 245. Modern religious curricula that claim to be in this mode abound. A recent example is Thomas H. Groome, *Christian Religious Education: Sharing Our Story as Vision* (San Francisco: Harper and Row, 1980). For a Jewish version, see articles in the *Melton Journal* (Jewish Theological Seminary, New York). For an interesting deliberation on this issue in the context of religious education, see Joseph J. Schwab, "The Religiously Oriented School in the United States: A Memorandum on Policy," *Conservative Judaism* 18 (Spring 1964):1.

8. See Margaret Mead, "The Comparative Study of Culture and the Purposive Cultivation of Democratic Values," in *Science, Philosophy, and Religion: Second Symposium* (New York: Conference on Science, Philosophy, and Religion, 1942). Dr. Mead and her discussants, writing during World War II, agonize over the right to indoctrinate democratic values.

9. Peter L. Berger, *A Rumor of Angels* (Garden City, N.Y.: Anchor Books, 1970).

10. In this light, it is fascinating to remember Freud's statement about his Jewish identity: "What bound me to Jewry was (I am ashamed to admit) neither faith nor national pride, for I have always been an unbeliever and was brought up without any religion though not without respect for what are called 'ethical' standards of human civilization. Whenever I felt an inclination to national enthusiasm, I strove to suppress it as being harmful and wrong, alarmed by the warning examples of the peoples among whom we Jews live. But plenty of other things remained over to make the attraction of Jewry and Jews irresistible—many obscure emotional forces, which were the more powerful the less they could be expressed in words, as well as a clear consciousness of inner identity, the safe privacy of a common mental construction. And beyond this there was a perception that it was to my Jewish nature alone that I owed two characteristics that had become indispensable to me in the difficult course of my life. Because I was a Jew, I found myself free from many prejudices which restricted others in the use of their intellect; and as a Jew I was prepared to join the Opposition and to do without agreement with the 'compact majority.' " Quoted by Erik H. Erikson, "The Concept of Identity in Race Relations: Notes and Quotes," in *The Negro American*, ed. Talcott Parsons and Kenneth B. Clark (Boston: Beacon Press, 1965, 1966).

11. Philip H. Phenix, *Education in the Worship of God* (Philadelphia: Westminster Press, 1966). For Phenix, religion is one of the "realms of meaning" without which man's apparatus for understanding the world is incomplete. See his *Realms of Meaning* (New York: McGraw-Hill, 1964). See also, Douglas M. Sloan, ed., *Education and Values* (New York: Teachers College Press, 1980).

12. James W. Fowler, *Stages of Faith: The Psychology of Human Development and the Quest for Meaning* (San Francisco: Harper and Row, 1981). Fowler's writing in general represents the most significant recent work on the psychology of faith development.

13. For an illuminating article on the teaching of community, see Joseph J. Schwab, "Learning Community," *Center Magazine* 8 (May-June 1975): 30-44.

14. Ibid. See also, Groome, *Christian Religious Education*.

15. David Purpel and Kevin Ryan, "Moral Education: Where Sages Fear to Tread," *Phi Delta Kappan* 56 (June 1975): 662. The entire issue is devoted to moral education.

16. The moral education movement has become an industry and a "religion" in its own right. For representative materials, see *Stage Theories of Cognitive and Moral Development: Criticisms and Application*, Reprint No. 13, *Harvard Educational Review*, 1978. See also, Brenda Munsey, ed., *Moral Development, Moral Education, and Kohlberg* (Birmingham, Ala.: Religious Education Press, 1980), especially the essays by Ernest Wallwork, Barry Chazan, and James M. Lee, who respond to Lawrence Kohlberg from the perspective of Protestant, Jewish, and Catholic education respectively.

17. See Craig R. Dykstra, *Vision and Character: A Christian Educator's Alternative to Kohlberg* (New York: Paulist Press, 1981).

18. The basic texts for the values clarification movement are: Louis E. Raths, Merrill Harmin, and Sidney B. Simon, *Values and Teaching: Working with Values in the Classroom* (Columbus, Ohio: Charles E. Merrill, 1966) and Sidney B. Simon, Leland Howe, and Howard Kirschenbaum, *Values Clarification: A Handbook of Practical Strategies for Teachers and Students* (New York: Hart, 1972). The critiques of values clarification are legion. See, for example, John S. Stewart, "Clarifying Values Clarification: A Critique," *Phi Delta Kappan* 56 (June 1975): 684-88, and Sidney B. Simon's reply (p. 688). Values clarification has become one of the most popular pedagogic strategies of religious education in all denominations. See, for example, Audrey Friedman Marcus, "Values Clarification," in *The Jewish Teacher's Handbook*, ed. Audrey Friedman Marcus (Denver: Alternatives in Religious Education, 1980). Analogous writings abound in Protestant religious education and even in Catholic settings.

19. In recent years, Kohlberg has expanded his own moral education approach beyond the discussion of hypothetical dilemmas to the development of what he has called "the just community." See his essay in *Moral Development, Moral Education, and Kohlberg*, ed. Munsey. In our opinion, the approach still is one-dimensional compared to what is possible in religious communities. Still, religious institutions ought to learn from moral education research in the latter's concern for developmental issues. This would enable the creation of more sophisticated *pedagogic* techniques, the pitching of Bible materials, say, at more appropriate levels without, at the same time, reducing them to moralistic tales. Concern for the "hidden curriculum," how the structure of an institution and the relationships in it teach, psychological sophistication about how "role models" function, and so forth are also necessary. Religious traditions have understood these matters intuitively, but the experience and research in these and other areas could be helpful.

20. The best anthology of articles that presents this approach and includes extensive additional bibliographies is Paul J. Will, Nicholas Piediscalzi, and Barbara Ann DeMartino-Swyhart, eds., *Public Education Religious Studies: An Overview*, American Academy of Religion (Chico, Calif.: Scholars Press, 1981).

21. *School District of Abington Township* v. *Schempp*, 374 U.S. 203 (1963).

22. Lawrence A. Cremin, *Public Education* (New York: Basic Books, 1976), p. 57.

23. See David R. Krathwohl, Benjamin Bloom, and Bertram B. Masia, *Taxonomy of Educational Objectives: Handbook II, Affective Domain* (New York: David McKay Co., 1964). One of the pernicious unintended effects of this book has been to influence educators to see the affective and the cognitive as two separate domains. It is incredible to hear this view in religious education circles.

24. See Richard A. Baer, Jr., "Cosmos, Cosmologies, and the Public School," *This World*, no. 5 (Spring/Summer 1983): np.

25. Robert N. Bellah, "Civil Religion in America," in *The Religious Situation—1968*, ed. Cutler, p. 331. See also, *Religious Education* 70 (September-October 1974), which is devoted to the theme of "Civil Religion" and has an extensive bibliography compiled by Boardman Kathan and Nancy Fuchs-Kreimer, pp. 541 ff.

26. Joseph Lukinsky and Stephen Brown, "Integration of Religious Studies and Mathematics in the Day School," *Jewish Education* 47 (Fall 1979): 28-35.

27. See Michael Polanyi, *Personal Knowledge: Toward a Post-Critical Philosophy* (Chicago: University of Chicago Press, 1958). See also, Bruno V. Manno, "Michael Polanyi and Erik Erikson: Towards a Post-Critical Perspective on Human Identity," *Religious Education* 75 (March/April 1980): 205-214.

28. Ian G. Barbour, *Issues in Science and Religion* (New York: Harper Torchbook, 1966). See also, Hans Jonas, "Jewish and Christian Elements in Philosophy: Their Share in the Emergence of the Modern Mind," in Hans Jonas, *Philosophical Essays* (Englewood Cliffs, N.J.: Prentice-Hall, 1974).

29. John Dewey, *Democracy and Education* (New York: Macmillan, 1916); idem, *School and Society* (Chicago: University of Chicago Press, 1900); idem, *A Common Faith* (New Haven, Conn.: Yale University Press, 1934).

CHAPTER IX

Youth-Serving Agencies as Educators

MARY CONWAY KOHLER, EDWARD L. FRICKEY,
AND DIXIE LEA

Introduction

In the United States, there are literally thousands of programs designed to provide out-of-school educational experiences for young people. A number of these are sponsored by schools; others are conducted by voluntary associations, some of which are affiliates of national organizations, such as the Scouts. In most cases, they have been established to fill a perceived gap in the learning environment of the community. The Youth Panel of the President's Science Advisory Committee spoke of the problem in terms of American youth being "information rich and experience poor." Schools offer "an incomplete context for the accomplishment of many important facets of maturation."

This panel and other committees and commissions have stressed the serious problem that many young people have today in making the transition from childhood to adult life. They have had few opportunities to assume responsibilities that are an important part of adulthood and to suffer or enjoy the consequences of their efforts to meet these responsibilities.

Although there are many programs that furnish opportunities for young people to learn in the world outside of school, a majority of youth are not participating in such programs. There are a variety of reasons. One is the lack of understanding among many community and school leaders of the significance and need for programs of this sort to provide essential learning experiences for all young people. This chapter is planned to furnish examples of two kinds of educational out-of-school programs. In the first section, Judge Mary C. Kohler outlines and describes programs that are often sponsored by schools. In the second, Edward L. Frickey and Dixie Lea describe and explain the programs of 4-H, which is sponsored by state and national organizations of the Land-Grant Colleges and U.S. Cooperative Extension Service. Space in this volume does not permit us to present a larger number of examples. These two, however, suggest the possibilities for important learning in the local community through programs which may be sponsored by schools or by volunteer groups or agencies.

1. Developing Youth Who Are Responsible and Caring

MARY CONWAY KOHLER

Some years ago, I was listening to the parent of a friend, a mother of many children—a woman considered learned and wise. She was telling me the facts of life about young people.

"Adolescent years are torn with conflict," she said. "We really can't get to these youngsters. We can't even understand them. I can't even understand mine. So, you'll just have to stop worrying about kids. The secret is to mentally bury them at fifteen years old and dig them up again at twenty."

She really believed that. So do millions of other parents like her who want their children out of the way during the adolescent years. Even most adults still give our young people the same message. We bury all that youthful energy, all that caring, all that potential. But instead of burying them at fifteen and digging them up again at twenty, we have extended the interment by six years. Today we bury our youth at ten and do not absorb them into adult society until about twenty-one.

During my seventeen years as Referee of the San Francisco Juvenile Court, I saw hundreds of young people who refused to be buried. Some had turned their energies in destructive directions, but many were just normal youngsters trying to understand and deal with their own potential. During all those years of work with young people in the Court, I saw many children and adolescents who felt rejected and unloved, yet they wanted to show their love and caring. Almost always, I could detect their desire to make a difference, but they seemed to be unable to make a difference constructively in their families and society.

Unfortunately, by treating young people the way we do in this country, we are wasting their potential. We keep postponing the time when we allow them to contribute to society and test their capacities for making important decisions for which they can assume responsibility.

We cannot expect young people to know intuitively how best to utilize their talents, skills, and other potential. Adults need to present them with constructive avenues in which to employ their abilities.

ORIGIN AND MISSION OF THE NATIONAL COMMISSION ON RESOURCES FOR YOUTH

In the early 1960s, I was a member of President John F. Kennedy's Youth Employment Committee, whose task was to design job opportunities for young people who were out-of-school and out-of-work, as well as for low-income youngsters still in school who needed part-time work to continue. Once the youth employment legislation had come into existence in the Youth Employment Act of 1962, the President's Committee went out of existence, but only officially. Many of us on the Committee continued to meet informally to discuss how we could work together to develop public interest in helping youth to develop into responsible, caring adults. To legalize our efforts, we incorporated. We became the National Commission on Resources for Youth.

Our mission, as we saw it then, was to figure out how to make America a better place for young people by giving them responsible and challenging roles. This, we thought, would involve three problems. The first was attitudinal. It was clear to us that our country desperately needed the caring and human services that youngsters could offer. Ironically, while the United States faced tremendous social and economic problems, as well as problems with youth, it also had in young people themselves abundant means for solving some of these problems. We Americans could provide a decent life for all our people. What we lacked was the commitment to change the present attitudes toward youth and enough people capable of providing the leadership to do this.

The second problem was how to create opportunity for young people to become full-fledged members of their communities. We wanted them to find social roles where people depended on them. This thinking led us to develop the concept of Youth Participation Programs. For such programs to help youngsters make the transition from childhood into responsible adult life, they would need to have certain essential elements such as opportunities to assume responsibility and to engage in challenging action. The action needed to be something that made a difference to someone. It had to meet a genuine need in the community. We also wanted young people to be able to participate in making decisions about what they did or did not do. Further, we realized that such programs should enable young people to reflect frequently upon their experience and discuss it. In this way, they could recognize and understand what they were doing, how effective it was, what consequences were involved when they made mistakes, and what should be done next.

The third problem was the most difficult. We were asking adults to invite youngsters to participate deeply in the life of their communities and to accept them as equals in that involvement. But it is very hard for adults to accept young people as equals, and it is a very revolutionary idea in today's world.

We thought we could easily sell the idea of youth participation to the government. Congress, however, was content with the Youth Employment Act. We realized that this movement could not be developed from Washington as a strategy for local communities; it would take long years to build up momentum in the states and localities. So we began the slow work of developing programs in a number of communities. We hoped these programs might become examples, if not models, that could be adapted in many places.

EXAMPLES OF YOUTH PARTICIPATION PROGRAMS

In developing youth participation programs, it is essential for local sponsors to take responsibility for the conduct and continuing improvement of the programs. We found that many local schools were interested in this sponsorship. We also found that churches and other local institutions concerned with youth were willing to take responsibility for youth participation programs. In a few cases, colleges and universities became sponsors. Teachers, other educators, guidance counselors, youth workers, psychologists, and psychiatrists have been frequently involved in developing these programs, with representatives of the National Commission on Resources for Youth serving local groups as advisors and a resource.

Our first experimental programs in youth participation followed three approaches: Youth Tutoring Youth, Day Care Youth Helpers, and Peer Co-Counseling. I shall briefly describe each of them.

Youth Tutoring Youth. In the mid-1960s, the states were receiving federal funds to administer the Neighborhood Youth Corps, which provided jobs, in school and out, for unemployed youth living in poverty. I found that few of the jobs being offered provided significant learning experiences. For example, the jobs usually included mowing lawns, cleaning up parks, emptying waste baskets, washing chalk-boards, or cleaning erasers. All of these jobs needed to be done. Yet we believed the projects should provide young people with jobs that would entail a helping service to others; in other words, jobs that would make these adolescents feel that their actions would make a difference in the lives of other people.

We were told that no such jobs existed. We would have to create them. This was how the Youth Tutoring Youth program began in Newark, New Jersey, in the summer of 1968. We wanted to begin with the most difficult situation we could find, believing that a program that could work against heavy odds should work in many other situations. In Newark, at that time, the dropout rate was extremely high and student literacy was very low.

We asked the school system to let us use a school during the summer in one of Newark's poorer neighborhoods. We were offered the South Side High School. Then we asked for about fifty of their poorest students who were at least fourteen years of age. These young people were to be the tutors of younger children in our program.

We were given students who were performing at least two years behind their grade level, but they were also considered the "worst kids" in the school. They were members of youth gangs, and many had delinquency records. When we asked the teachers why delinquents and gang youth were selected, they said, "You wanted us to find fifty poor students in a hurry, and we knew for sure that these kids were poor students. They stuck out in our minds like sore thumbs because of the trouble they had given us."

We brought the fifty young tutors into the school for a few days of orientation. We explained to them that their job would be tutoring young children sent to summer school because they were failing to learn to read. Each tutor would have two students, one in the morning and one in the afternoon for four days each week. The fifth day would be a training session for the tutors. At the end of each day, they would meet with us and with the supervisors to discuss their insights and to share with each other what they had learned.

Instead of training the new tutors in the usual methods of drills, quizzes, and tests, and assigning them to work with an already manufactured textbook, we simply explained the skills that their academically struggling children needed to learn. Instead of telling a tutor what to do, we might say, "Mary, Charles is now in your charge. He seems to have a problem reading. Maybe you can find out what bothers him and find a new way to teach him."

Standard textbooks—from first grade to college level—were made available in a room set aside for the students. We also provided paper, paints, scissors, masking tape, old magazines, tin cans, scraps of fabric, shells, straws, empty paper cartons, yarn, string, glue, and assorted other construction materials for the use of the new tutors in developing materials to teach reading.

On the very first day, some of the young tutors rose to the occasion by inventing creative teaching methods. Their successes were eagerly shared in the review meeting at the end of the day and this sharing inspired other tutors to develop ingenious responses to their task. Predictably, some of the youngsters did not quickly develop creative teaching methods. They experienced a few days of trial and error and meandering around the task. Some of the adult supervisors were tempted to take over and show the young tutors how to do it. But we assured them that the young tutors were taking the necessary time to discover the interests and motivation of their tutees.

It soon became evident to the tutors that each child had some strong interest, whether it was in cars, dogs, airplanes, cats, horses, or dolls. The tutors worked long into the evening to invent materials and tailor them to the individual interests of their tutees. We were astonished to see tough gang youth, who as students had been uninterested in classroom learning, gradually become competent teachers of younger children and adult models for their tutees. Like ideal educators, they were inventing teaching tools personally designed to meet the needs of each of their students.

The academic objectives we had set at the beginning of the summer concerned both the young children and their tutors. We hoped the young children's language skills would increase and that they would improve their attitudes toward school and themselves. This was achieved. As for the tutors, we hoped that they would improve their own language skills and increase their interest in school. When we compared test results on the Iowa Silent Reading Test before and after the weeks of summer school, we discovered that the average tutor had advanced three years and five months in language skills.

To the Commission, even more important than the academic scores were the new attitudes we saw developing in the young people. Among the attitudes were improvement in self-image, an increase in self-confidence, a renewed interest in school, and a more positive role identification.

During the next five years following the summer of 1968, Youth Tutoring Youth programs grew by leaps and bounds, and came to be a common practice in many school systems across the nation. We summarized the results of the Commission's five years of work in a book entitled *Children Teaching Children.*[1]

Day-Care Youth Helpers. Ever since my days as a Referee in Juvenile Court, one thing has bothered me almost obsessionally: the lack of nurturing in the lives of these youngsters who get into trouble. Recent studies show that the number of children who have not experienced much love and concern is increasing markedly. At ages fifteen or sixteen, these young people still need nurturing, but by then they have little chance of getting it from their families. My hunch was that if these young men and women could give nurturance to children, their caring attention would reflect back upon themselves, and their unfulfilled need for care and attention might possibly begin to be satisfied. This was the idea behind our Day-Care Youth Helpers program. We hoped to expose adolescent youth to nurturing by letting them be the nurturers.

Our plan was to work with a school in a disadvantaged neighborhood. Students who so desired could elect to serve as auxiliary staff at a nearby day-care center for a few hours on certain school days. Afterward, when they returned to the school, they would attend a class in child development where they would discuss the problems they could not understand about the children's responses, or their own. In such a reflective discussion, the adolescent might observe, "I can't understand why Jenny sits in a corner and sucks her thumb. I can't seem to interest her in toys or anything." To this, another youngster might respond, "Have you ever thought of putting her on your lap and rocking her?"

We felt that questions and comments like these would offer the classroom teacher an opportunity to talk about interpersonal situations that generate strong emotions such as fear, anger, resistance, or violence, and how the need for nurturing might be one of the roots of the problem.

During the summer of 1972, we started our first Day-Care Youth Helper pilot programs in a number of cities. The main objective of the program was to offer disadvantaged youngsters a chance to show and experience the nurturing of younger children in a real setting. As they built a foundation of knowledge about the physical, intellectual, social, and emotional development of the children, the Day-Care Youth Helpers were able to try out in real-life situations what they were learning in class. But more important, as I saw it, was that both the students and their charges were experiencing the kind of nurturing that only comes when two people care about each other and show it.

As I observed the program in Newark, I noticed that each day when the junior high school students arrived at the day-care center, there was a rush of excitement as the little children ran to greet the older students. Clearly, a fond relationship had been established in the few days that the programs had existed. When the Youth Helpers first came, they had to work with the little children to build rapport, perhaps by sitting on the floor with a child and playing together.

I remember one young helper, a girl who came from a public housing development for the poorest families in the neighborhood. She formed a great affection for a particular child who had been bruised by being thrown around by irate parents. In one of the center's closets they found a doll. It was a very fragile thing, but the child loved the doll, and the older girl sewed a dress for it. At the housing project where she lived, she collected scraps of material that had been thrown into the trash, and from them she made an entire wardrobe for the doll. She learned the art of sewing in the process, but more importantly, in fantasy she imagined she was making all the beautiful clothes she herself wished she could own. The day-care situation gave her the opportunity not only to nurture the young child, but also to nurture her own dreams and wishes.

After two years of trying to establish Day-Care Youth Helper programs across the United States, we realized that we could not provide sufficient staff to offer the constant follow-up and support the programs needed in order to succeed. There was no way we could develop general rules to make the necessary adjustments and maintain continued cooperation between the two separate institutions—the schools and the day-care centers.

In the meantime, certain youth-serving agencies, including the Girl Scouts and other girls clubs, picked up the idea of youth working in day-care centers as a way of learning parenting and implemented it in their programs.

Peer Co-Counseling. The idea of young people helping others in the community has been the central focus of the Commission since its inception. But the idea of youth counseling their peers has a special history.

During my court years in San Francisco, I often noticed spontaneous co-counseling taking place among the girls at the detention home, and I was impressed by a certain kind of earthy wisdom in these young women. Although at times one girl might try to lead another astray, more frequently one youngster would guide another into a healthier attitude toward life or into more appropriate conduct.

I once overheard a former prostitute counseling another girl. As she spoke, I was impressed by her lack of preachiness and her sense of wisdom. "Do you realize," she said, "it just depends on us? I mean, whether we stay in prostitution or whether we choose to go through the kind of struggle it takes to finish high school? It might mean staying at home and taking the beatings our fathers give us, but in the end we'd be able to support ourselves and be independent. Otherwise, we just become the property of some pimp." These two girls were both runaways trying to support themselves. They had found their way to one of the more popular houses of prostitution in San Francisco. I think it first dawned on me, when I heard such young people trying to help each other, that peer counseling could work.

However, I did not think of it as a possible Commission program until I saw large-scale peer co-counseling in action in a very successful youth participation program under the leadership of Dr. Robert Petrillo, counselor in the Woodlands High School in Hartsdale, New York. He was the only counselor on the high school staff, and he realized that he could not singly reach all the young people who needed help. He asked the administration for the use of a room where students could come and talk about their problems. Word soon spread that if anyone needed help with a personal problem, he or she could go to RAP Room for that help. It was open during school hours on Mondays, Wednesdays, and Thursdays. I visited the RAP Room many times, and I observed that there was a socioeconomic mix of Woodlands students who participated. Some were children of upper- and middle-class professionals; others came from modest homes or from a nearby public housing project. As I listened to the youngsters airing their problems and supporting each other, I became intrigued with peer counseling. In that RAP Room, I observed a sincere caring on the part of those adolescents who were sharing their problems with their peers. Dr. Petrillo served as their facilitator. He seldom spoke, and the young people seemed to have no inhibition as they talked to each other in his presence.

One youngster might say, "I've got a problem I wish we could discuss." The problem might be feeling unfairly treated by a teacher, or worry about a pending divorce between parents, or anxiety about a recent sexual involvement with some girl or boy. Alcoholism and drugs were much discussed. But whatever the problem, the youngsters openly reacted, expressed their opinions, made suggestions, and truly co-counseled.

The foundation of RAP Room and the key to its success was trust. Because the students felt assured of confidentiality, they were free to speak about deeply personal matters such as parental problems, conflicts with siblings, jealousy, anger, sexual anxieties, and racial prejudices. In this atmosphere of trust, self-disclosure was encouraged, and the youngsters would draw out the student who was speaking by asking sensitive questions.

In order to promote peer counseling in the schools, the Commission sponsored a number of workshops across the country where adult counselors could learn how to initiate and maintain peer counseling.

We pointed out the many possibilities for its use, such as suggesting that peer counseling could provide an easy way to introduce new pupils into the mainstream of the school, how it could be used to break up cliques in the school and widen the possibilities of friendship, and how it could help integrate students who felt isolated from the mainstream because of poor English or being the "new kid in town."

The program became tremendously popular with students in both junior and senior high schools. Youngsters who took the peer-counseling training were encouraged to volunteer for in-school counseling. Their supervisor arranged various types of assignments. They included providing one-to-one assistance on adolescent problems, working with physically handicapped peers, teaching social skills, orienting new students, or serving as teaching assistants in psychology classes. In addition, the young counselors were often sought out informally by other students as advisors to help meet a wide variety of problems.

Many schools reported that the peer-counseling process had been an instrument of growth for hundreds of students. For example, a scientifically studied peer-counseling program in Libertyville, Illinois, reported that both peer counselors and counselees improved in seven categories: self-confidence, school attendance, school performance, classroom behavior, family relationships, coping with daily problems, and providing mutual support among students. Though control groups showed some gains in some of these areas, they were much smaller in amount.

Despite the many differences in peer-counseling programs throughout the country, all of them contained a training component, adult supervision, and backup. The emphasis in peer counseling is on listening, caring, empathizing, and being a friend. "In this way," explained Dr. Norman Sprinthall, the director of the peer co-counseling program in Minnesota, "we ward off the possibility that the trained teenagers will begin to think of themselves as junior psychiatrists. Instead, the students begin to realize that helping relationships can be formed with friends."

Other examples. I have described these three examples of youth participation programs in some detail to give the reader a sense of the deep involvement of youth in the various activities and their intellectual and emotional development in the process. A brief description of several other programs will give the reader some indication of the variety of programs that the Commission has identified.

Some students in the Berkeley, California, East Campus High School established a Career Center for the benefit of their fellow students. Some of the student body were from low-income backgrounds and therefore were in need of jobs. But they did not know where to look for work. The students who staffed the Career Center located paying jobs for youngsters who were interested in working. They learned the requirements for various careers and then counseled their schoolmates. Even more important, the Center staff learned job-seeking skills, such as collecting references, writing résumés, and being interviewed. They then passed these skills on to other students who came to the Center.

In neighboring Marin County, California, the emphasis for involving young people was not focused on finding paying jobs but on volunteer service. Here, a Youth Participation program, called the "Switching Yard," was sponsored not by the local high school, but by the Volunteer Bureau of Marin County. The Switching Yard became the Youth Placement Branch of the Volunteer Bureau, which trained students and paid them to act as volunteer coordinators in their high schools. In this way, students interested in community service were referred to agencies and programs that needed volunteers.

The Switching Yard also operated projects of its own. In one such project, they organized a group of high school students to lead therapeutic play groups for emotionally disturbed children. The idea for this began when some members of the Switching Yard group noticed that there was inadequate after-school care for physically and mentally handicapped children. In order for school buses to accommodate the mainstream of students, the handicapped children were taken home much earlier and often left at a home where no adult was present until he or she returned home from work several hours later. In a number of cases, the emotionally disturbed children would become anxious and frightened when left in front of an empty house.

"This can't go on," said one of the Switching Yard team. "We've got to provide some kind of care for these kids." So these high school students found quarters near the school where the children could be left. They developed a program and were responsible for its management and for providing good playtime.

In San Diego, California, a group of young women, aged thirteen to eighteen, wrote, designed, produced, and distributed a community-based newspaper that dealt with high school women's issues. These same young women journalists also did public speaking about women's issues at area high schools and community youth forums.

As another example, teams of young women from nine Massachusetts high schools met together and were trained to become alert to sex-role conditioning in their communities and to learn the provisions of the state's equal education laws. They then returned to their high schools to plan and carry out programs to deal with the sex-stereotyping they identified in their own schools.

Programs such as the two described above take young people out of the fundamentally passive structure of the typical classroom and place them in active roles in which they directly interact with the school and the community. The challenging and responsible action these young women performed helped to overcome the limiting and negative self-image that so many of them seemed to have.

Another similar program was operated in Salt Lake City. It helped low-income, young women, who had dropped out of high school, to learn nontraditional job skills. A number of the program's activities focused on energy conservation and the use of solar energy. The young women assumed responsibility for major program decisions. They worked in community building projects and did jobs such as weatherizing low-income homes and constructing solar greenhouses. They also received training in assertiveness and communication skills. While the schools they attended might have encouraged conformity, dependence, and passivity, their work in the program challenged them to be creative, cooperative, and active, and offered them a way to make a difference in their community.

A final example of the variety of Youth Participation is the Barefoot Doctors program of New York City, located at one time at the Dewitt Clinton High School. It involved sixty male high school students who provided health screening and information to their peers and other community members. They ran a screening clinic at the high school, where they checked for venereal disease symptoms, tested urine and blood pressure, measured height and weight, took temperatures, and did some dental screening. They also provided training in venereal disease prevention and treatment in many high school classes and provided screening and information to community members at a variety of sites. Participants in this program received some training and firsthand experience at the North Central Bronx Hospital.

These examples are but a few of the several thousand described in the files of the National Commission on Resources for Youth. They demonstrate not only that schools and communities can establish and carry out programs that utilize the energies of youth and aid them in their constructive development, but that thousands of localities are already doing so.

DEFINING YOUTH PARTICIPATION

As the Commission worked with local groups in developing programs, a definition of effective programs gradually evolved. We stated it in the following words:

Youth Participation means the involvement of young people in responsible, challenging action, that meets a genuine need, with young people having the opportunity for planning and decision making that affects others, in an activity that has an impact on others (people or community), but definitely goes beyond the young people involved.

This definition became the norm by which the Commission selected projects for inclusion in its files and described them in the Commission's Clearinghouse and newsletter.

In addition to the four essential components of the definition, there are two other features that will enrich Youth Participation programs. The first is a seminar that offers a chance for young people to reflect critically on their experiences and on the program and its processes. The seminar should also include the adult learners. The second feature is that the program should provide opportunities for a group effort on the part of young people toward a common goal.

John Dewey reminded educators that experience alone does not automatically produce learning. There is a need to link practice with reflection. It is necessary to reflect upon and examine one's experience if its meaning is to be consciously grasped and understood. Often the reflection relates the experience to relevant subject matter the students are dealing with in their classes. The purpose of having students reflect on what they do is not primarily to pass judgment on the activity, but to enable them to discover significant meaning in it and to see its importance in the lives of both themselves and others. In this way, they can find ways to act more effectively and caringly in the future.

Participating in group efforts toward a meaningful social goal is an important developmental experience that adolescents often miss. It is a special privilege and a strongly motivating experience to be part of a team committed to carrying out a project that makes a difference in the lives of other people. Though highly desirable, this component is not necessary to every successful Youth Participation program. Much worthwhile experience can result from individuals working alone on a program. Being able to work effectively as a team member, however, is a quality that prepares young people for the team work that takes place in adult life in families, business, and many other situations.

In the nearly twenty years of the Commission's efforts, it has become clear that Youth Participation programs can provide young people with vital experiences that complement their academic learning and can greatly assist in their development toward responsible adulthood.

2. Education in 4-H

EDWARD L. FRICKEY AND DIXIE LEA

While opportunities for most American youth to engage in constructive educational activities outside the school have been sharply curtailed by changed conditions in American society, the 4-H program continues to furnish these opportunities. 4-H is the informal youth education program of the Cooperative Extension Service, conducted on a cooperative basis by the United States Department of Agriculture, state land-grant universities, and county governments. Federal, state, and local Extension employees and volunteer leaders staff the program. Participants are primarily between the ages of nine and nineteen and reside in every demographic area: farm, city, and places in between. The program is open to all interested youth, regardless of race, color, sex, creed, national origin, or handicap.

Young people participate in 4-H through a variety of programs.

These include organized 4-H clubs, special interest or short-term groups, school enrichment programs, instructional television series, camping programs, or as individual 4-H members.

A dynamic growing organization, 4-H has expanded steadily over the years. The most recent statistics indicate that there are approximately 5 million boys and girls involved in this youth educational program. Of the total current enrollment, 65 percent are girls. Since 1914, over 40 million youth from all states, plus the District of Columbia, Puerto Rico, Virgin Islands, and Guam, have participated in 4-H.

THE ORIGIN AND DEVELOPMENT OF 4-H

4-H had its beginning at the turn of the century. School administrators saw the need for technical training in agriculture beyond the traditional curriculum. This technical training was needed in agricultural production to enable farmers to increase their income. In 1904, the first "corn club" was organized to teach youth about raising corn. This modest beginning expanded into other 4-H clubs, which placed a similar emphasis on agriculture and home economics. 4-H was started by formal educators in the school and designed to supplement the schools' curriculum. 4-H still maintains this close tie with the schools and in many cases uses school facilities for club meetings and teachers as volunteer leaders.

In the early 1900s, over half the country's population was engaged in farming, and 4-H clubs were organized to serve this part of the American scene. However, as agricultural production increased and became more efficient, the population shifted to the cities. The 4-H program was mandated to expand its emphasis to where people were living. 4-H clubs now operate in Chicago, Detroit, Newark, and many other urban areas of this country. Traditional 4-H Club program models have been adapted to meet the particular environment and needs of urban dwellers, and the clubs continue to grow.

Joan Lipsitz, Program Associate for Adolescence with the Learning Institute of North Carolina, and a consultant to the Ford Foundation, explains this continuing growth of 4-H as follows:

When we look at the various institutions that serve these kids, there is a terrible lack of fit between the institutions and the early adolescent group. Generally, I think that we don't know who these kids are and who we want them to be. However, I do believe there is hidden 'gold' in voluntary organizations because they serve young adolescents in ways that strictly bureaucratic organizations cannot. *Yet, most national voluntary youth organizations are suffering from serious image problems. 4-H doesn't have the precipitative drop off in enrollment at this age level that some of the national organizations have.* I think 4-H has the answer: 4-H involves youth in the sharing of decision making and program policy—in other words, doing *with* instead of to or for. *4-H has strength not only in its learning by doing*, but also for involving young people in power.[2]

4-H PROGRAMS

In developing a local educational program, the club members, as well as the club leader, participate in examining possible projects, in deciding on one or more to undertake, and in selecting learning goals for the programs. This participation contributes greatly to the motivation of the club members. The following are a few examples of projects and learning goals.

In a rural county in western Wisconsin, a 4-H club leader became concerned with the influx of snowmobiles into the area. Young people with little or no training were driving snowmobiles into fences, trees, ravines, and other vehicles. He found the club members also concerned with this problem. With the help of parents and snowmobile merchants, the club organized a special interest group on snowmobiles. As goals to learn, they selected proper driving habits, methods of maintenance, and care of the machines. Through this project, they also learned first-aid and safety skills, how to conserve natural resources, and some of the attitudes and skills involved in good citizenship and leadership. The 4-H club built several miles of snowmobile trails and two bridges, and posted signs warning of potential dangers. The program resulted in a significant reduction in snowmobile accidents. Several hundred young people were trained in the proper use of mechanical vehicles. The club leader and 4-H members have been recognized by the community with several awards for their efforts.

This club's attack on a current problem closely parallels early 4-H club efforts to learn improved cropping techniques, food preparation and preservation, and tractor maintenance. Because such projects focused on problems in the communities, they obtained the cooperation of many local people.

4-H clubs may not only devise their own projects, as in the development of the snowmobile project; they are also aided by lists of exciting activities. For example, Indiana 4-H members may choose from the following offerings or develop their own interests:

Aerospace	Flower	Potato
Alfalfa	Food Preservation	Poultry
Aquatic Science	Foods	Rabbit
Arts and Crafts	Forestry	Recreation
Automotive	Garden	Shooting Sports
Beer	Geology	Soil and Water
Beekeeping	Health	Conservation
Bicycle	Home Environment	Soybean
Child Development	Home Furnishings	Strawberry
Clothing	Home Grounds	Swine
Corn	Improvement	10 x 10 Garden
Dairy	Horse and Pony	Tractor Program
Dairy Record	Junior Leadership	Veterinary Science
Dairy Goat	Lamb	Weather
Dog	Oats	Weed
Electric	People in My World	Wheat
Engineering	Personality	Wildlife
Entomology	Photography	Windowsill Garden
	Plant Science	Woodworking

Record keeping is an important part of each of these projects, and the project is finished only when the record is completed and the project work is evaluated. This data gathering, analysis, documentation, and reporting of facts help members learn basic knowledge and skills and reinforce the formal education experiences of the 4-H member.

As we mentioned earlier, 4-H clubs are to be found not only in rural areas and towns, but even in the inner cities. In Detroit, Michigan, thirty 4-H clubs have been established on the East Side. These clubs were organized to serve the needs of youth in a part of the city with the second highest crime rate. Young people in this program selected a variety of activities designed to teach them a skill, improve their self-image, enhance their community pride, and bring about closer ties with their families. An impact study of the area showed that youth who joined 4-H exhibited less asocial behavior and a significant reduction in juvenile offenses. The program had its greatest impact on teenage boys. In addition to its impact on youth, the program was very attractive to adult volunteers who gave freely of their time even though many of them did not have children in the program.

Over 9,500 4-H members in the urban areas of Pennsylvania annually attend county, regional, multicounty, or local 4-H day camps. Formerly called "street camps," these day camps meet special needs of inner-city and low-income youngsters. Programs are held close to home, often in streets, on sidewalks, or in vacant lots. They feature programs on preparation, quality, safety, and storage of food; recreation; citizenship; crafts; and conservation or recycling. Parents also become involved in these programs as short-time volunteers and contribute some of their resources in exchange for food information. Practices are adopted to improve family nutrition in the process.

In Luzerne County, Pennsylvania, 523 youth participated in twenty-nine summer "street" camps, under the leadership of two summer assistants and thirty-eight volunteer teen leaders. Local citizens contributed $900 to fund the "street" camps. The camps involved 499 youth who were not 4-H members.

EDUCATIONAL ACTIVITIES IN 4-H

There are a number of learning components to 4-H activities. For example, the emphasis on projects chosen by the participants not only furnishes a strong motivation but the projects involve "real life" activities so that transfer is greatly facilitated. Participants usually recognize that they are engaged in real tasks and not in practice exercises, although most projects entail a great deal of practice and feedback. A few more examples will indicate some of the learning experiences involved in the projects undertaken.

In Haywood, California, over 100 young people belong to a community 4-H club. Six volunteer leaders and fifteen team leaders work with the members in this racially mixed club. Members learn by growing and managing vegetable gardens, by preparing, serving, and preserving vegetables, and by marketing surplus produce. A similar program, the 4-H Green Market in Milwaukee, Wisconsin, has been supported financially by the Milwaukee Downtown Business Council. Produce managers from local supermarkets teach the youngsters how to grade, weigh, price, and display their products. In addition to produce, members sell home-made crafts, baked goods, and toys. They demonstrate how to can and freeze fruits and vegetables to market goers. The Green Market is also a showcase for 4-H talent: members sing, dance, and provide music and plays for city workers who lunch in the park.

The Willing Workers 4-H Club in Indiana identified leadership skills as an objective for each member. Instead of electing one set of officers, they select new presiding officers for each meeting. This gives each member of the club an opportunity to learn how to lead. In this process, members learn how to recognize the need for leadership, and the democratic process is respected, encouraged, and used to the benefit of the entire club. This involvement by the 4-H member in the decision-making process gives a feeling of accomplishment to every member of the group.

Virginia's 4-H Business Management, Economics, and Manpower Careers Program assists 4-H youth and volunteers to understand business management and economic principles. As new program materials are developed, information on careers becomes a part of various 4-H projects. A Business Management Workshop conducted in each of Virginia's six districts involves about 300 youth and adult volunteers. Participants are organized into small companies where they produce a simple object to be sold at a trade show. Follow-up to the workshop includes a 4-H marketing project, "Let's Start a Business." As a direct result of participation in this program, a 4-H community club on business was organized in one area involving fifteen teen members and three adult volunteer leaders. This group conducted monthly income-producing projects. Applying the information they had learned, they generated approximately $1,000 for the club in their one year of operation.

Experience in working with others and taking on club responsibilities helps members become better citizen leaders in their club and in their community. In fact, citizenship and leadership have become the by-products of the 4-H learning experience.

This by-product may very well be the continuing strength of all out-of-school educational activities. Activities, such as the "project" in 4-H or the "merit badge" in Scouts, can teach specific subject matter skills. However, while these skills are important, the additional citizenship skills and leadership skills that young people learn in the educational process may well form the most solid foundation for their growth and development.

VOLUNTEER LEADERS

There is another important factor that may help to explain the continuing growth of a 4-H, namely, the opportunity it provides for adults in the communities to share in its activities by being volunteer 4-H leaders. 4-H participation is satisfying to both youth and adults. The Extension Service has long recognized that the adult volunteer leader is the foundation upon which the 4-H is built. It spends a great deal of effort in identifying, recruiting, training, evaluating, and providing continuing education for volunteers. Local, state, and national recognition is given to superior accomplishments of volunteers, thereby enhancing their satisfaction and maintaining their strong motivation.

Moreover, because volunteers are supported by the equivalent of 4,372 professional and 1,225 paraprofessional 4-H staff members in local, state, and national offices, it is possible to recruit, train, and maintain continuing supervision and development of volunteers. The land-grant universities provide important intellectual resources for volunteer leadership, and nearly all of the approximately 16,500 Extension workers give some time to 4-H programs.

Volunteers also give the program continuity over the years and contribute thousands of hours of time working in a variety of roles. They assist youth in 4-H educational projects and activities. Many serve on local 4-H advisory committees. State or district planning groups are expanding roles of volunteer leaders to include middle management responsibilities, including recruiting and training other volunteers.

In recruiting volunteers, 4-H gives major attention to the motivation of the prospective recruit. The motivation to help others is a powerful resource when it is identified in the community and channeled through the 4-H organization. In recent years, the value of such volunteers has been widely recognized, and volunteers are sought by many groups.

The average 4-H volunteer donates 220 hours per year in preparing for teaching and teaching. Thus for each hour the salaried staff member spends in 4-H, a volunteer spends twelve hours. He or she drives 300 to 400 miles for 4-H in a personally owned car and spends $50 to $60 on teaching materials. Estimated value of the total time volunteers devote to 4-H plus their out-of-pocket expenses is about $1 billion annually. There is also substantial involvement and assistance to 4-H programs by community resource people, business, industry, agricultural, and civic groups. This assistance is not included in a Gallup survey of volunteer leadership.[3]

SOME PROBLEMS OF 4-H

In spite of continued growth, success, and community support, a number of problems confront 4-H today. Some of these problems are similar to those experienced by other youth-serving groups; some are unique to 4-H.

The strong rural image of 4-H is one of these unique problems. Even though 4-H programs have been conducted in urban areas for over twenty years, many people still consider 4-H a "farm" program. County 4-H fairs and grand champion steers often generate considerable media coverage, and the message they communicate to urban youth and their families is that 4-H is for young people who live on farms. The anomaly in this is that the majority of 4-H members live in large cities, suburban areas, and small towns. In 1982, 4-H enrollments indicated that 3,062,020 members came from towns and cities with populations over 50,000; 890,798 members came from towns and cities with populations under 50,000; and only 810,203 members lived on farms. While this strong rural image may have a restricting influence, it is still a strong base for future expansion.

The strong influence of the agriculture complex of the land-grant university on the 4-H program is another problem unique to 4-H. The land-grant university is a rich resource to the 4-H program, but it tends to restrict expansion in subject matter available to 4-H members. Traditional programs in agriculture and home economics do appeal to some youngsters. However, if 4-H could offer more programs in computer literacy, aerospace, communications and media, fine arts, cultural education, and other current high interest areas, it could appeal to an even broader clientele.

The problem that 4-H shares with other youth-serving agencies is the focus on competitive activities. Society's desire to convert activities into contests keeps many young people from actively participating.

Young people who are achievement oriented are successful in these contests. But youth who are less competitive feel inadequate and tend to drop out. In today's youth-serving programs, greater emphasis is being placed on participation. The focus tends to support cooperation and keeps competition in perspective with the overall growth and development of the child.

A second problem 4-H shares with other youth organizations is the potential for adults to dominate the program. Although parents and leaders grow and thrive in their 4-H leadership roles, there is often a need to remind them that many young people today have limited opportunities to make major decisions and to learn from their consequences. To remedy this, current 4-H leadership programs encourage parents and leaders to use "Shadow Helpership" techniques with 4-H members. Rather than deciding or doing things for members, leaders are encouraged to be on hand when help is needed, but to give members the opportunity to learn from their *own* decisions and experiences.

4-H plays an important role in the total educational program of the community. The neophyte learner is first exposed to education informally in preschool and kindergarten settings. Growth into more formal educational experiences occurs in the primary grades. Outside the schools, youngsters participate in many family-centered learning activities—camping, sports, peer relationships, and others. The 4-H program enters the learning arena at this point with organized, informal learning experiences. It offers the youngster the opportunity to belong, make choices, learn by doing, and learn leadership and citizenship skills.

The significance that 4-H plays in the growth and development of a person is elusive. There have been impact studies such as the one in Detroit, surveys like the Gallup Poll conducted in the 1970s to determine people's understanding of out-of-school activities, and some very sophisticated research designed to indicate causal relationships. They all support the value of informal educational experiences. However important 4-H becomes in any person's life, it is not a panacea. So much depends on the individual person and how he or she assimilates the varied learning experiences and grows as a result. One thing is clear: the 4-H experience reinforces the learning process and helps to provide productive citizens for the growth of our democratic society.[4]

Successful out-of-school educational programs will need to modify their efforts if they are to maintain and strengthen their role in educating children. They must provide specialized programs needed by youth and maintain flexible program requirements that are in keeping with today's needs, interests, and life-styles. In addition, programs must have current educational materials that relate to expressed needs of their clientele and permit goals to be set cooperatively by participants, parents, and leaders.

Youth organizations cannot do all things for all people. They need to choose an area of expertise and pursue it vigorously. They will need to identify, recruit, and train the rich reservoir of potential volunteers in this country. The burgeoning population of older Americans possesses skills and abilities to be shared with others. Large numbers of senior citizens can be recruited and involved in youth programs. American workers, moreover, are spending fewer hours on the job. Informal education organizations like 4-H can offer ways to involve them with others and satisfy many of their human needs.

Youth need a variety of experiences, both in kind and number, if they are to achieve their potential. This potential is at the very root of our democratic process. If we are to continue with the American way of life, we must take advantage of constructive learning experiences that can complement and supplement the school in the education of our children.

FOOTNOTES

1. Alan Gartner, Mary Kohler, and Frank Riessman, *Children Teaching Children* (New York: Harper and Row, 1971).

2. Joan Lipsitz, in an address to Youth Development Professionals, National Curriculum Project, Washington, D.C., November 12, 1978.

3. Gallup Survey, "The National Poll on Volunteers" (Unpublished report, 1981).

4. United States Department of Agriculture, *4-H Educational Goals and Objectives: 1983* (Washington, D.C.: Extension Service Printing Office, 1983).

CHAPTER X

Media and Technology as Educators

NEIL POSTMAN

All culture is a conversation. More precisely, it is a conglomerate of conversations, which may take a variety of symbolic forms. The differences among ordinary conversations are easy to identify. They may be constructive or aimless, amicable or belligerent, controversial or canned. We can characterize conversations in these ways and be more or less sure of what we are talking about. But when it comes to the mass conversation we call culture, categories like these are too glib to tell us much. Yet differences between cultures are as real, indeed as glaring, as those that separate different conversational tones. We cannot label them, but we should be able to account for them. How?

In the case of a conversational conversation (as opposed to a cultural one), we can account for variations in three ways: according to the occasion at hand, according to the participants present, and according to the subject under discussion. When I speak of cultural conversations, however, these three variables cease to be of much use in explaining differences. For one thing, the occasion of the cultural conversation is always and everywhere the same—it is simply the generalized quest for coherence, for harmony in a shrill universe. Second, the participants—the cultural conversationalists—are equally invariant. They comprise anyone who happens to be engaged in that quest, which, if we are to accept the foundation of all modern theories of mind, means everyone. The final variable naturally concerns the content of cultural conversations, and it is there that an explanation of differences usually begins. For surely it is what we talk about as a culture that characterizes our collective sensibility, just as, on a more intimate scale, a conversational content such as "breakfast foods" will lead in one direction, while one like "the nature of evil" will head in quite another.

But there is a problem. When we widen our scope to encompass culture-as-conversation, the matter of direction becomes curiously complicated. The reason why is quite simple, really. All cultural conversations are preoccupied with startlingly similar "subjects." We tell each other now—as we have always told—the same old stories: of our relationships to those in our midst (including ourselves); of our relationship to the physical, temporal, and spatial world surrounding us; and of our relationship to possible ultimate worlds that subsume us. But the ways in which different cultures frame these relationships can and do vary wildly. The reason has very little to do with who is doing the talking, or why we are talking, or even what we are talking about.

The answer resides in a fourth variable: the *way* we talk. Cultural differences may be impressively accounted for by considering how "the conversation" proceeds, or what we are talking *with*. It is, in brief, the symbolic forms in which cultural conversations are encoded that are largely responsible for our peculiarities of style, of scale, and of substance as inquirers. Or, to put it even more strongly, our means for conversing may very well define our ends as a culture.

Within any culture, it is the task of educators—their vital role in the conversation—to monitor these forms of talk. To understand the biases of various forms of discourse is to possess the means both for conserving what, in our culture, we deem of ultimate worth and for subverting what is hostile to it. It is a peculiar trust, really. It requires us to be extraordinarily attentive to the most ordinary phenomena: the means by which our culture talks to itself, better known perhaps by the term "communication media." Each new medium makes possible a new mode of discourse, requiring a refashioning of intellect and consciousness, and the evolution of this consciousness is mostly the history of our means for conversing.

The study of the technology of the intellect, I would like to note, was not invented by Marshall McLuhan. It has a long, if discontinuous, history that extends back at least to Socrates and Plato, both of whom made observations and prophecies about the influence of alphabetic writing on Athenian culture. Plato, for example, comments in his Seventh Letter that "no man of intelligence will venture to express his philosophical views in language, especially language that is unchangeable, which is true of that which is set down in written characters." Nonetheless, he wrote voluminously, and understood better than anyone else that the setting down of views in unchangeable language would be the beginning of philosophy, not its end.

Plato knew that writing changes the nature of criticism. Once thought is transcribed, it becomes the object of a continuous and concentrated scrutiny that is not possible with speech, which is to say that Plato knew that writing required a shift from the ear to the eye as an organ of language processing. (There is a legend that to encourage such a shift Plato insisted that his students know geometry before entering the academy.) He also knew that in an oral culture, the main task of the intellect is *to remember*: to remember its history, poetry, rituals, traditions. He knew this was an exhausting agenda that does not leave much time for or inspire any inclination toward philosophic invention. Writing, he believed, would release the intellect from its preoccupation with mimesis and would provide unprecedented opportunities for intellectual novelty and creativity.

Socrates disagreed. To him, only orality could express serious ideas, beautiful poetry, and authentic piety. He distrusted the disembodied, visual word, and nothing seemed more unnatural to him than the silence one encounters when posing a question to a text. Without immediate feedback, there could be no dialectic. Writing, Socrates held, forces a student to follow an argument rather than to participate in it. But more than this, he worried that writing would undermine the power to memorize, would destroy privacy, depersonalize audience, debase communication itself.

We can continue to discuss the views of Plato and Socrates. The point is, from the attention they paid to the nature of conversations, we can extract the three major problems that new technologies pose, problems that scholars to the present day have addressed and that educators now ignore at their peril.

To begin, we know that new technology may create novel preoccupations for the intellect and new social contexts in which the intellect must function. Therefore, we must ask: how does this occur and under what circumstances? Second, we know that such changes will result in both enabling and disabling consequences. The widespread use of writing in the fifth century B.C. is a paradigmatic example of the Faustian bargain that media change imposes. But, because we know more about it, the invention of the printing press with movable type is an even richer example. Typography created prose but made poetry into an exotic and elitist form of expression. Typography made modern science possible but transformed religious sensibility into mere superstition. Typography assisted in the growth of the nation-state but thereby made patriotism into a squalid if not lethal emotion. Every new form of conversation gives and takes away, although not necessarily in equal measure. Thus, the question is: are we getting more than we are yielding? And, assuming we have some answers to the previous questions, we must then ask: what, if anything, can we do about our situation?

No group of people has more reason to inquire into these matters than educators. The creation of the modern idea of school was, in fact, a consequence of the invention of the printing press. Prior to its invention, learning was unsystematized and informal. Knowledge was acquired mainly by ear, through sermons, drama, narrative poems, stories, and ballads. Certainly there was no need for what we call elementary schools, since all human beings are genetically programmed to learn to speak, and speech was the only conversation medieval culture required. But human beings are not genetically programmed to read. After the printing press, knowledge not only became systematized; it also became intimately associated with book learning. To be educated meant to be literate. For this reason, the school was consciously invented as a mechanism to promote literacy. And for three centuries it has devoted itself to teaching the skills and attitudes demanded by a book culture. This includes not only teaching the young how to decode letters but also teaching them how to remain immobile for long stretches, how to delay their responses (as well as their need for immediate gratification), how to analyze expository prose, how to think sequentially, how to learn in isolation.

Yet, as we move toward the twenty-first century, typography is clearly being moved to the periphery of our culture and the electronically produced image is taking its place at the center. We have entered the Age of Television—ready or not. For this reason alone, it is essential that educators consider carefully the nature of the changes this new environment will bring; just as typography brought schools into being, television may bring them to an end, at least in their present form. Or, if not that, the schools will survive only by establishing a harmonious relationship with the new biases of a new communication environment. In short, we need to know what we are up against.

A young graduate student I know returned to his small apartment the night before an important exam to discover that his only lamp was irremediably broken. He turned on the television set, turned off the sound, and with his back to the set used its light to read his notes. This is one educational use of television: as a source of illuminating the printed page.

But the television screen is more than a light source. It is also a smooth, nearly flat surface on which the printed word may be displayed. I have stayed at hotels in which one's television set has a special channel for describing the day's events in letters rolled endlessly across the screen. This is another educational use of television: as an electronic bulletin board.

Many television sets are also large and sturdy enough to bear the weight of a small library. Indeed, the top of an old-fashioned RCA console can handle as many as fifty books, and I know one woman who has securely placed her entire collection of both Dickens and Flaubert on the top of a twenty-one-inch Westinghouse. This is still another educational use of television: as a bookcase.

I mention these quixotic uses of television to ridicule the hope harbored by some people that television can be used to support the literate tradition. I have, in fact, heard English teachers maintain (indeed at a National Council of Teachers of English conference) that television can help children become literate because quite often words appear on the television screen. Perhaps they had in mind such phrases and sentences as CBS NEWS, AVIS TRIES HARDER, and SUPER-BOWL. There are even people who, possessed of an equally emaciated idea of what literacy is, believe that programs like "Sesame Street" advance its cause. In this belief, the National Education Association has bestowed honors on Joan Gantz Cooney, the creator of "Sesame Street"—a gesture somewhat akin to the National Railroad Workers of America celebrating the birthdays of Wilbur and Orville Wright.

Unfortunately, all such hopes represent perfectly and poignantly what McLuhan called "rear-view mirror" thinking: the assumption that a new medium is merely an extension of an older one—that an automobile, for example, is only a fast horse or an electric light, a powerful candle. To make such a mistake in the case of television is to misconstrue entirely how it educates the young. What is television? What kinds of lessons does it teach? What are the intellectual tendencies it encourages? Indeed, what sort of person does it produce?

These are compelling questions. To answer them, we must begin by making a distinction between a technology and a medium. We might say that a technology is to a medium as the brain is to the mind. Like the brain, a technology is a physical apparatus. Like the mind, a medium is a *use* to which a physical apparatus is put. A technology becomes a medium as it employs a particular symbolic code, as it finds its place in a particular social setting, as it insinuates itself into an economic and political context. In other words, a technology is merely a machine. A medium is the social and intellectual environment that a machine makes possible.

Of course, every technology has an inherent bias; that is, it has within its physical form a predisposition toward being used in certain ways, toward amplifying certain kinds of symbols. The printing press, for example, is a technology with a clear bias toward being used as a linguistic medium. It is *conceivable* to use it exclusively for the reproduction of pictures. And, one imagines, the Roman Catholic Church would not have objected to its being so used in the sixteenth century. Had that been the case, the Protestant Reformation might not have occurred, for the Reformation took its impetus from the spread of the printed *word*, not the picture.

Luther himself remarked that printing was "God's highest and extremest act of grace, whereby the business of the Gospel is driven forward." But in fact there never was much chance that the press would be used solely for the duplication of icons. From its beginning in the fifteenth century, the press was perceived as an extraordinary opportunity for the display and mass distribution of written language. Everything about its technical possibilities led to its being used in this way. Indeed, one might even say it was invented for that purpose. The technology of television has a bias as well. It is conceivable to use television as a lamp, a bulletin board, a bookcase, even a text. But it has not been so used and will not be so used—at least in America.

When we consider that virtually every American home has a television set; that more than half of our homes have two or more sets;

that television operates around the clock, seven days a week; that the average American youth has clocked about 5,000 hours of viewing before entering school; that sleeping is the only activity that occupies more of an American teenager's time than television viewing—when all of this is considered, the most obvious conclusion is that television is the major educational enterprise now being conducted in the United States.

Television has become our primary means for conversing on a cultural scale. It is our new form of talk. Consequently it is among the first and inarguably the most pervasive of the messages reaching the minds of our children. Television has become for American youth a curriculum. Indeed, if one may define a curriculum as a specially designed information system whose purpose is to train or cultivate the character of the young, then television, which does all this with a relentlessness of purpose no single human being could dare to equal, has become *the* curriculum.

For those who think I may be exaggerating the problem, here are some more figures to ponder: in the first twenty years of his or her life, an American child will see something approaching one million television commercials, at the rate of close to 1,000 per week. According to studies by Daniel Anderson of Harvard University, children begin to watch television with sustained attention at thirty-six months, at which time they are able to interpret and respond to the imagery of television. They identify with characters, sing television jingles, and begin to ask for products they see advertised.

Television, in other words, needs no equivalent of the McGuffey Reader. It is almost immediately accessible to the young and requires no prerequisite training. Unlike the school curriculum, television does not give its students time off for weekends, summer vacations, or holidays. Indeed, according to Frank Mankiewicz's book on television, *Remote Control*, every day of the year approximately two million children are watching television between 11:30 P.M. and 1:30 A.M. But the bad news does not stop here; it only gets more specific.

There are five characteristics of television that set *its* curriculum in direct opposition to what educators have always construed as *theirs*.

The first characteristic is the most obvious one and certainly the one from which most of the others are generated. It is simply that the basic mode of discourse of the television curriculum is the visual image. People *watch* television; they do not read it. What they hear is almost always subordinate to what they see, and what they see is millions of pictures. It is sometimes said that one picture is worth a thousand words. But we must not take this to mean that one picture is the equivalent of a thousand words. Or two hundred or twenty or even one. A word is a creation of the imagination in a way that a picture can never be. A picture, for example, cannot convey the idea of "cat" or "work" or "wine" or "book." A picture can merely give you an example, a particularity, whereas a word gives you a concept, a generality. There is no such thing in the universe as "cat" or "work" or "wine" or "book." Words, even of the more specific kind, are always several levels removed from reality. Words are abstractions and are therefore entirely responsible for whatever intellectual superiority we may claim to have over baboons. Thus, a curriculum based on pictures, such as we have with television, is very different from one based on words, such as we have in school. Moreover, the pictures seen on television are in constant motion and are continuously changing their aspect. The average length of a shot on a network show is 3.5 seconds. This means that every three and a half seconds, more or less, there is a new point of view or angle of vision and a new pictorial image to process. On commercials, the average length of a shot is 2.5 seconds. A child watching television must process as many as 1,200 different shots every hour. That means about 30,000 per week for your average eight-year-old. In brief, the television viewer is immersed in a world of pictorial representations, not linguistic concepts.

The second characteristic of television is related to the first. Because it consists of pictures and stories, television's curriculum is mostly nonpropositional. Pictures do not make assertions about the world, as language does. Pictures are presentations of experience, not commentary about experience. Thus, the television is largely irrefutable. You can dislike television programs, but you cannot disagree with them. There is no way, for example, for us to refute Laverne and Shirley, or an Ajax commercial, or Carl Sagan's turtleneck sweater, or Dan Rather's good looks. There is no way for us to show that the feelings evoked by the imagery of a McDonald's commercial are false or, indeed, true. Such words as "true" and "false" come out of a different universe of symbolism altogether. They are applicable to the world of exposition, in which we confront statement and counterstate-

ment, hypotheses, reasons, refutations, contradictions, explanations—
above all, where we confront ideas expressed in the form of subjects
and predicates. School, of course, is a world dominated by subjects and
predicates. Television is a world dominated by picture stories. It
makes exposition irritating to students and renders them increasingly
incapable of attending to it for long periods of time. In other words,
the television curriculum does not encourage the development of
analytical abilities, which is the central purpose of most school
subjects.

This leads me to the third characteristic of the television curriculum:
it is easy. As I implied earlier, watching television requires no skills; in
fact, it develops no skills. This is why we will never hear of courses in
remedial television viewing. It is also why we are no better today at
watching television than we were ten years ago. I am not about to
argue that easy things are necessarily worse than hard things. But, in
this case, the fact that no learning is required by the television
curriculum means that it is nonhierarchical, nongraded, and nondiffer-
entiated. "Sesame Street" is not easier to watch than "Cosmos" or
"Little House on the Prairie." Unlike books, which may be scaled
according to their lexical and syntactic complexity, and unlike school
subjects, which may be scaled according to their conceptual complexity, television has no idea of the prerequisite, or of sequential learning,
or of intellectual and emotional growth. Television is the most
egalitarian curriculum ever devised. Everything in it is for everybody,
simultaneously. For viewers there can be no standard of excellence or
competence or even improvement. The consequences of such an
education should be clear. It is enough to say that it mocks the ideas of
deferred gratification, self-discipline, and intellectual achievement.
Without these, education is mere entertainment.

This leads me to the fourth characteristic of the television curriculum; namely, that it is almost always entertaining. Television is an
attention-centered curriculum. It has no purpose that takes precedence
over keeping the attention of its student viewers. Unlike the school,
which selects its subject matter first and then tries to devise ways to
attract interest, television first selects ways to attract interest, then
shapes content accordingly. In the school curriculum, if the student
repeatedly does not pay attention, the teacher may remove him or her
from class. In the television curriculum, if the student repeatedly does

not pay attention, the teacher is removed from class; that is, the show is cancelled.

What television teaches is not merely that learning is fun, which quite often it is not, but that learning and entertainment are indistinguishable from one another. This is a very dangerous idea, not only because it is untrue but also because it makes teaching school increasingly difficult. Students expect to be charmed and amused by their studies and, above all, expect that what they are to learn ought to be instantly accessible to them. This situation is painful and perplexing to their teachers, who, naturally enough, want to engage their students' attention but to do so must model their lessons on television. It is not impossible in the years ahead that, if television is allowed to proceed unchecked, most teachers will be singing the entire curriculum to their students, interrupting their songs every eight minutes for a string of commercials. What all this implies for the state of learning in the years ahead is painful to contemplate. When there is no distinction between the tasks of the mind and the action of the viscera, we have, by definition, come to the end of education. The conversation is over.

The last characteristic of television I want to mention is that its curriculum is entirely fragmented and discontinuous. Nothing on television, for example, has very much to do with anything else on television. There is no theme or coherence or order to what is presented. Both the school curriculum and the television curriculum are windows to the world. Yet, the world as revealed through television is made up largely of discrete events having no connection to anything that has gone before or will come after. We need only glance at the weekly syllabus as found in *TV Guide* to see this confirmed.

The television curriculum in this respect stands in sharp contrast to the school curriculum, which even at its worse has a rational order to it. If the television curriculum has any organizing principle, it is merely the immediate, short-term psychological gratification of the viewer. What is shown on television requires no continuity and need have no implications beyond itself. That is one of the reasons why a commercial message, as it is called, can be inserted anywhere during a program—even a program that might be thought of as "serious." On any news show, for example, one may find a commercial for a detergent or a soft drink sandwiched between a story of mass murder and an earthquake in Chile. Now, if I had paused every few paragraphs in this article to insert a word or two in behalf of the United Airlines or Jordache jeans, you might rightly think I have no respect for my subject or my audience. Or, if you were in a less generous mood, you might believe I had lost my mind. Why, then, do we not think the same about those who design television presentations? The answer is that we do not expect or require that there will be any logical, emotional, or ideational connections among events shown on television. Each event stands alone, as each program stands alone, as each commercial stands alone.

Make no mistake about it: television's curriculum has a clear and powerful philosophy concerning the nature of reality. Its axioms include that history is bunk, hierarchies are arbitrary, problems have no antecedents, the future is not worth dwelling upon, randomness is uncontrollable. The word for these beliefs in philosophical discourse is nihilism. In aesthetic discourse, the word is Dadaism. In psychiatric circles, it is known as chronic depression.

The teachings of television are hostile to language and language development, to vigorous intellectual activity, to both science and history, to social order, and in a general way to conceptualization. Television is a curriculum that stresses instancy not constancy, discontinuity not coherence, immediate not deferred gratification, emotional not intellectual response. These are the values of television, the rules according to which it conducts its conversation. The question is: what can we do about it?

Perhaps the most important contribution schools can make is to provide youth with a sense of purpose, meaning, and interconnectedness in what they learn. At present, a typical, modern school curriculum reflects the fragmentation one finds in television's weekly schedule. Each subject, like each television program, has nothing whatsoever to do with any other. There is no longer any principle that unifies the school curriculum and furnishes it with meaning, unless it is simply that education is to provide jobs—hardly a moral or intellectual theme. One treads on shaky ground in suggesting a plausible theme on which to build an education. Nonetheless, I would propose as a possibility the theme that animates Jacob Bronowski's *The Ascent of Man*, a book and a philosophy filled with optimism and suffused with the transcendent belief that humanity's destiny is the discovery of knowledge. Although Bronowski's emphasis is on science, he finds ample warrant to include the arts and humanities as part of our unending quest to gain a unified understanding of nature and our place in it. Thus, to chart the ascent of man, which I will here call the ascent of humanity, we must join art and science. We must also join the past and the present: the ascent of humanity is above all a continuous story.

The virtues of adopting the ascent of humanity as a scaffolding on which to build a curriculum are many and various. For one thing, it does not require that we invent new subjects or discard old ones. The structure of the subject-matter curriculum that presently exists in most schools is entirely usable. For another, it is a theme that can begin in the earliest grades and extend through college in ever-widening and deepening dimensions. Better still, it provides students with a point of view from which to understand the meaning of subjects. Each subject can be seen as a battleground of sorts, an arena in which fierce intellectual struggle has taken place and continues to take place. The curriculum itself may be seen as a celebration of human intelligence and creativity, not a meaningless collection of diploma or college requirements.

Best of all, the theme of the ascent of humanity provides us with a nontechnical, noncommercial definition of education. It is a definition drawn from an honorable humanistic tradition and reflects a concept of the purposes of academic life that goes counter to the prejudices of television—namely that to become educated means to become aware of the origins and growth of knowledge and knowledge systems and to be familiar with the intellectual and creative processes by which the best that has been thought and said has been produced. To learn how to participate, even if as a listener, is what Robert Maynard Hutchins once called The Great Conversation. (Does it ring a bell?) Such a definition of education is not student-centered, not training-centered, not skill-centered, not even problem-centered. It is idea-centered and coherence-centered. It is also otherworldly, in that it does not assume that what one learns in school must be directly and urgently related to a problem of today. In other words, it is an education that stresses history, the scientific mode of thinking, the disciplined use of language, a wide-ranging knowledge of the arts and religion, and the continuity of the human enterprise. It is a definition of education that provides an excellent corrective to the antihistorical, nonanalytical, nonsequential, immediately gratifying biases of television.

As an example of what I mean, let us consider history. In some ways, it is the central discipline of all of this. As Cicero puts it, "To remain ignorant of things that happened before you were born is to remain a child." History is our most potent intellectual means of achieving a "raised consciousness." But some points about history and its teaching require stressing, since they are usually ignored by educators.

First, history is not merely one subject among many that may be taught in school. Every subject has a history, including biology, physics, mathematics, literature, music, and art. Therefore, every teacher should be a history teacher. To teach, for example, what we know about biology today without also teaching what we once knew, or thought we knew, is to reduce knowledge to a mere consumer product. It is to deprive students of a sense of the meaning of what we know, and of how we know. To teach about the atom without Democritus, to teach about electricity without Faraday, to teach about political science without Aristotle or Machiavelli is to refuse our students access to "The Great Conversation." It is to deny them knowledge of their roots, about which no other social institution is presently concerned—least of all television. To know about your roots is not merely to know where your grandfather came from and what he had to endure. It is also to know where your ideas come from and why you happen to believe them, and to know where your moral and aesthetic sensibilities come from. To complete Cicero's thought, begun before: "What is a human life worth unless it is incorporated into the lives of one's ancestors and set in a historical context?" By "ancestors," Cicero did not mean your mother's aunt.

I recommend that every subject be taught *as* history. In this way, our students can begin to understand that knowledge is not a fixed thing but a stage in human development, with a past and a future.

The teaching of subjects as studies in historical continuities is not intended to make history as a special subject irrelevant. If every subject were taught with a historical dimension, the history teacher would be free to teach what histories are—hypotheses about why change occurs. Of course, in one sense there is no such thing as "history." All historians, from Thucydides to Toynbee, have known that their stories must be told from a special point of view that always reflects a particular theory of social development. Historians also know that they write histories for some particular purpose—more often than not either to glorify or condemn the present. Thus, there is no definitive history of anything; there are only histories, human inventions that do not give us *the* answers, but give us only those answers called forth by the particular questions that were asked.

Historians know all of this; it is a commonplace idea among them. Yet it is kept a secret from our youth. Their ignorance of it prevents them from understanding how "history" can change and why the Russians, the Chinese, the Lebanese, and virtually every other people see historical events differently from the authors of history school books.

The task of the history teacher, then, is to become a "histories teacher." This does not mean that some particular version of the American, European, or Asian past should remain untold. A student who does not know well at least one history is in no position to evaluate others. But it does mean that at all times a histories teacher will be concerned with showing how histories are themselves a product of culture.

Some educators may object that this idea—history as comparative history—is too abstract for students to grasp. But this is one of several reasons why comparative history should be taught. If we teach the past simply as a chronicle of indisputable, fragmented, and concrete events, we merely replicate the bias of television, that is, we largely deny our youth access to concepts and theories and provide them only with a stream of meaningless events. Whatever events we may include in the study of the past, the worst thing we can do is to present them devoid of the coherence that a theory or theories can provide, to present them as meaningless. The histories teacher must go far beyond "events" into the realm of concepts, theories, hypotheses, comparisons, deductions, and evaluations. The idea is to raise the level of abstraction at which "history" is taught.

This idea should apply to all subjects, including science. I have already mentioned the importance of teaching the history of science in every science course. But this is no more important than teaching its "philosophy." Science should be taught as an exercise in human imagination, something quite different from technology. Is it an exaggeration to say that not one student in fifty knows what "induction" means? Or knows what a scientific theory is? Or a scientific model? Or knows what are the optimum conditions of a valid scientific experiment? Or has ever considered the question of what scientific truth is? Because our students do not address these questions, I would propose that every school—elementary through college—offer and require courses in the philosophy of science. Such courses should include a consideration of the language of science, the nature of scientific proof, the sources of scientific hypotheses, the role of imagination, the conditions of experimentation, and especially the value of error and disproof. They would emphasize that science is not pharmacy or technology or magic tricks but a special way of employing human intelligence. Students must learn that one does not become scientific by donning a white coat or by manipulating substances (which is what television teaches) but by practicing a set of canons of thought, many of which have to do with the disciplined use of language.

In addition to courses in the philosophy of science, every school should offer a course in semantics—the processes by which people make meanings; in other words, the relationship between language and reality. Like history, semantics is an interdisciplinary subject. It is necessary to know something about it in order to understand any subject. If our youth had available special courses in which fundamental principles of language were identified and explained, it would be extremely useful to the growth of their intelligence. Such courses would deal not only with the various uses of language but with the relationship between things and words, symbols and signs, factual statements and judgments, and grammar and thought. Especially for young students, these courses ought to emphasize the kinds of semantic errors that are common to all of us and that are avoidable through awareness and discipline—the use of either/or categories, misunderstandings of levels of abstraction, and confusion of words with things.

In using the ascent of humanity as a theme, we must also elevate to prominence such subjects as literature, music, and art. Their subject matter contains the best evidence we have of the unity and continuity of human experience and feeling, which is why, in our teaching of the humanities, we should emphasize the enduring creations of the past. In my opinion, the schools should stay as far from contemporary works as possible. Because of the nature of the communications industry, students already have continuous access to the popular arts of their own time—its music, rhetoric, design, literature, and architecture. Their knowledge of the form and content of this art is by no means satisfactory. But their ignorance of the form and content of the art of the past is cavernous. That is one important reason for emphasizing the art of the past. Another is that no subject is better suited for freeing us from the tyranny of the present than the historical study of art. Painting, for example, is more than three times as old as writing and, in its changing styles and themes, contains a 15,000-year-old record of the ascent of humanity.

In saying this, I do not mean to subsume art under the heading of archaeology, although I certainly recommend that the history of art forms be given a serious place in the curriculum. But art is much more than an historical artifact. To have meaning for us, it must connect with levels of feeling. But "is it possible for students of today to relate, through feeling, to the painting, architecture, music, sculpture, or literature of the past?" The answer, I believe, is: only with the greatest difficulty. Students, and many adults, have an aesthetic sensibility of a different order from what is required to appreciate a Shakespeare sonnet, a Haydn symphony, or a Hals painting. To over-simplify the matter, a young man who believes Led Zeppelin to have reached the pinnacle of musical expression lacks the sensibility to distinguish between the ascent and the descent of humanity. However, it is not my intention to blacken further the reputation of popular culture. My point is that the artistic products of the popular arts are amply provided by the media. There is no excuse for the schools to sponsor rock concerts, when students have not heard the music of Mozart, Beethoven, Bach, or Chopin; or for students to have graduated from high school without having read Shakespeare, Milton, Keats, Dickens, Tolstoy, or Balzac; or for students not to have seen at least one photograph of paintings by Goya, El Greco, David. It is not to the point that many of these composers, writers, and painters were in their own times popular artists. What is to the point is that they spoke when they did, in a language and from a point of view different from our own and yet continuous with our own. These artists are relevant because they established the standards with which civilized people approach the arts. And they are relevant because television tries to mute their voices and render their standards invisible.

Finally, I would include the subject of religion in the school curriculum. It is, after all, intertwined with so much of our painting, music, architecture, literature, and science. Specifically, the curriculum should include a course in comparative religion. Such a course would deal with religion as an expression of humanity's creativeness; that is, as a total, integrated response to fundamental questions about the meaning of existence. The course would be descriptive, promoting no particular religion but illuminating the metaphors, literature, art, and ritual of religious expression itself. I am not unaware of the difficulties such a course would face, not the least of which is the belief that the schools and religion must on no account touch each other. But I do not see how we can claim to be educating our youth if we do not ask them to consider how different people of different times and places have tried to achieve a sense of transcendence. No education can neglect such sacred texts as Genesis, the New Testament, the Koran, the Bhagavad-Gita. Each of them embodies a style and a worldview which tell as much about the ascent of humanity as any book ever written.

Before ending, I feel obligated to add the following cautionary note. This essay has been written only thirty-five years after television assumed a dominant place in the American communications landscape. Anyone who has seriously studied the history of communications media knows that thirty-five years is not enough time to allow for accurate prognoses about what a new medium will, in the long run, mean to a culture. For four hundred years, the alphabet was used by the Greeks mainly to facilitate business transactions; it was not until the fifth century b.c. that its value as a means of intellectual discourse was fully grasped. For sixty-five years, the machine-made book flourished throughout Europe before anyone thought of numbering the pages. That simple idea added a new and enduring function to books—as scholarly sources of reference.

Because people are more aware of media today, it does not take so long as it once did to arrive at reasonably good guesses as to the social and intellectual consequences of media change. Nonetheless, it is possible that someone may have just been born who will think of a function for television that will take everyone by surprise and that will make television an ally, not an enemy, of the literate tradition. Even among those of us who were not born yesterday, certain possibilities have occurred that do not seem entirely implausible. Television has the potential, for example, of becoming a true theater of the masses, bringing into every home the best, the most demanding, of the Western theatrical heritage. It is also possible that a television art will emerge—something quite different from either theater or cinema, an art that need not be literary, yet capable of enriching and extending our aesthetic experience.

We often hear that television played a role in amplifying—if not generating—the antiwar movement during the Vietnam years. To see the real "enemy" on the nightly news, as against seeing him in fictionalized Hollywood versions, tends to diminish one's appetite for killing. Is it possible that television makes the taste for war unpalatable? We also hear that television may yet make some of the more simpleminded forms of racism obsolete. Television specializes in showing faces, and racism, like war, depends on the "other" remaining faceless.

All of these things are possible, and we must keep them in view as we proceed in making our plans as educators. I stand behind what I have said in this essay, not because I cannot see the possibilities but because I see much more clearly the realities.

Part Three
RELATING SCHOOL AND
NONSCHOOL SETTINGS

Introduction

Americans have traditionally held an abiding and even a touching faith in education—not only in its value to the individual but to the future welfare of the nation. Nowhere is this faith more evident than in our attempts to solve some of the nation's most persistent social, economic, and political problems through the schools. Lawrence Cremin once quipped that "in other countries, when there is a profound social problem, there is an uprising; in the United States, we organize a course."

In recent decades particularly, we have made extraordinary efforts to improve schools in order to correct a variety of national ills. Moreover, we now ask schools to provide a staggering array of functions that in previous generations were assumed by families, churches, employers, and a variety of community agencies. Indeed, the school today has become an ambitious social service agency. It has also become a beleaguered institution as it attempts to meet a wide range of goals at a time of dwindling resources. Ironically, efforts to improve the situation, to "reform" schools, have only brought more responsibilities to their agenda. Clearly, tinkering will no longer do.

While the school must educate the whole child, it cannot do the whole job. As the chapters in the previous section make clear, there are a variety of institutions and agencies within society that are powerful educators in themselves. We suggest that now is the time to look at the full panoply of functions that schools are being asked to perform, and identify which of those the school is best equipped to handle and which of them can best be handled by other institutions and agencies. But the challenge is not simply to divide, to parcel out responsibility. There must be a reconception of the role of the school and a new relationship between schools and society—a relationship in which the function of education is seen as a joint one, involving responsibilities

201

on the part of school and society that may be distinct or shared or complementary.

In this section, we examine how to relate school and nonschool settings and describe some of the specific ways in which schools can collaborate with other institutions and agencies in the educational process. Specifically, essential conditions for learning in both school and nonschool settings are described, ways to create and combine learning environments that enrich education are examined, and the dynamics of collaboration between schools and other social agencies are explored.

Schools can no longer afford to "go it alone." At the same time, as these chapters make clear, collaborative efforts between schools and other community sectors require careful attention to the proper conditions for learning, to the nature and use of educational settings, and to the relationships between school and nonschool personnel. Instant collaboration may bring instant gratification, but it is less likely to bring any lasting success. Instead, careful planning, combined with thoughtful use of people and places, is the essential ingredient for successful school-community collaboration and improved education for all children and youth.

In sum, our challenge is to examine the whole cloth of education rather than to view it as "a tissue of small jealous principalities incapable of cohesion." We must develop a relationship—a configuration, if you will—in which schools and all sectors of society see education as a common cause and a common task. The chapters in this section are intended to move the relationship that is necessary for quality education in these times closer to reality.

CHAPTER XI

Conditions for Effective Learning

RALPH W. TYLER

The conditions required for conscious human learning are the same whether the learning takes place in school or in nonschool settings. Learning is a universal characteristic of all human beings. Behavior that is instinctive, that requires no practice or previous experience to carry on effectively, is very limited in the human species. No child could survive the first year of life without learning many things. Learning is as natural and universal among humans as respiration or digestion. There are no nonlearners.

Some children are called nonlearners, but close observation reveals that these children are learning. They may not be learning what the school seeks to teach. They may be learning to play basketball, to gain friends, to do other things that seem important to them, and appear to be impervious to teaching in the classroom, or in the home, or in the Scout meeting. But they are learning. The task of the educator, the parent, or other teachers is to stimulate and guide young people to learn what is educationally valuable.

We know something of what takes place when human beings learn. They carry on some behavior that they have not done before. If they find it satisfying, they repeat the behavior; if it continues to provide satisfaction, it becomes part of their repertoire which they use in those situations where it is appropriate. When this occurs, we say the behavior has been learned.

Behavior is used in this sense to include all kinds of reactions an individual is capable of carrying on. One can acquire a new skill, or new habit, a new interest, a new attitude, a new way of thinking, a new way of perceiving some complex phenomenon—all of these are illustrations of human learning.

Conditions for Learning

1. MOTIVATION

Certain features of this description of learning require elaboration and further explanation. The first question that comes to mind is what gets learners started in carrying on new behavior? Since learners must first direct their attention to the new behavior and put forth the effort required to carry it on, motivation is an essential condition for learning. Fortunately, many sources of motivation exist within both school and nonschool settings. When we see another person doing something that appears significant or enjoyable, we may try to emulate that behavior, and in this way we get started in the learning process. Or we may believe that a certain behavior is essential to something else that we desire, and so we try it. These are common sources of motivation, but they are not the only ones. When parents, friends, teachers, or other persons whom we respect tell us that a certain behavior is something worth learning, it can be a motivating force. Once students find initial learning experiences satisfying, the desire to repeat them furnishes continuing motivation.

2. CLEAR LEARNING OBJECTIVES

In trying to carry on the behavior to be learned, we need to have a clear conception of what it is we are trying to learn. Young people who want to learn to play baseball or to dance can manage by simply watching games or dances. This gives them at least a rough notion of the behavior so that they can emulate those who are carrying it on successfully. If we cannot see clearly some of the intricacies of the movements, the leader or teacher may slow down the movement or focus attention on certain parts of the action. For behavior that is not easily observable, like ways of thinking or feeling, learners often have difficulty in perceiving the learning objectives. In such cases, the parent, leader, or teacher may need to show learners what the "invisible" behavior is and how meaningful and satisfying it can be. Conscious human learning requires that students perceive something to be learned that is attractive to them. Moreover, they must see it clearly enough so that it guides their initial steps in emulating this behavior.

3. APPROPRIATE LEARNING TASKS

Initial attempts to learn a new behavior should involve a task that requires learners to put forth a real effort, one that they find hard to do but not so difficult that they are unable to accomplish it. If the learning is too easy, learners are likely to perceive it as mere busy work or a Mickey Mouse activity. As a result, they will neither give it careful attention, nor will they find their success in carrying on an easy task to be rewarding. Learners gain great satisfaction from accomplishing a task that they found difficult. Hence, an appropriate learning task is one that demands a good deal of attention and effort from learners, yet is one that they can complete successfully when they devote real effort to it.

4. CONFIDENCE THAT SUPPORTS WILLINGNESS TO ATTEMPT THE TASK

Lack of confidence is a possible factor that may inhibit one from attempting a learning task even though one would like to try it. Learners need confidence that they can complete the task successfully and not be perceived as failures by their peers. We can develop confidence in learners by encouraging them and by providing preliminary learning tasks that appear to be only slightly more difficult than those that they are now doing successfully.

5. REWARDS AND FEEDBACK

As learners successfully carry on the behavior that they are seeking to achieve, their incentive to continue comes from success, that is, the satisfaction they obtain from successful performance. Many possible rewards are satisfying, but in a democratic society the nature of the reward system itself should be consistent with the role of a self-directive, responsible person. We need to help young people to discover the satisfaction that comes from having acquired and used new understanding, interests, attitudes, and skills, rather than depending largely on rewards that are extraneous to the learning process itself and depend on the favor of others. Those teachers of children who use techniques of conditioning commonly place great reliance on rewards that gratify appetites in contrast to those rewards the importance of which derives from intellectual or social influence. Here it is important to keep in mind that habitual respónses to physical gratification make a human being more dependent on those who can use force and material power. Our goal instead should be to develop self-directive learners.

In addition to the satisfaction that comes from having learned something we wanted to learn, there are numerous rewards that we can receive from successfully completing a learning task. A very important reward for most people is the approval of peers, especially friends. Whether one is a parent, a club leader, or a teacher in school, it is an important feature of teaching to see that learners gain these rewards.

Some learners will have difficulty with a learning task and may not carry it out satisfactorily. If we reward such efforts, it will result in their learning the wrong things. We need to inform them instead that they did not complete the learning task successfully and that they need some information about what the difficulty seems to be. In short, they need what is commonly called "feedback." Next, they need to be encouraged to try again either the same learning task or another one that may be more appropriate for their present stage of learning. With the help of feedback and encouragement, most learners having difficulty with a learning task successfully complete it (or a similar one) on the second or third attempt.

6. SEQUENTIAL PRACTICE

It is also extremely important to provide learners with opportunities to practice the new behavior until it becomes part of their usual repertoire. Availability of opportunities means that learners have many chances to carry on the behavior and also that they have time for necessary practice. Too often, learning situations require learners to spend most of their time passively, while the leader or teacher performs, rather than having learners actively engaged in thinking, feeling, and acting what they are expected to learn.

Another aspect of providing opportunities for practice is that they should be sequential, that is, each subsequent practice goes more broadly or more deeply into the learning task than the previous one. Sheer repetition is quickly boring to the learner and has little or no further effect. Only as each new practice demands the learner's attention because of new elements in it, does it serve adequately as a basis for effective learning. This means that concepts and principles are brought in again and again, but each time there are new and more complex illustrations. As a result, the learner, whether in school or out-of-school, has to think through the way in which these concepts and principles help to explain or to analyze the illustration. In developing a skill, we need to ensure that each new practice of the skill provides the learner with the opportunity for greater variety or complexity in using it. Sequence is also important in developing appreciation, for it means that each new work of art should demand something more of perception and provide opportunity for a greater variety and depth of emotional response.

Opportunities for sequential practice are important for other learning objectives: new attitudes, interests, problem solving—in fact, all kinds of complex behavior. Sequential practice is too often neglected in classroom activities and assignments and in nonschool programs and projects.

The textbook materials for the middle grades are one current example of neglecting sequential practice. In the past, the reading curriculum for the primary grades was designed to enable children to gain the basic skills of reading and word attack that they would then employ in the subject fields of the middle grades. As they used the skills, the reading materials in social studies, science, and other subjects would present an increasing range of vocabulary, complexity of syntax, and concepts.

During the back-to-basics movement, however, many schools demanded textbook material for fifth-grade subjects at third-grade reading level and for sixth-grade subjects at fourth-grade reading level. This appears to account for the fact that the results of the National Assessment of Educational Progress at that time showed that 9-year-olds had improved in reading since earlier assessments but 13-year-olds showed a decline. The need for reading materials that furnish opportunities for sequential practice seems to have been overlooked.

7. TRANSFER

Transfer has always been a matter of potential difficulty in guiding learning. Too often, what we learn in a particular context is used only in that context. Fair play may be learned in athletic activities, but some of the players do not practice fair play elsewhere. Some students learn things in school, but rarely, if ever, do they use them outside. To overcome this lack of transfer, teachers, parents, and other leaders need to see that young people have opportunities to practice in other contexts what they are learning at home, in school, and in other institutions.

Teachers and parents can use various ways to furnish these opportunities. For example, parents should encourage children to learn to read to the family at home. Children can bring arithmetic problems from home or playground to the school for the class to solve. Students learning to write may take turns in ordering supplies, writing thank-you letters, writing to a sick friend, and the like. Students should be encouraged to bring to class various kinds of curious phenomena they have observed or to describe various social problems they are facing. Students should use these examples for practice to develop understanding and problem-solving skills. Simulation is frequently employed in some school subjects to develop understanding and skills, as it is in athletic games and in the operation of complex machinery. To assure transfer, we need to see that learners use what they are learning in a variety of contexts and circumstances, bringing to their attention the ways in which they can use what is being learned, and illustrating how helpful it is.

We may need to provide other conditions for conscious human learning to achieve certain kinds of behavior in certain particular situations. These seven, however, comprise the essential conditions for most learning that have been identified through millennia of educational experience and a century of experimentation.

Illustrations in School and Nonschool Settings

The general conditions for learning described above may seem overly abstract. In that case, the reader may find it helpful to review the following examples that suggest how to apply these learning conditions in both school and nonschool settings.

POSTPONING IMMEDIATE GRATIFICATION

One of the most important kinds of behavior we must develop to become a self-disciplined person is the ability to defer immediate self-gratification. Learning tasks in school, work of children in the home, projects of members of youth organizations, and educational activities in other nonschool settings—all these require concentration of attention and effort, some degree of thought and planning, and postponing desires that conflict with these activities. These behaviors must be developed, for they are not characteristic of very young children. Infants shift rapidly from one activity to another as their attention is caught by changing objects in their environment. They have a very limited span of attention and respond immediately to attractive stimuli.

In the home, parents can begin to develop self-discipline in children by establishing a regular schedule of feeding rather than continuing to provide food whenever they cry, seeing that they pick up toys before coming to the meal, requiring that they make the bed before leaving home for school, and so forth. The child obtains rewards for this behavior from the parent's show of love and pleasure and also by his or her observations that this behavior is the same as the parent's behavior that the child wishes to emulate. As the child grows older, the practice of planning for important events—a trip to a museum, the library, a picnic, or other family events—can be shared by the entire family. After the event is over, a family discussion can help the child to see how much more satisfaction came from a planned event than from events hastily carried out without thoughtful consideration.

The school can build on the development in the home by: (a) establishing a schedule that gradually increases the time in which children work without serious interruption of important learning tasks; (b) encouraging student projects and activities that are thoughtfully planned; and (c) conducting children's discussions of their own experiences, ones in which hasty impulsive actions are contrasted with those thoughtfully considered in advance. Similar opportunities to contribute to the young person's development exist in such out-of-school settings as Scouts, 4-H, religious organizations, recreation groups, and science clubs.

For this kind of development, motivation may need to depend initially on the coercion of parents and organizational rules, or on pleasing the parent, teacher, or leader, or on gaining the love or respect of the one in charge. We need, however, to help the child see increasingly that impulsive actions prove less satisfying in their results than planned ones and that most impulsive people are not attractive models for emulation.

In most cases, the learning objective is clear to the young people involved. If, in a particular situation, it is not clear to the learners what they are being asked to postpone or forego and why, time should be taken to discuss this objective until they perceive the objective clearly.

The appropriateness of the learning task requires that we consider carefully the intensity of the stimulation that must be postponed and the length of time of postponement. A child coming home from vigorous play may have an intense desire for food. In that case, postponement may need to be only long enough to get cleaned up before a snack. On the other hand, a child's urge to play with a favorite toy is not so intense, and it is appropriate to require that school assignments be done first.

The initial steps families take at home to help children learn to postpone or inhibit impulsive action are likely to require some coercion. As children get older, however, their learning efforts should be voluntary, fueled by their desire to avoid rash actions and to be guided by thoughtful plans.

Even when motivation is strong, learners may hesitate to attempt something that they cannot complete successfully. For example, "Can I give up enough of my unnecessary expenditures to save the money needed for college expenses? If not, why try, and then be the laughing stock of my friends?" In such cases of lack of confidence, the parent, teacher, or other leader can help the learner see that the earlier efforts at giving up certain gratifications have been successful and the next learning requires only a little more self-control than these previous successful ones. This is merely an illustration of the various ways by which we can build up confidence in learners so that they are willing to undertake this kind of learning task.

The rewards for postponing or inhibiting impulsive actions can be the satisfaction learners receive from the thoughtfully planned activity, from the approval of people they respect, and from perceiving that they have lived up to their self-image. Feedback will, of course, depend on the factors involved in the failure to postpone or inhibit the impulsive actions. After children understand their impulsive actions, they should be encouraged to try to postpone or inhibit this behavior until they are successful in these efforts.

Sequential practice of thoughtful planning in place of impulsive action requires a continuous progression of practice opportunities. Each new opportunity should involve either or both postponing gratification for a longer period of time or taking into account more complex considerations. Beginning with the brief postponement of food until the child has cleaned up, the opportunities for practice should progress so that, as a high school student, he or she will sacrifice to save the money needed to prepare for a career that has been thoughtfully identified.

Transfer is provided when parents, teachers, and other leaders understand the importance of this educational objective and see ways in which they can help the young people with whom they live or work to practice postponing impulsive actions and to substitute thoughtful planning of constructive activities. By bringing to the learner's attention the variety of situations in which such behavior is desirable, we can help to overcome the obstacle to transfer that arises when the learner initially perceives that this desirable behavior applies only to the circumstances in which he or she has practiced it.

DEVELOPMENT OF ORAL LANGUAGE

The learning of oral language serves as another illustration. Since everyone who is not physically handicapped or brain-damaged speaks, we often assume that mature oral language development can take place without giving it serious attention. True, almost everyone speaks, but many people do not use oral language effectively for the purposes that it could serve. Often children cannot communicate orally all that they wish to convey to others. Although their oral expressions of feeling may be adequate, their descriptions of their experiences are still very limited. Frequently their explanations of a phenomenon are clear only to those who already understand it. Some have a very small vocabulary, too limited to include all that they want to talk about. Strangers judge us by our speech as well as by our appearance, and those who fail to use conventional speech are considered ignorant or unintelligent.

Finally, we need to stress good listening habits. In any conversation, there must be listeners as well as speakers. Many people are so intent on what they wish to say that they give little attention to the speech of others. To develop effective oral speech, learning should begin in infancy and continue for many years.

Children begin to develop oral speech by imitating the speech of those close to them, usually the mother, but also the father, siblings, and others in the home. How accurately children imitate this speech depends on how adequately they judge their own efforts and by the response the mother or other person makes to their attempts. Children keep trying to imitate what they hear, seeking sounds as close as possible to those they are imitating. They also try to make sounds that bring a satisfying response from the other people. This analysis of how children begin to learn oral speech indicates the great importance of speech models in the home. Not only is the form of speech important but also the nature of the content. The conversation of uneducated parents is often a kind of free association of events—one sentence leads to another without furnishing a clear description of the event or the phenomenon mentioned. It is hard to identify from such disorganized conversation the answers to such questions as: What went on? Why? How? Who were involved? What were the outcomes?

In the home, as the child begins to use oral speech, family members can help by talking with the child to describe things clearly and explain things in terms of purpose and process, cause and effect. The family can also provide opportunities for conversations in which adults listen carefully to children and children in turn listen to adults as well as to one another. This means that the conversations should be about matters of interest and concern to the children, where they have a chance to tell what they are thinking and doing, and also about matters on which they seek greater understanding and guidance for their actions. These experiences with oral language in the home are also very helpful to the child in his activities in school.

School and other community contexts should furnish many more opportunities for meaningful use of oral language. Teachers are often conscious of a child's inadequate vocabulary and conventional forms of language. In such cases, certainly the school has a responsibility to help the child overcome these problems. But responsibility must not stop with that. The school should also help the child develop effective oral expression in description, exposition, persuasion, and in aesthetically enjoyable utterances. In each of these kinds of expression, children need help in becoming attentive listeners who gain information, understanding, social involvement, or aesthetic enjoyment from what they hear.

The nonschool contexts also furnish many opportunities for oral communication. Educational leaders in these situations need to listen to children, converse with them, and try to identify their strengths and weaknesses in speaking and listening. Often, opportunities for developing better oral language habits are greater within the projects and activities of the out-of-school organizations than in other settings. If children are given a meaningful task involving the use of oral language, they will often put forth more effort to express themselves clearly and to listen closely than they will for a learning task in the school which may seem to have less meaning or importance to them.

The motivation for children to work on improving their oral language largely depends on their involvement in activities in which effective oral language is important. Through encouragement, parents, siblings and friends may help children to make the necessary effort. For most people, however, the idea of improving one's speaking or listening is not particularly attractive. What does provide motivation occurs when children realize that they are speaking in a way that commands attention and respect from others—parents, siblings, and friends.

Many efforts to improve oral language fail because learners do not see clearly what they are to learn. In this event, their difficulties should be analyzed and particular activities developed to help them overcome one or more of these weaknesses. The trouble may be in their own vague perception of what they are trying to describe. It may be in their failure to organize the explanation they want to make. It may be in having no words in their vocabulary to express some of the things they want to say. By helping children analyze their difficulties, we also help them to see more clearly the particular objectives of the learning activities they can carry on.

Appropriate learning tasks are those that focus on one or more of the learners' difficulties under conditions that require real effort to overcome them. These conditions, however, should not be so difficult that learners will fail even when putting forth great effort. For example, if the child's difficulty is in organizing a presentation, the task might involve observing a simple activity such as the game of tag and explaining how it is played. If the child's difficulty is being bashful when talking to a group, the remedial task could be speaking to a few friends on a subject of mutual interest.

The confidence to undertake learning tasks in oral speech often requires that learners attend primarily to what they want to say and how the audience is reacting. To overcome the learner's self-conscious timidity in this way, the teacher may need to remind the learner of recent situations in which he or she was not embarrassed, or it may require the learner to speak without an audience a few times until confidence in speaking is established. When learners see most of their learning tasks as being interesting and meaningful, activities that they like to carry on, they obtain their reward when they perceive that they have completed the learning task successfully. Approval by members of the group and the leader further enhances the reward. Feedback should be given as soon as possible after the learning task so that learners know almost at once what the inadequacies were in their performance and can be immediately encouraged to try again.

Sequential practice in oral language requires the leader, parent, or teacher to record or keep in mind the progress of learners in overcoming difficulties they are having. As one difficulty after another is overcome, a new learning task can then be devised that involves practice on other aspects with which the learner has difficulty. Transfer is greatly facilitated when parents, teachers, and educational leaders in other settings are all giving some attention to the oral speech development of the young person. This development is so central to communication, and to clarifying perception and thought, that it deserves the attention of educational leaders in all settings. In addition, learners should be advised to observe their own use of oral language in all the arenas of their lives and to try to improve their language in all appropriate situations they encounter.

READING

Learning to read illustrates the complementary and supplementary relationships among the various learning contexts. In homes where stories are often read to preschool children, and where parents and siblings often engage in reading and commenting on their reading, the motivation to learn to read is usually well established before the child starts school. In most cases, these experiences help children to perceive the educational objectives of primary reading and to develop confidence that they can carry on successfully a learning task that does not appear too difficult to them. Less frequently do parents reward the successful performance of the learning tasks by asking the child to read to one or more of the family members and by showing approval of what the child has accomplished. Yet, as a reward and to facilitate

transfer, opportunities for children to read to their parents are important aids to their development in reading. These activities in the home
not only motivate and help clarify reading objectives for preschool
children, but they also help to extend their vocabulary and develop
familiarity with the sentence structure of narrative writing.

Other organizations involving young children can help the learning of primary reading by having members read simple reports,
directions for constructing toys and furnishings, and other printed
materials used in the organizations. These are useful ways to help
children attain the objectives of primary school reading—namely, to
master the so-called mechanics of reading.

Yet, according to the findings of the National Assessment of
Educational Progress, not all American youth learn the mechanics of
reading. Among 17-year-olds, 18 percent have not attained these
skills. Most of them come from homes where the parents have had
little or no education. Most likely, few, if any of them, had stories read
to them when they were very young. They probably saw few, if any,
adults who read, in their family or even in the neighborhood. Hence,
they lacked the motivation to learn to read.

Today the workplace offers some of the most successful efforts to
develop the mechanical skills of reading among older youth and adults.
They cite the demands of the job and opportunities for advancement as
the two most common motives for their desire to learn to read. In
various parts of the nation, employers and educational leaders have
developed successful programs for primary reading that are either
carried on with a promise of employment as soon as reading skill is
demonstrated, or in cases where learners are already employed, with
the promise of promotion.

Whereas reading in the primary grades concentrates on developing
the mechanics of reading, in the middle grades and beyond the
objectives are more complex. In these years, the purposes are to gain
new information, and to guide thinking about problems in science,
mathematics, social studies, literature, and the arts. This shift requires
students to develop vocabularies in these different subjects, an expanded and more complex sentence structure, and modes of thinking
stimulated by the reading material and useful in helping them derive
greater meaning from what they are reading. From the process of the
primary grades, the child learns to translate the symbols of the printed

page into the words and sentences with which he is familiar orally. In the middle grades and high school, reading becomes a process for gaining new information, then a process for interpreting meanings, then a process for weighing and evaluating what is read, and a process for consciously deriving emotional satisfaction as students appreciate literature of various types.

We recognize these shifts of educational objectives in reading only in the vague phrase "becoming a mature reader." But these more complex objectives of reading beyond the primary grades are not easily attained. They require not only clarification by teachers and other educational leaders, but their development also requires the cooperative support of nonschool settings. Surveys of adults show that they devote the largest amount of their reading time to fiction which presents few, if any, examples of important new information, ideas, problems, or principles. Fiction, instead, is filled with stereotypes, familiar scenes, and interpretations. Such material requires adults to use little more than the reading skills acquired in the primary grades.

Family reading sessions should use literature, books or articles in science, politics, economics, sociology, religion, and the arts as material for oral or silent reading, followed by thoughtful discussions. Or it is possible for community groups to be formed, like the Great Books groups, to stimulate and assist people to learn to read at the secondary school and college level. The development of reading at this level is very important if we are to become increasingly a civilized and humane society, but it requires that a considerable fraction of the learning be carried on in nonschool settings. The school alone is not enough.

DEVELOPMENT OF COOPERATION AND ALTRUISM

As a fourth example of learning conditions, consider the development of cooperation and altruism. The continued existence of a society requires a binding force that holds people together and largely inhibits conflict among its members. In a society seeking to be democratic, the binding force to be developed is not that of fear or coercive power of rulers, but common concern for the well-being of every member as a human being deserving of respect. This binding force is enhanced when everyone participates in planning and conducting common activities and when there is a practice of helping others in need. Such a society needs to educate its young people in the attitudes and practices of cooperation and altruism.

When public education was rationed and only a small fraction of young people were expected to complete secondary school, competition was an important source of motivation for completing school tasks successfully. From the earliest grades on through high school, each child was given a mark representing excellent, good, fair, or unsatisfactory work. As children moved through the grades, they usually discovered from their marks whether they were being encouraged to go on or to drop out. Most students recognized this sorting process and felt themselves in competition with other members of the class.

In the United States today, our public policy is to encourage everyone to complete secondary school. The sorting function of the schools is minimized. At the same time, however, we have not made a corresponding effort to emphasize cooperation in the academic work of the school, although it is strongly emphasized in some athletic programs and other extracurricular activities. Attention is now turning to developing cooperative learning tasks in school subjects. Research on cooperative learning has been pioneered at the University of Minnesota by two brothers, David and Roger Johnson. They have also developed demonstration activities in which students working on cooperative learning projects make substantial progress in acquiring academic objectives.

Many of the projects of out-of-school organizations depended heavily in the past on the motivation of competition and the rewards of achieving more than others. More recently, certain of these organizations such as the Scouts, 4-H, and Junior Achievement have been developing cooperative learning projects while reducing the emphasis on competition.

Schools rarely give major attention to altruism, the desire and practice of helping others. The focus of classroom activities is on cognitive learning and individual disciplined behavior. An accident to a child in school or a serious illness of a classmate is commonly used to encourage children to send greetings, flowers, or other signs of their caring, but these activities are not frequent and do not involve sequential practice so important in learning.

Programs of youth participation in nonschool settings offer many opportunities to develop altruism. The National Commission on Resources for Youth has collected thousands of examples of such programs, most of which are sponsored by the school but carried on in various nonschool settings. The program most widely known is "Youth Tutoring Youth" in which older children assist younger children having difficulty in school work. These child tutors report great satisfaction with this helping relationship and especially enjoy the increased school success of their tutees. They are discovering the rewards of altruism without having to depend on the approval of adults. There are many other successful participation programs as reported in chapter 9 of this volume.

Many nonschool settings can furnish opportunities to practice altruism and develop altruistic interests and attitudes. The school can provide an important supplement in assisting students to understand the needs of human beings for help from others and to recognize that being in need is not necessarily a sign of carelessness, laziness, or sinful behavior. The experience of helping others can also be used to discuss dependence and independence. The ideal of a democratic society is that every member will be an independent, autonomous person, not meekly subservient to others. However, the satisfaction one gets from helping others may consciously or unconsciously lead to continuing this dependency rather than helping one in need to become independent and able to meet his or her own needs. This matter is an excellent topic for school learning.

Because learning tasks that help to develop cooperation and altruism usually appeal to young people, little special attention needs to be given to motivation and to rewards. However, selecting the appropriate learning task and developing sequential practice opportunities are conditions that are often overlooked. Students usually find activities like Youth Tutoring Youth, or Day-Care Helper, or assisting in a Senior Citizen's Residence initially attractive and rewarding. But the duties may soon become routine and their learning value lost.

Teachers or leaders need to sense the points at which student interest and attention decline and try to provide learning tasks that are more difficult or demanding. This does not necessarily require an entirely different activity. Adults working on the program can direct the learner's attention to new skills, or new problems, or new emotional aspects that have not been in focus previously. For example, in Youth Tutoring Youth, the tutor's attention can be turned to diagnosing the particular difficulties of the tutee, whereas previously the attention has been focused on monitoring the tutee's practice. As another example, the Day-Care Helper's attention can be directed to observing the child who appears isolated in the Day-Care Center, thereby helping the young person to understand the reasons for self-selected isolation. As a final example, the assistant in a Senior Citizen's Residence can be asked to observe more carefully the infirm and ill residents. This provides information on whether the youth can control his or her emotional reactions to the suffering of a resident so as to decide thoughtfully what help can be given. In every situation involving interpersonal relations, there are so many facets that it is not difficult to develop a number of sequential assignments.

Experiences in life are usually chaotic; that is, one event follows another without easily apparent connection. The child's reactions are largely determined by the need for survival, security, acceptance, and by achieving some previously selected purpose. Unless there is frequent opportunity for children to reflect on these experiences and discuss their meaning, educational gain will be limited. Although all organizations that seek to help educate young people should provide for this reflection and discussion, the school is the agency that should recognize the importance of these seminar-like sessions and arrange for them under competent leadership. Otherwise, many of the experiences will be seen by the child only as fun, or boring, or revolting rather than being understood and challenging to the child's thought and action.

MATHEMATICS

Another illustration of learning conditions can be found in mathematics. Elementary school mathematics deals with the most common problem of learning to use computation in appropriate situations outside of school. The National Assessment shows that about 90 percent of all American 17-year-olds can add, subtract, multiply, and divide accurately with whole numbers but only 45 percent can use computation appropriately in the kind of situations commonly encountered in purchasing, measuring, computing taxes, and the like. Through student projects and simulations, the school can do more in providing opportunity for students to deal with these kinds of situations. But nonschool contexts afford a wider variety of applications that students perceive as real. For example, when a child is learning to add, he or she can be asked by the parent to compute the cost of purchases of food and clothing that are being planned. There are many other family situations where computations need to be made and when the child should be asked to make them. In so doing, the parent enhances motivation, clarifies the objectives and provides some appropriate learning tasks. Encouragement by a parent should also help the child to develop the confidence to understand the tasks, while the approval of the parent and other family members serves as a reward and is likely to produce continuing motivation.

It is not so easy for parents to establish sequential practice for arithmetic problems in the home. Other organizations can furnish more complex and difficult applications of mathematics to provide sequential practice as the student's mathematical skills develop. The school can supplement the others through simulation of meaningful activities that involve mathematical analysis and computation. Most organizations have activities and problems involving numbers, income, costs, per-person expenditures; quantities needed for construction, ordinary consumption, group parties, and the like. If the leaders of these organizations know about the mathematical development and needs of its members, they can develop learning tasks that can greatly facilitate the mathematical learning of their young people.

During the middle school, a decreasing proportion of girls express interest in mathematics, and fewer 17-year-old females do as well as the average of males in the National Assessment of mathematics. To increase girls' interest and achievement in mathematics, the school needs to assign learning tasks that are interesting and meaningful to females in the home and other nonschool settings.

SCIENCE

Learning conditions for science education serve as another example. Currently, the public has been aroused by reports of the declining achievement of Americans in science. An examination of the results of the science tests given in the 1970s in the International Evaluation of Educational Achievement indicates that in all the thirteen developed nations participating in the International Achievement studies, the top 5 percent of the students performed similarly regardless of the variation in educational conditions among these nations. Apparently, most young people who get deeply interested in a subject learn a great deal when there are opportunities for learning in families, schools, libraries, and so forth.

A second finding was that the lowest quartile among the American children in achievement did about as well as the average children in the other nations. Since the 1960s, the United States has focused great attention on the so-called "disadvantaged children" with considerable success in aiding their school achievement.

However, the science achievement of the middle group of American young people falls in the lowest third of the thirteen developed nations. When this fact is coupled with the results from the National Assessment, some possible interpretations become evident. In 1969, the first National Assessment of Science was made. At that time, the American astronauts were reaching the moon. The American public was thrilled by the scientific and technological exploit. Science was very highly regarded.

By the second National Assessment of Science, the mass media were playing up the perils of pollution and science; technology and industry were pictured as the chief villains. The science achievement of 17-year-olds dropped considerably from that of 1969. In contrast to the American public attitude toward science, the Japanese consider it the major source of their economic recovery and put great emphasis on their children learning science. This analysis supports the accepted view of anthropologists that the younger generation will learn whatever the adults they respect consider important.

The school can take a number of steps to improve science education. To achieve maximum results, however, the home and other organizations in nonschool settings need to give attention to science learning. In *clarifying learning objectives*, students need to understand that science is not simply a set of facts or answers to questions about physical and biological phenomena. Science is a continuing quest for understanding the phenomena of experience. In each case, questions arise: What is it? How does it happen? Why does it happen? How is it related to other phenomena? Can human beings use this understanding? How?

Science involves curiosity, openness to possible explanations and to modifications of earlier ideas, and a search for order and unity in matters observed. In this large sense, the home and other agencies can develop motivation and clarify objectives by stimulating and encouraging imaginative inquiries, and by emphasizing the continuing development of science understanding in contrast to fostering the idea that we now have final answers to important questions in science.

Science clubs are excellent settings for developing student interests, attitudes, skills, and understanding in science. The school can encourage projects that assess community problems related to science, such as air and water pollution, waste, conservation of energy, and maintenance of parks and wildlife areas. In order to understand the purpose and procedures used, the workplace can encourage questioning about the industrial and commercial processes employed. Organizations like the 4-H Clubs have many projects in which significant achievements in science are possible. But above all, community leadership needs to take responsibility for developing a positive attitude toward science and technology.

CITIZENSHIP AND SOCIAL STUDIES

Illustrations of learning conditions can be seen in the social studies. In American society, where everyone is expected to be a responsible and informed citizen, the primary function of education is to develop essential interests, attitudes, and skills needed for citizenship. Furthermore, with the increasing complexity of the political, economic, and social institutions, the school has the difficult task of helping students understand these complexities. We would hope that students would see the educational program in citizenship and social studies as vital and important. Yet many surveys of student interests find that most students report social studies to be the least interesting of their school subjects. The National Assessment indicates that the average American 17-year-old achieves less adequately in social studies and citizenship than in reading and mathematics. In the International Evaluation of Educational Achievement, the average scores for American students were in the lowest third of the thirteen developed nations participating. Interviews with high school graduates of Project Talent conducted by American Institutes for Research indicated that most students did not relate what was taught in the high school social studies courses to the "real world" outside of school.

The school itself can work to improve this situation. Under the leadership of Lawrence Kohlberg of Harvard University and Edward Fenton of Carnegie Mellon University, a dozen demonstrations are being conducted in which the high school community itself becomes a participatory democracy, with students learning the responsibility for decisions and actions of importance. However, most schools that attempt to improve education for citizenship and the social studies turn to nonschool contexts where students participate responsibly in various organizations and settings. The National Commission on Resources for Youth has in its files more than a thousand such programs. As I have observed these programs in various parts of the nation, I have noted several educational objectives to which youth participation projects might make a contribution. These include helping students to:

1. Understand the reality of social experience and connect this reality with the concepts and principles that help to make sense of what they are observing and experiencing.

2. Understand and appreciate the values and limitations of social institutions in serving individuals and groups in our society. Many students have not examined city governments, police departments, courts, fire departments, churches, health agencies, schools, and other social institutions in terms of the need for their service, the effectiveness of these services, and particularly the extent to which they furnish opportunity for individuals to participate effectively in society and achieve self-fulfillment.

3. Develop interest in working with others for a common social purpose.

4. Develop the social skills that are useful in working effectively with peers and adults.

5. Develop the skills and attitudes needed to assume responsibility for important social actions. Most students have not had responsibility for making decisions that significantly involve and affect others. Decisions are frequently made without careful consideration of alternatives and the probable consequences of each alternative course of action. Participation projects can be a major arena for developing these skills and attitudes.

6. Develop appropriate emotional and cognitive reactions as students enjoy the satisfactions of successful activities and bear the consequences of those that fail. Many students have been protected from feeling responsible for either significant failures or successes that

involve others who suffer or benefit from the activities. Projects that students have had a major role in planning and carrying out will usually result either in obvious social benefits or losses or both. They afford opportunity for young people to observe, question, and face the facts of success and failure.

7. Discover the satisfactions that are obtained when one shares efforts, ideas, and possessions with others and can empathize with them in their different moods. Most students have few occasions in which they share matters of importance with people other than relatives and close friends. Hence, it is hard for them to appreciate what it means to give as well as to receive, particularly with people of other ages or of different home and cultural backgrounds. Youth participation projects can involve students in face-to-face relations with nonschool persons who need help and to whom students are able to give assistance. These situations can be used to aid students in developing sensitivity to people of different backgrounds and to empathize with them in joy and sadness.

8. Discover the satisfactions that are derived from understanding puzzling social, economic, and political phenomena. Many students find the social world complex, and significant phenomena appear contradictory to them in their limited perceptions. Participation programs frequently provide a perspective on social situations that help the students identify the previously hidden factors that are needed to explain the ways people behave in these complex situations. If they are helped to examine and analyze these experiences, they are often excited about the way they can understand matters that were previously confusing.

9. Discover the different roles they can successfully play in working with others. One of the obstacles to cooperation and teamwork among children and youth is the lack of clear ideas of the different roles played by different members of the group in making an effective team. They need to learn that not all team members can be quarterbacks and that a team without linebackers and other roles would be a sorry spectacle. Moreover, as in any good team, all members get satisfaction from the success of the team itself. Many participation projects involve the students in interdependent roles, all of which contribute to the success of the project.

Objectives like these represent a considerable educational task. It may require many years for most students to obtain them adequately. No one project is likely to furnish the educational experiences necessary to contribute to all of these objectives, but many can be devised that will provide experiences likely to help students' progress toward several of them. This requires careful planning by the organization developing these experiences. Every student's present development in each major objective should be appraised when selecting an appropriate learning task. Motivation is rarely a problem for projects of this sort, but in many of them the students need help in understanding their learning objectives. The rewards for successfully completing the learning task are in the satisfaction the students feel in accomplishing what they attempted.

Sequential practice is often overlooked. Students gain satisfaction from their early experiences and want to continue them rather than attempting something different or more difficult. Hence, the teacher or leader needs to consider activities that can provide sequential practice for students rather than permitting their efforts to become routine.

The transfer problem is rarely acute since participation projects are in the "real world." However, the organizations must give attention to finding a variety of situations in which learning can be applied so that students will use what they learn wherever that behavior is appropriate. Reflection on the experiences and discussion to help to understand them and derive maximum meaning are essential. Without this component of participation, projects have little educational value.

LITERATURE

The field of literature furnishes illustrations of learning experiences. The reading of literary works is for most people primarily a recreational activity. In school and college literature courses, however, it is an educational activity with several important objectives. Good literature produces an illusion of reality that enables the thoughtful reader to explore human experiences in imagination and thus gain an understanding and feeling for them. In many cases, the experiences depicted are not available in the student's environment. In most cases the understanding and the emotional reactions developed in the actual life experiences would require more time and suffering than is necessary for a person to learn the consequences of various alternative actions. Hence, education in literature is often used to explore human potentials, problems, possible life-styles, and the like. In this sense, literature is good when it appears to thoughtful critics to have dealt with important facets of life in depth; that is, the writer has selected important human situations and has presented them so that the reader is able to delve beneath the surface of events to expose some of the significant underlying factors, and the work is skillfully written so that the reader has the illusion of reality.

If school classes are the only context in which students are encouraged to explore human experience through good literary works, many of them will not develop sufficient interest, skill, and practice in this kind of reading. The home, too, can furnish such experiences: family members can read the same book and discuss its meaning. The home can also purchase or borrow books that are worthy of such treatment. These activities will contribute to motivation, reward, and transfer.

Organizations of peer groups can make the reading of relevant literature, coupled with reflection and discussion, an important part of understanding interpersonal relations. Young people are often amazed at the ways in which their own amorphous feelings are clarified by reading a book in which a character experiences similar confusion and seeks to understand it.

Motivation for such learning is easily established when one or more such books are selected that appeal to students. However, learning to read and appreciate a wider range of literature requires careful selection of books and of learning tasks. They should represent sequential development of interest, skill in reading literary works, and complexity of behavior to be understood and appreciated. The wider the circle of nonschool settings in which literature is used, the more likely will be the transfer to all appropriate situations.

AFFECTIVE EDUCATION

In current educational writing, affective education is frequently mentioned. This is an area where illustrations of learning conditions are needed. The analysis of human behavior into three categories—cognitive, affective, and psychomotor—is a construct roughly similar to the age-old distinctions of thinking, feeling, and acting. Few, if any, human reactions fall completely into one of these categories. In fact, almost all human learning involves an affective component. To develop into mature, responsible, loving, caring, happy adults, children require an education of feelings. They must learn to express emotions in socially acceptable and satisfying ways, as well as learn to find elements in their environment that can arouse interest, enhance pleasurable emotions, and serve continuously as stimuli for enjoying life rather than being bored.

Emotional reactions are both means and ends in education. Children's interests provide important motivation to learn. Their patterns of satisfaction and enjoyment are the major bases for the rewards that are experienced when they are successful in learning. Emotional reactions are also among the ends of education. Teachers commonly try to develop students' interest in reading, science, art, and other school subjects. They hope to help their students develop a positive attitude toward education and learning. They hope that students will come to cherish values that involve feelings of compassion and fellowship rather than selfish ones, values of beauty rather than ugliness, intellectual values rather than only physical pleasures.

There are two overall objectives of affective education. One is to help the students discover an increasing range of learning experiences that elicit interesting and pleasant emotional reactions. The other is to help students learn ways of feeling about art, music, and other aspects of culture that give them new pleasures in living. The objectives of affective education also include helping students learn to express their strong emotional reactions in ways that are socially acceptable and do not tear them apart. Intense anger, fear, hatred, and humiliation are examples of affective reactions that can seriously upset bodily systems and distort reason. When a child expresses these intense feelings through temper tantrums, aggressive outbursts, and crying spells, it can be repulsive to others as well as injurious to the child. It is not wise to attempt to suppress these feelings, but it is possible to learn to express them in ways that are less devastating to the child and are more socially acceptable. Students should also learn how to produce positive moods when they find themselves overcome with a sense of disappointment or disillusion.

As with most important educational developments, the home provides the initial experiences in affective education. In the home, children first find satisfaction in a variety of activities and begin to control outbursts of anger, aggression, and fear. The family can help each child explore areas of potential interest in physical activities, the arts and crafts, and activities with language and music. In the home, children also have their first opportunities to discover the satisfactions of helping others and the joys of successfully completing difficult tasks.

Most of the educational activities in organizations serving children and youth furnish opportunities to satisfy interests involved in the activities of the organization, such as athletics, cooking, science demonstrations, singing, dramatics, raising a crop. The affective outcomes of these organizations can be increased by helping members learn to enjoy experiences new to them.

Although contemporary writing emphasizes the attitudes of workers who do not like their work, the Follow-Up Study of Project Talent found that 80 percent of this sample of high school graduates reported their work as a source of satisfaction. In the workplace, attention can be given to helping young people find new aspects of their work interesting. The pleasurable emotional reactions of life need not be limited to times when one is at home or on the job. In all settings where children are in groups, it is possible to help them learn to control violent emotions and to find satisfaction in a variety of associations with other children and adults.

Coordination

This review of the learnings of children in school and nonschool settings indicates the interdependent relationships among them. In some cases, for example, the role of the home is to arouse interest in the learning, while the learning tasks are developed in school or in other settings. Reading and mathematics are examples. In these subjects, the home can also furnish some of the rewards for successful achievement and opportunities for transfer.

In some cases, the work setting is the source of original motivation to learn, as in mathematics for some youth, while in other cases, youth participation activities stimulate initial motivation, as in biology for a Day-Care Helper. The clarification of the learning goal takes place in different settings depending on the educational objective. The same diversification is found in selecting appropriate learning tasks and developing confidence to undertake them. The rewards for successful learning may be obtained in a variety of settings, and this is also possible for sequential practice. But the school and the workplace are the settings most often concerned with this gradual development of increasing skills. All of the settings can promote transfer.

Unless attention is paid to coordination, these possible interdependent relations will not take place and are often overlooked by those organizations responsible for particular learning objectives. Parents could coordinate their children's learning experiences if they possessed enough information about the available opportunities, but few do. To facilitate coordination and to maximize the learning experiences in a particular school and its community, a council should be set up with representatives from the school, the homes, and all of the organizations providing educational activities in the community. This council need not be formally established, but it should involve people who care about improving the educational opportunities for children in the community and have or can obtain relevant information about the community organizations.

This council should try to identify the ways in which the various organizations are providing conditions for learning and thus are helping children learn. It should know about their successes and their problems. The council should also identify unmet educational needs and suggest alternative ways these needs might be met. An active and concerned council can help greatly to increase learning for the children of the community by fostering interdependent contributions by home, school, and other community organizations.

CHAPTER XII

Curriculum Connections: Combining
Environments for Learning

ROBERT L. SINCLAIR AND WARD J. GHORY

In the United States, public elementary and secondary schools are a necessary yet single part of a larger network of learning environments that are important for education in a democratic society. Most of the primary educating institutions of contemporary life—the family, the media, the school, the peer group, the religious institutions, the workplace—have, in important ways, extended their influence and effectiveness as component parts of the public educational system during the current century.[1] The parts of the system showing the greatest strain—religious institutions, family, and schools—may have suffered more from their loss of primacy within the changing system than from internal deficiencies.[2] To the degree that this is so, curriculum change within schools alone will not produce hoped for improvements, unless we make adjustments in the ways the school curriculum connects with other agencies that educate.

The increased influence of different agents for learning and additional sources of knowledge have obscured the position of school curriculum in the larger configuration of educational settings. For example, radios, telephones, records, movies, and microcomputers have opened up more ways of gaining skills and attitudes than were previously available in a self-contained community in the early part of this century. These gains—too simultaneous, novel, rapid, and loosely controlled—created unanticipated friction with the curriculum and with the role of the teacher.[3]

No longer can the relatively well-educated teacher, as guide to the mysteries of the printed page, offer the school curriculum as the primary gateway to information about the broader community. Nor

230

can the teacher act, in most cases, as the primary monitor of the attitudes, beliefs, and values students need to participate successfully in the culture. With confidence and with confusion, our young crisscross a conflicting set of curricula embedded in institutions occasionally working at cross purposes and rarely working deliberately in tandem.[4]

Nevertheless, the school curriculum still teaches unique skills, habits, and information that are today, more than ever, indispensable to productive life in an information society. Sparked by a series of studies of the public high school curriculum, national attention is being drawn with renewed concern to identifying more carefully the knowledge and skills needed for effective participation in a changing society and to developing educational means for preparing more young people for the future. The first reports are emphasizing ways in which the existing high school curriculum does not provide appropriate content or high standards of instruction for many students. For example, the Carnegie Foundation report estimates that 15 percent of our youth receive a superior high school education while 25 percent do not complete high school, leaving 60 percent of the young people to muddle through an amorphous curriculum not carefully related to their future needs.[5] Indeed, we have had a long history of unequal opportunity in which only the students who have been most successful in school were provided with truly adequate opportunities for learning. But while the need for reforming the high school curriculum is being carefully clarified, we should avoid the fallacy of directing attention to one part of the educational network without considering the full context in which schools operate. Our view is that the weak connections that exist between school learning and life experience outside school are an important reason for the difficulties many adolescents have in responding to the high school curriculum.[6] To provide a more rigorous academic curriculum to all students and to construct more satisfactory transitions from youth to adulthood, school reformers have to pay attention to the points that connect their curriculum to the curriculum in other institutions of educational importance.

Points for Connecting School and Nonschool Environments

Although building a coordinated curriculum that spans several settings can become a necessary priority for leaders from many institutions, teachers hold the pivotal responsibility for blending the school curriculum with outside resources in a way that brings the best conditions to bear on the learning of young people. Our purpose in this chapter is to suggest where teachers can direct their energies if they want to provide leadership for expanding the school curriculum to incorporate opportunities for learning beyond the confines of the school. We recognize that teachers can also use their position as the ones closest to the learner to resist or ignore opportunities for improvement. Indeed, in the coming reconstruction period, we suspect that teachers will frequently be placed in a position of responding to outside initiatives that change their status and function. Yet, at the instructional level, where the school curriculum (no matter how revised) has to be converted into meaningful opportunities for individual children to learn, the teacher has the power and the responsibility to make those connections among school and nonschool experiences that bring vitality to learning.

There are three major ways teachers can make curriculum connections. First, teachers can make those curriculum decisions that capitalize on experiences already taking place in the learner's life outside school. Young people acquire and accumulate an unorganized reservoir of knowledge from daily experience and sheer exposure to various community environments. In an "informal" way, teachers draw upon and extend this untapped pool of knowledge by connecting it with the school curriculum. The second point of productive connection is the deliberate combining of school and nonschool environments to promote learning. In this "formal" approach, the teacher supplements classroom learning by deliberately organizing opportunities for short-term exposure to people, places, and things from the community. The third way teachers establish connections across curricula is to assist in placing individual students in other settings for specific experiences in a set time period. This "nonformal"[7] approach creates opportunities for learning systematically related to the school curriculum but taking place under the authority of a nonschool agency. The possible ways that teachers can use these approaches are now described in turn.

Improving Learning by Using Existing Conditions in Nonschool Settings

If curriculum is confined only to the current resources within the walls of the school, the opportunities for promoting learning are unnecessarily limited. To each learning task set in school, young people bring incredibly varied backgrounds that can stimulate or interfere with school learning, depending upon the ways in which these backgrounds are tapped.

Classroom observations reveal that teachers can refer to external experiences to illustrate how what is being learned in school links with out-of-school life. By simply discussing and explaining the association between what is being studied and its application to everyday situations that students experience, teachers can give some sense of usefulness and satisfaction about what is being learned. For example, when students are asked to explain how their family decides what to do on weekends, the decision-making skills of defining a problem, proposing alternative solutions, determining the benefits or costs of a particular solution, and selecting a decision from a number of options can take on added meaning. Such informal connections rarely appear on lesson plans. Perhaps since they do not systematically plan to do so, teachers often do not encourage students to make the simple yet necessary associations that lead to desired learning.

Again, one can observe teachers who are more sensitive to clues provided by student comments or actions that show particular learning is taking place outside of school or reveal special student interests. The teacher can use this information to promote learning by building on students' previous accomplishments and by using their interests to increase the desire to learn. This approach keeps students involved in sustained, challenging efforts. It makes sense, moreover, for teachers to be properly informed about the nonschool life of students. Teachers having a greater understanding of the informal experiences of students can interpret, motivate, and guide their behavior, because they can productively respond to values and habits that were developed outside school as part of the family and cultural heritage.

By giving attention to the interchange between school and nonschool settings, the teacher can take educational advantage of natural happenings in the life of the student. Too often teachers do not plan and implement a curriculum that encourages students to make those necessary associations between both school and nonschool settings that lead to desired learning.

Combining School and Nonschool Resources
for Learning

Collaboration with agencies or individuals beyond the school walls involves a short-term sharing of responsibility for learning, in which the teacher works with outside groups to plan combined efforts to accomplish a school objective. Teachers view such coordinated efforts in an ambivalent way. On the one hand, they view the outreach efforts as representing extra work and an additional set of logistical complications. On the other hand, teachers who harmoniously blend outside resources into their instructional program are acknowledged as providing a service that is both beneficial to and popular with students.

With greatest frequency, teachers bring resources and people from outside the school into the classroom to further or enliven a lesson. Teachers develop a style for using nonschool resources: a treasured collectible is borrowed and presented to the class for its special significance for a lesson; an appropriate tape recording or film is checked out of the library; a speaker willing to address students is scheduled. Student imagination and memory are fired by exposure to concrete examples of the viewpoints and skills being taught. Teachers organize speakers, special paraphernalia, and media to arouse the affective dimension of students as an aid to their cognitive development.

Another popular way to combine school and nonschool resources appropriately occurs when the teacher takes students into nonschool settings for specific experiences. Field trips offer supplemental cultural experiences for learners who lack easy access to such opportunities. Examples might include witnessing a trial during the study of the Bill of Rights, attending a play by an author studied in literature class, or taking industrial arts students on a tour of an assembly line. But these ventures beyond school walls need not involve large groups, buses, and fund raising. Giving a student a ride to the library or bookstore; accompanying a senior on his first college visit; requiring children to get a library card—these represent opportunities for constructive involvement in the "adult" world. In that sense, they are preparatory experiences in which students practice and experimentally assume behaviors expected of full participants in social life. If students perceive such experiences as superficial, it is most often because the teacher has underestimated the sophistication they have already gained outside the school. That some such ordinary gestures of interest and concern by a teacher get magnified in importance by a student speaks again to the key role of the teacher as a guide to the learner's search for a personal way to connect with society outside the school.

Also, teachers or parents can take a leadership role in tailoring environments in two or more settings to correct the weaknesses or stretch the strengths of a learner. One model for initiating this collaboration is the conference required in planning individual programs for special education students. Parents and teachers may be joined by a consulting psychologist and a doctor, to assess how a student's visual learning disability can be not only recognized and considered in the classroom, but also improved through a coordinated program of visual exercises in the home with periodic checkups by the doctor to monitor progress. Similarly, educators regularly collaborate with parents in correcting behavior problems evident at both home and school. For example, to control a student's hyperactivity, teachers and parents might give attention to dietary habits, agreement about expectations and limits, and consistent application of rules and consequences in both settings.

Finally, teachers combine environments in an effective blend for learning when they assign tasks to complete after school that promote a more conscious involvement by the learner in the out-of-school setting. Charting the family tree, conducting oral history interviews, working with the advice of a science teacher to stock a neighborhood pond—such purposeful activities suggest ways to initiate and apply skills developed in school that enrich student lives. Not only do such challenges extend the time and effort the student devotes to the task, but they also offer intermediate steps in developing skill and interest in pursuing learning independently. In all these examples of combining environments for learning, the school curriculum is connected by the teacher in a delicate and deliberate way with the student's afterschool experience. What is learned, then, in one setting is likely to be better understood, supported, and reinforced in the other.

ARRANGING FOR LEARNING OUTSIDE OF SCHOOL

A third option for curriculum connection is for the teacher to take the lead in organizing learning opportunities outside school in which the responsibility for instruction is assumed by the outside agency. Apprenticeship or internship programs place the student in a nonschool setting for an extended period of time. What students learn and how they perform is monitored and evaluated by a supervisor in the workplace. A frequent concern over such programs—that the student may become involved in unproductive tasks—stems directly from the transfer of major responsibility from the school to the outside agency. However, particularly at the preprofessional level in engineering, medicine, architecture, and education, a "cooperative" program is an established part of the school curriculum. In essence, this differs little from study abroad programs in which the educational institution arranges for lodging and course work in a foreign institution. Schools and parents sanction a parallel type of opportunity when they agree to a student's leave of absence from school to pursue work experience or travel. Special programs for the gifted, summer computer camps, sports clinics offered by successful high school coaches—all these offer connections with the school curriculum through arrangements for learning outside school.

Often, however, such arrangements take on the character of a less restrictive or less rigorous alternative to the school program. They are turned to when a student is not satisfied with or fully successful in the opportunities for learning available within the current institution. This unfortunately demeans the arrangements for out-of-school learning. There is a subtle competitive flavor that can surround such attempts at nonformal education. There is an underlying concern that the alternative offering may supplant or undermine part of the school curriculum. Yet it is sometimes through this sharing that the school curriculum has changed to incorporate opportunities for which a growing demand is discerned. Clearly, the initial marketing and educational strategies of microcomputer firms that aim at the home market and offer training in programming at the business location appear to be playing this angle to convince school officials to expand their curriculum to incorporate computer literacy. Since the essence of this kind of curriculum connecting is the transfer of responsibility for instruction outside the school's immediate control, these programs will create a sense of uneasiness and lingering suspicion over educational quality among those imbued with a school-centered vision of public education.

Remnants of Outdated Thinking

The identification of where teachers and others can create productive curriculum connections is a necessary and important part of the total effort to improve education through joining school and nonschool settings. Yet, the progress made by determining connecting points will not result in constructive action unless teachers establish a way of thinking that encourages rather than hinders the actual development of coordinated environments for learning. It is our view, then, that teachers have to maintain a certain perspective in order to entertain ways to form curriculum connections. Creating and combining environments for learning is not prevalent for all students because ways of thinking that are counterproductive to making necessary associations persist in the minds of too many teachers. Our intention here is not to imply that by altering what many teachers think we will easily combine curriculum existing in various settings. Rather, our purpose is to suggest that creating a proper mind-set toward collaboration for improved education is a necessary beginning point.

Recognizing and systematically capitalizing on the educational potential of the community is not primarily a technical problem. It is a psychological and perceptual one. It makes little sense to change school organization and curriculum if those who make the institution work do not understand the need for these changes. Fortunately, although the following views that hinder collaboration do indeed exist, they are slowly being altered to make combined school and nonschool settings an important part of the delivery of quality education to more learners.

WHAT TEACHERS THINK

Rationalizations that protect current practice are important clues to the working assumptions held by teachers. Research on school innovation makes it clear that most ideas for change are greeted with resistance, and that the specific views voiced in this resistance must be taken seriously as a source for dialogue that can lead to constructive improvements.[8] In our work with teachers regarding the need to relate school curriculum to other institutions that educate, we encountered the following viewpoints that block progress toward building connections.

Viewpoint 1: *Teachers see the need to limit their responsibilities rather than expand collaboration among environments for learning. The initial emphasis is placed on what teachers will and will not do, more than on what learners need.*

Teachers feel beleaguered. They first probe ideas about collaboration with nonschool settings for signs that it will mandate more work. They are apt to respond to suggestions about a revised role for the teacher by asking if what is being proposed can be carried out within the already established way the school functions. For example, a proposal to contact parents by telephone to report successful student progress may be initially assessed to determine its impact on teacher time, instead of its potential benefit for learners.

One result of this limiting viewpoint is an unfortunate distortion of goals, in which the educational system is conceived primarily as an employment system for members of the teachers union. At a time when close cooperation among educators in and out of school is essential to the resolution of learner difficulties, the focus can too easily shift from the learner to issues involving the power and autonomy of the professional employee. These defensive reactions are among the reasons why teachers are accused of appearing dull and unresponsive to new ideas.

At hand here is a basic confusion over means and ends. The case has to be made with teachers that learning and the school curriculum can improve through cooperation with the other institutions shaping the child's experience. Without this broadening perspective, teachers will continue to react to problems with short-term, stopgap means. The persistent desire on the part of too many teachers to look prematurely to easy solutions before considering desired ends for learners must be challenged, for it is one source of the proliferation of add-on tasks that do not relate directly to student learning. Instead, sufficient time must be taken to consider whether learning can be significantly improved through collaboration. If this approach becomes accepted, some of the responsibilities teachers have might need to be limited to make room for others implied by collaboration. Teachers can provide leadership in this effort, but first they must hold off negotiating over means until they can agree upon ends.

Viewpoint 2: *Teachers think curriculum exists primarily in schools.*

Their major responsibility is conceived as presenting and covering required course content.

Dating back to the time when the school curriculum was the primary means of providing information about the outside world to the child, teachers have viewed their major responsibility as covering the course content. Indeed, they typically saw curriculum change as being the adoption of a new textbook. This overemphasis on specific subject matter, organized in courses with lists of objectives and approved printed materials, created a delivery system for imparting concepts, values, and attitudes that was available only in school. This orientation to curriculum bred a limited view of instruction that emphasized the teacher's delivery of information.

In today's information-rich environments outside of school settings, many teachers are questioning the predominance of the traditional function of the curriculum. They realize that teachers who emphasize only the linear coverage of course content without promoting a fertile mix of ways to process or internalize this content are likely to have more learners who experience difficulty in tuning in to the school's instructional wavelength. As Dewey notes, the teacher's job is to create environmental conditions that connect the experience of the child with the concepts, skills, and attitudes intended by the curriculum.[9] Without expanding the points of connection between the many environments the child experiences, the teacher creates classroom conditions that favor only a narrow band of learners comfortable with the passive incorporation of printed and verbal information through reading independently and listening or answering teacher questions in a large-group setting.[10] Thus, the number of learners who do not achieve predictably increases whenever the curriculum emphasis swings to covering the content without teaching the child. We believe that recognition and use of the connections among learning environments is one way to resolve this problem.

Viewpoint 3: *Teachers see themselves as primarily responsible for decisions about the academic (mainly cognitive) growth of children in school. Parents, physicians, politicians, and religious leaders are expected to make the major decisions about the physical, social, and emotional development of students.*

One cause for the general failure of parents, teachers, and community members to work jointly on improving education is the assumption that these groups have basically different responsibilities.[11] The teacher's job is to develop academic competence by directing the successful completion of learning activities in the classroom. The parent's role is to provide for the physical, emotional, and spiritual needs of a young person, in consultation with medical experts and religious leaders. Politicians organize to provide the economic means and the legal safeguards necessary for education. In effect, this view of how responsibilities are divided leaves the impression that there are few decisions which these groups can or should make together.

This way of thinking leads each group to retreat and defend its own separate sphere of territory and control instead of cooperating for improvement. By tradition, few outsiders can influence what happens behind classroom doors. In the same way, parents, churches, and businesses create an inviolate space within their own spheres, with customs and traditions that teachers are generally not encouraged to view, much less question. As a result, parents and community persons often refrain from visiting school, and teachers rarely visit families at home or seldom use the community as a resource for serious learning.

The resulting segregation of the school from the community can in part be traced back to the religious origins of schools as the institution to which young people were sent to be trained for the clergy. Conventional religious thinking held that these young people needed to be cloistered from the distractions and temptations of the riotous city. Once inside school walls, the young had to be insulated, as well, from the debilitating influences of their own emotions and physical needs. When today's teachers argue that to engage in nonschool settings would water down the basic skills emphasized in the school curriculum, they often speak from within these traditions.

As the once seemingly separate spheres of influence merge, teachers start to recognize the influence home environment has on developing language skills, and design home packets and summer assignments. More teachers also recognize the interconnected role of the cognitive, affective, and psychomotor domains in the act of learning, and create programs to take advantage of these associations. Businesses form partnerships with the schools and produce the technology needed to make the home a more powerful educational station. State governors, senators, and even presidential candidates campaign on plans for curriculum development. Thus, parents and community persons are increasingly being viewed as having important information and resources for children. Further, the educational potential of nonschool settings is gradually being developed in a coordinated fashion with the school curriculum. The foundation for a new basis for working together is being formed.

Viewpoint 4: *Difficulties with school learning are seen as ultimately the child's problem. Such problems are still assumed to have their source in deficiencies in the child's world outside of school. There is no reason to alter or expand the school environment for learning since the problem is essentially in the learner.*

Fragile coalitions among teachers, parents, and community persons naturally come under the greatest strain when the children involved are not succeeding according to expectations. Our achievement-oriented, rugged-individual, white middle-class-centered culture persistently views lack of success in school in terms of a moral failure that becomes part of the very character of the person in difficulty. Reflecting this assumption, many efforts of teachers to assist failing students, as well as many programs of school collaboration conducted by foundations and corporations, are still conceived at one level as acts of compassion or concern for the child's (or the school's) problem. A variation of this missionary approach to the flawed person or institution is to reach out with aid as compensation for social forces that have placed some children (or public schools) at a disadvantage for learning the information and skills required for achievement tests.

If we view the school difficulties of learners as givens resulting from their cultural background, socioeconomic status, or IQ, we must then assume that learners would bring those same intractable problems to every environment, no matter how altered or combined. On the other hand, if we view learning difficulties as arising from the interaction between learners and the particular features of their learning environment, we can more reasonably define the role of the teacher as one which alters and adjusts the classroom and school environment to encourage learning. From this revised viewpoint, it also follows that it is appropriate for teachers to seek ways to expand the classroom environment by drawing on the resources from the learner's nonschool experiences.

More people are accepting this alternate way of viewing the

promotion of learning. As Benjamin Bloom has noted, for years study after study of the sources of academic achievement and intelligence attempted to correlate academic success or failure with relatively unalterable variables like cultural background, socioeconomic status, family size, sibling order, and so on. However, in the last twenty years, researchers are finding that interactions between adults and children and the specific activities children undertake in a learning environment influence their academic competence. Some of the variables that have been studied include: verbal encouragement of children to learn well, teacher expectations, parental aspirations, questioning strategies, verbal reinforcement techniques, provisions for special assistance in learning, and organizing time and space for study.[12] The family and school variables measured by these studies are alterable. They have been identified, for example, as aspects of the family environment that can readily be influenced by school programs to support parent efforts to improve family settings.[13] Similarly, family-based reinforcement of desirable school behaviors is proving to be an efficient and effective method for motivating children to overcome some of their most persistent learning difficulties.[14] More educators are now accepting that all children can learn given sufficient time and appropriate environments. Success in learning depends not only on what is inside the child but on the ability of educators to create exciting and stimulating conditions for promoting learning.

Our intention in presenting the above teacher viewpoints is less to convert others to our position than it is to stimulate the dialogue necessary for improving public education. We think replacing outdated ways teachers think with more constructive viewpoints is central to creating a curriculum that spans school and nonschool settings.

Concern for Reform

In the developing agenda to reform school curriculum, the need to restore stronger connections across the various institutions that educate has a way of drifting to a secondary status. At the same time, criticism of education persistently dwells on activities taking place inside schools as if their environments are unconnected to other settings. For this reason, it is essential for professional educators to encourage a quality dialogue by working to ensure that important concerns about combining environments for learning gain a more prominent spot on the agenda for reform. As school people join the movement to reform education and give it direction, their contribution to this dialogue might be enhanced by understanding the concerns addressed in this chapter, namely, the need to determine the fruitful places where school and nonschool life can be connected, the need for a leadership role for the teacher in promoting these connections, and the necessity to analyze critically and transform outdated thinking that hinders teachers from collaborating with other institutions.

Simply put, one fundamental answer to the persistent calls for improvement in education is a curriculum and a program of instruction that better connects school and nonschool environments for learning. This direction for reform is crucial to ensure that excellence in education is no longer a privilege for the few but a goal shared by all institutions that are responsible for educating children and youth in our society.

FOOTNOTES

1. Lawrence Cremin, *Public Education* (New York: Basic Books, 1976).

2. Christopher Lasch, *Haven in a Heartless World* (New York: Basic Books, 1977).

3. Neil Postman, *Teaching as a Conserving Activity* (New York: Delacorte Press, 1979).

4. James Coleman, ed., *Youth: Transition to Adulthood* (Chicago: University of Chicago Press, 1974).

5. Ernest K. Boyer, *High School: A Report on Secondary Education in America* (New York: Harper and Row, 1983).

6. Ward J. Ghory, "Alternative Educational Environments" (Doctoral dissertation, University of Massachusetts, Amherst, 1977). In this study of over 1,760 high school students in thirty-one public high schools in six New England states, the perceptions of marginal learners differed significantly from those of nonmarginal learners. In particular, marginal learners perceived greater interference from responsibilities outside the school, and were less likely to see relevant connections between their school work and their present and future problems in nonschool settings.

7. Our use of the terms "formal," "informal," and "nonformal" follows the definitions advanced in Philip H. Coombs with Manzoor Ahmed, *Attacking Rural Poverty: How Nonformal Education Can Help*, a research report for the World Bank prepared by the International Council for Educational Development (Baltimore and London: Johns Hopkins University Press, 1974), pp. 7-9.

8. Paul Berman and Milbrey McLaughlin et al., *Federal Programs Supporting Educational Change*, vol. 6 (Santa Monica, Calif.: Rand Corporation, 1975).

9. John Dewey, *The Child and the Curriculum* (Chicago: University of Chicago Press, 1911).

10. Bruce Joyce, *Models of Teaching* (Englewood Cliffs, N.J.: Prentice-Hall, 1972).

11. Sara Lawrence Lightfoot, *Worlds Apart: Relationship between Families and Schools* (New York: Basic Books, 1978).

12. Benjamin S. Bloom, *All Our Children Learning: A Primer for Parents, Teachers, and Other Educators* (New York: McGraw-Hill Co., 1983), chap. I.

13. Lawrence Dolan, "The Affective Consequences of Home Support, Instructional Quality, and Achievement," *Urban Education* 13, no. 3 (1978): 323-43.

14. Richard Barth, "Home-Based Reinforcement of School Behavior: A Review and Analysis," *Review of Educational Research* 49 (Summer 1979): 436-58.

CHAPTER XIII

Demand for Excellence and the Need for Equity: The Dynamics of Collaboration

JAMES P. COMER

Today, those Americans who are able to acquire a quality education have a greater chance of social and economic opportunity in our society. In view of this, it should not be surprising that the demand for educational excellence for all students is greater than ever. One important way to promote excellence in education and to improve individual and group opportunity for social equity is through collaboration—among disciplines such as social and behavioral science and education; among educators; and among educators, parents, and other community groups.

Until the 1940s, reasonable social equity and a good education were not inextricably linked. Most uneducated and unskilled people with marginal social skills could find employment that permitted them to care for themselves and their families and, in turn, to experience a reasonable sense of social equity. In other words, except in the case of several minority groups, reasonable social equity was a possibility without educational equity.[1] That situation has changed dramatically. After the 1940s and particularly in the last several decades, science-based and technology-based changes, and related social changes, have made educational and social equity largely interdependent.

Change and Social Equity

Over the past several generations, beginning before the 1900s, America has moved from a preindustrial society through the peak of the heavy industrial age (or "smoke stack" period) to the 1960s and to our current postindustrial period. Heads of households who were able to acquire better employment opportunities in one generation were in a better position to carry out successfully family functions and, as a result, were better able to prepare their children to participate in the educational, social, and economic environment of the next generation. In fact, many families (and their groups and communities) underwent a three-generational pattern of development roughly paralleling the development of the American economic system.[2]

This pattern, however, was not entirely predictable. The culture and other social arrangements made it possible for some families in less favorable economic situations to be successful, while personal problems and unique social situations interfered with the functioning of some families who were relatively well off economically. Nonetheless, employment opportunities generally played a major role in enabling families to feel they were a part of the American mainstream and in motivating them to embrace its attitudes, values, and ways. As a result, children from such families had access to social networks of experience, information, and opportunities that facilitated good education and future opportunities for them. It also put them in the best position to adjust to the social changes and conditions that scientific and techno-logical development brought about.

Developments in science and technology, however, have changed the current nature and location of much work. In the recent past, most work was based in the neighborhood and community. Today this is more often the exception. Physical labor is also the exception today as opposed to a generation or two ago. Less than a third of today's workers are in the manufacturing or goods-producing sector of the economy. Today's work force requires social, technological, and academic skills more than physical skills. And even where this is not the actual case, job entry requirements now demand technological and academic skills.

In addition, massive, rapid, visual communication has interrupted the knowledge monopoly held until quite recently by important authority figures, such as parents, teachers, ministers, and others. Young people today are bombarded with information and knowledge from many sources. Moreover, improved transportation and the subsequent move to the suburbs by many, have decreased the oppor-tunities for such people to interact. As a result, there has been a weakening of the sense of community and a decline in trust of authority figures. While these developments have been liberating, particularly when they have changed unfair attitudes, values, and ways, at the same time they have created confusion and uncertainty about what constitutes and how to establish just attitudes, values, and ways. Young people have many more options for life-styles and behavior, as well as the opportunity to act on them, than they did in the past.

In the face of this change and uncertainty, all American families have experienced stress. Drug abuse, an epidemic level of mental health problems, unacceptable crime rates, and a number of other social indicators apparent across the socioeconomic spectrum attest to this fact. But the most adversely affected of all are those groups whose members were closed out of the political and economic mainstream of the society before science and technology drastically changed the nature of work.

Many adequate and potentially adequate families have become isolated from the benefits of better job opportunities. Prior to this century, a strong sense of community and certain specific cultural supports such as church or religion enabled many such families to function well despite their economic marginality. Some continue to do so. And segments of all groups have undergone the typical three-generational development experience of most families. But when the effects of mass communication and transportation began to weaken the sense of community and cultural supports of all groups, the greatest adverse affects were on those groups relying most heavily on community and cultural supports in the absence of economic and educational opportunities. A disproportionate number of such families began to function less well from generation to generation. They were and are least prepared to enable their children to meet the social and academic demands of modern society.

In addition to isolation, several minority groups—blacks, American Indians, and Hispanics—were deliberately excluded from better job opportunities.[3] These three groups were more vulnerable to exclusion and the adverse effects of economic marginality because of severe cultural insult (experiences such as slavery and other violations) and a high level of racism. Certain segments of the Asian-American population also experienced severe cultural insult and a resulting social vulnerability and disadvantage. But cultural continuity and support remained relatively intact for many Asians during the crucial economic transition period that took place in the first half of this century.

Ironically, in the late 1950s and the 1960s, improved education and social opportunities for black Americans intensified and precipitated their determined quest for social and thereby educational equity. While this was a reaction to injustice, the probability of their continued economic marginality as a result of the growing link between educational and economic opportunity was a prime moving force. Other minorities and women quickly joined the stepped-up national quest for social equity and academic excellence. At the same time, growing international economic competition, concern about national defense, and the apparent decline in the achievement levels among both affluent and economically disadvantaged Americans further increased the demand for academic equity and excellence for all Americans.

At the same time, changes in science and technology, as well as directly and indirectly related social changes, have created tensions between groups that now represent significant obstacles to providing good school programs. Thus, in our efforts to improve schools, we must address these intergroup tensions—between home and school; among school staff; between staff and students; between races, income groups, and professions.

Change and the School

Prior to World War II, America was a nation of small towns and rural areas. And even large cities, in effect, were collections of small towns. Parents, teachers, administrators, and other authority figures often interacted in informal but socially and psychologically supportive ways. They sometimes attended the same church, often met while shopping or at recreational and social events. This made school people and the school a natural part of the community. And school people were generally valued, respected, and trusted, at least more so than today.

Under these circumstances, the authority of parents could be transferred to the school staff. This permitted staff members to serve as powerful mentors, helpers, and guides. These relationships fostered identification with the mission and program of the school and a motivation for adequate social and academic performance. Without being fully conscious of their role, school staff helped young people to develop in ways critical to school learning—socially and ethically, psychologically, cognitively, and linguistically.

This is not to say that social practices in and outside the school were always fair. Indeed, they often were not, particularly for minorities, low-income people, and women. But expectations were clear. Neither high mobility nor mass communication significantly challenged the local social order. Parents and school people reinforced each other, a reinforcement promoted by the nature of the social setting. Under these circumstances, student acceptance of authority was great, and behavioral problems were minimal.

Students who could not adjust to the expectations of the school left and entered the job market. Most were able to earn a living sufficient to care for themselves and their families, and they experienced a sense of well-being and belonging. Changes in employment requirements after the 1940s, however, forced many such youngsters to remain in school. As a result, schooling had to be organized and managed in ways that were not fully appreciated.

Two developments—improved transportation and mass communications—greatly changed school and community relationships in America. High mobility allowed school staffs to live long distances from the neighborhoods in which they worked. Mass communications and the struggles for social equity to which the media gave high visibility, again while liberating in important ways, also broke consensus and the pattern of established relationships—race to race, social class to social class, home to school, administrator to teacher, student to staff. Distrust, suspicion, and disrespect are more possible under current conditions. For example, the authority of parents is not automatically transferred to the school. Indeed, school people and the institution itself can be—and often are in communities most marginal to the mainstream of the society—viewed as "the enemy."

With more information, stimulation, and behavior options to integrate into their developing persona, *all* young people need to interact more with mature, trusted adults than in the past. But circumstances have decreased the number of such people in school and elsewhere in their lives. As a result, there is more confusion, testing of authority, acting up, and acting out on the part of young people today. Again, families under stress in the past are the most adversely affected today. These families are more likely to send children to school with similar aspirations as other families. But these children are under-developed along pathways critical for school success. Some have been well cared for and have social and other skills that are useful and effective in other settings—but not in school. Unfortunately, the number of such familes is on the rise.[4]

Most schools are not prepared to help young people in general to deal with the complexities of the modern age. And even fewer are prepared to assist underdeveloped children or children who lack effective school skills. This is so because the education establishment—colleges, government, and private support systems—responded to scientific and technological changes by putting an increased emphasis on technical and academic content, teaching methods, and more course requirements and credentials for educators. Recently there has been increased attention to standards for student performance and, in some cases, for staff performance. But there is still limited recognition of the importance of preparing teachers to deal with student relationships and behavior issues. Unfortunately the roots of such problems are usually thought to be located in individual students or their families—based on the medical model—rather than systems-based or interactional or ecological in nature.[5]

Oddly, even with the focus on the individual, most educators are taught very little about child development. Where attention to child development and behavior exists at all, it is often theoretical rather than applied. And without a systems perspective, understandably most educators are not asked to consider the consequences of school organization and management on staff, student, and parent intra-personal and interpersonal relationships in a school building. Consequently, teachers and administrators are not prepared to collaborate with social workers, psychologists, special education teachers, and parents, who are the first teachers. Teachers are not prepared to collaborate with administrators and vice versa. And all are ill prepared to address the developmental needs of children, particularly those from stressful conditions.

Most schools use an organization and management approach that was adequate in pre-World War II America when they were a natural part of the community. That model is generally hierarchical and authoritarian: the principal is charged with providing leadership at the building level; teachers are expected to teach as directed and to offer little input to building management and program development.

In most places, parents are still excluded—or at best minimally and superficially involved—in the process of education. Social workers, psychologists, special education teachers, where they exist, operate in reactive ways after the problem develops rather than in proactive, preventive ways. The arts, athletics, and other programs are conducted as add-ons to the curriculum, more often considered unnecessary distractions or "frills" rather than integrated components of the curriculum used to aid social, psychological, cognitive, speech, and language development. And finally and most importantly, there is generally no mechanism, other than the principal, to coordinate the many programs and people needed in the modern schools or to react in an ongoing and systematic way to the specific problems and opportunities in a particular building.

Schools receiving families and children from the social mainstream often do not adequately meet their needs. But most such students are able to acquire adequate academic skills because of prior preparation and, in later school, because of the motivation of future opportunities. Schools, however, are often overwhelmed by children who come from families under past and present stress, who are often underdeveloped or with different skills, and who are without the incentive of future opportunities. With inflexible and inappropriate organization and management, without the necessary preservice training, most school staff respond to underdeveloped children as if they are "dumb" or have low academic potential, just as they respond to difficult behavior as if it is willful and "bad." These low expectations and efforts to control "bad" behavior often lead to conflict and a downhill social and academic course for students.

In turn, conflict between student and staff often leads to conflict between home and school and among staff people. The conflict often takes on overtones related to racial, social, or other differences. Parents often have mixed feelings about schools: hopeful, doubtful, some outright antagonistic. The teachers are often not successful at a level that is professionally rewarding and, as a result, frequently "burn out," "hang on" by any means necessary, or leave education entirely. In-service efforts to improve education are very similar to preservice programs in that they generally do not address process, child development, and relationship issues. For these and other reasons, the quality of education in the nation's schools, public and private, continues gradually to erode.

There are many problems in primary and secondary education. But critics point to almost everything except what is probably the most critical dynamic—the way scientific and technological change, with related social change, has broken the natural collaboration between home, school, and community.[6] Yet there is good and growing evidence that an emphasis on collaboration among the disciplines of education and behavioral and social science, among various education groups, and among community, home, and school can significantly improve the quality of education. We will not fully understand the effects of many of the factors cited as problems in education until we have put in place school organization and management approaches that facilitate collaboration among these critical players. Many of the apparent problems will drop away when this is the case.

Collaboration

We need collaboration at many levels to improve the American school system. At least four levels of collaboration are critical: collaboration between educators and social and behavioral scientists; collaboration between colleges and universities and primary and secondary schools; collaboration between the central office of a particular school system and its individual schools; collaboration among the participants in the educational process at the building level—parents, staff, and students. But while collaboration at these various levels is important, there are significant pitfalls.

OBSTACLES TO COLLABORATION

Social and behavioral scientists often look at problems from a psychosocial dynamic perspective. The discipline tends to be theoretical and favors long-range, structural changes to address problem situations. Social and behavioral scientists attached to academic institutions are often interested in research with a preference for experimental designs, the findings of which are usually too fragmented or isolated to be of great value in system-wide change or improvement. Social and behavioral scientists rarely look at schools and systems as a whole. Yet educators must or should take comprehensive or systems-level approaches to school improvement. Indeed, some of the difficulty of school improvement programs may be due to the influence of researchers who study pieces of educational programs in isolation.

Educators are under extreme pressure for system improvement. This too often leads to innovation or action in the academic and behavior area that is not based on sound social and behavioral science principles; that is, it is content- rather than process-oriented. What results is a cycle of innovation, enthusiasm, and the emergence of a "movement," marginal to no sustained success with the innovation, and then disappointment and abandonment of the approach, and the introduction of a new innovation. This cycle predictably results in hopelessness and apathy on the part of education practitioners and a loss of confidence on the part of the public.

Collaboration between colleges and universities and precollegiate schools has its own special problems. Society assigns higher status to colleges and universities. Yet the work of precollegiate schools is equally important, if not more so, in maintaining and improving society. College and university personnel often propose and implement programs in primary and secondary schools, but primary and secondary school personnel are rarely asked to contribute to the work of a college or university. Because precollegiate school personnel are generally in cooperative arrangements with colleges and universities but rarely in true collaboration, there is potential distrust and conflict. In addition, while there is often only limited project success in the school, college and university personnel often publish accounts of the project to their own career advantage, leaving many school people feeling "used" and with greater distrust and anger.

Central office and building-level collaboration is hampered by the hierarchical structure and authoritarian style of many educational systems and administrators. Every aspect of many school programs—operations, curriculum, staff development, extracurricular activities, and the like—is often planned at the central office level. Communication is generally top-down. Input and decision making from teachers, social workers, principals, parents, and others actually working with students are too often token or nonexistent. For example, staff development programs are frequently city-wide (even external to a system), planned centrally, and totally unrelated to the social and academic objectives, goals, and needs of a particular school.

Central office directives and expectations often interfere with building-level programs. Its services to academic subjects—mathematics, language arts, and so forth—and to arts, athletic, and mental health programs are often poorly coordinated and do not directly connect with what is going on at the building level. This is generally not because central office and building-level staff are incompetent or deliberately uncooperative. It is generally because the hierarchical, top-down, authoritarian organization and management of school systems do not permit effective and efficient communication, coordination, and program articulation.

Building-level collaboration is difficult for a number of reasons. First, as mentioned, central office directives often prescribe the building-level program whether it is appropriate to meet its needs or not. In many cases, collaboration with teachers, parents, and students is discouraged, and principals are punished or considered weak when this is the case. Even where central office staff, parents, and students want to work in a collaborative fashion, few central office personnel and building-level administrators and staff are trained in doing so.

Thus, establishing a collaborative process appears to be long, difficult, and risky. Simplistic curriculum changes and behavioral management approaches promise improvement in school behavior and achievement in less time, with less risk. But because these approaches do not address underlying problems in the modern American social system, their effect is minimal or unsuccessful.

Successful Collaboration Requirements

Successful collaboration between educators, behavioral and social scientists, colleges and universities and precollegiate schools, central office and building-level personnel, and building-level participants must begin with central office administrators who understand the need and support the concept. Equally important, they must understand the obstacles and be disciplined and creative enough to overcome them. Efforts at changes made without support and at a pace beyond the ability of most involved to adjust will result in excessive resistance and even rebellion. With effective central office leadership, structures can be created that permit collaboration by behavioral and social scientists, educators from outside and inside a school system, central office personnel, building-level staff, and parents.

Successful collaboration requires top-down (central office) and bottom-up (individual building) communication, planning, and program implementation. It requires that school personnel be taught the skills of collaboration through instruction and practice with appropriate supervision and support. It requires an organizational structure that preserves power and responsibility for administrators and at the same time permits parents, teachers, and students, where appropriate, to influence program management significantly.

A collaborative approach is successful at the building level when it improves communication, trust, and respect among all involved; provides a sense of program direction, ownership, and responsibility among all; permits parent, teacher, student participation in program planning, implementation, and evaluation; reduces conflict; allows adequate time on tasks; and improves the school performance on the part of students, parents, teachers, and administrators.

One model of collaboration designed to address the issues described above was developed in the New Haven, Connecticut, school system. A description of how this model works will illustrate the dynamics of collaboration for improved education for all students.

The New Haven Model

In the late 1950s and early 1960s, the New Haven school system began to try to adjust to its changed population (more low-income and minority group students).[7] It developed a number of approaches—community schools, busing in-town and into suburban areas for racial balance prior to court-ordered programs, enrichment approaches, and a variety of other innovative programs. While these efforts often required various kinds of collaboration, and were often instructive and helpful to the students involved, they did not constitute a comprehensive plan to improve the New Haven school system. Without such an approach, academic excellence and social equity could not be a reality for most students.

In 1977, Dr. Gerald Tirozzi was selected Superintendent of Schools. After a review of the innovative programs in the system over the past twenty years, he proposed the creation of an Urban Academy. The Urban Academy was designed to permit collaboration between behavioral and social scientists and educators, universities and the public school system, central office personnel and individual schools,

and among the parents, staff, and students at the building level. The
Urban Academy was also designed to build on what was learned from
previous innovation and to avoid the pitfalls common to collaborative
efforts.

The Urban Academy was instituted in 1980 and is composed of a
steering committee headed by the superintendent of schools, and, on a
daily basis, by a coordinator. The current coordinator is a principal on
special assignment. Central office, building-level, and university representatives plan the Urban Academy program. There is an introductory
level program for all the elementary school principals, entitled Tier I.
A more comprehensive program, Tier II, initially involved a six-
school subset of the total system. Tier II participation increases by two
to three schools per year. It will eventually involve middle and high
schools. As Tier I schools indicate a readiness to be involved in a more
comprehensive program of change, and as personnel to support the
more comprehensive approach are available, they can become Tier II
programs.

The Urban Academy permits the entire school system to begin to
work in a collaborative fashion necessary for successful school improvement, but at a pace and with the support that makes improvement
more likely and resistance and failure less likely. The approach permits
each school to tailor its change to its peculiar needs. At the same time,
the Tier I and Tier II programs are based on what was learned from
the many innovative programs in New Haven, particularly two such
programs: one by a behavioral and social science group; the second by
a university school administration group.

In 1979, Dr. John Brubacher, Head of the Department of Educational Administration at the University of Connecticut, and his
colleagues began to work with elementary school principals in the
New Haven school system to develop an Instructional Plan for
Improvement (IPI). The essential element of this program is an
administrator and teacher assessment of school academic achievement
and needs and a systematic plan for improvement based on the
findings. All elementary school principals participate in workshops
designed to assist them in carrying out this program. A two-day,
preschool planning session in the fall allows them to initiate the
process. Principals eventually submit improvement plans, and a periodic

review of their implementation is carried out over the school year. The emphasis in this approach is on academic achievement.

Tier I program schools are guided largely by the IPI process. In addition, Tier I, or all elementary school principals, attend a program of monthly seminars designed to introduce them to leadership skills, behavior and systems management approaches, and reading and mathematics improvement programs. On request the leaders of these seminars give a limited number of follow-up presentations in individual schools. These seminars and other activities prepare Tier I principals for a more comprehensive school improvement program in their buildings, or the Tier II level of involvement.

The more comprehensive building level collaboration model, Tier II, is based largely on the work done by myself and my colleagues, a four-person behavioral and social science (mental health) team from the Yale University Child Study Center.[8] Academic, social, and behavior issues are addressed in this approach. This project began in 1968 in two schools with the lowest academic achievement in the city. Students in these schools also presented severe behavior problems and had very poor attendance records. The project is a systems-level intervention approach.

The two Yale Child Study Center-New Haven school system project schools were among the first six in the Tier II group of schools. While the four other schools developed building level programs peculiar to their needs, the essential program elements of the original two project schools are expected to be developed in all of the Tier II schools.

The crucial project element is a representative governance and management body at the building level. The school principal heads this group, and it is made up of two to three teachers selected by the teacher group, two to three parents selected by the parent group, and initially a behavioral and social scientist or mental health team person from the Yale Child Study Center. In the 1983-84 academic year, mental health staff from the New Haven School System Pupil Personnel Services group provided the mental health input. All members of the governance and management group act as advisors to the principal. But because decisions are usually made on a consensus basis, they all have genuine decision-making roles.

The governance and management team identifies problems and opportunities in the academic (curriculum, achievement, and staff development) and social climate areas; plans and implements programs of improvement or delegates the responsibility to other groups in the school; evaluates the outcome of these programs and modifies them as indicated. This approach fosters communication, coordination, and a sense of psychological ownership of the school program by all involved. The mental health staff person on the team provides child development, behavioral, and social science knowledge to this management effort. In this way behavioral and social science knowledge is applied to every aspect of the school program and not just to student behavior or family problems. And the mental health team effort is preventive and not just reactive.

The mental health team also consults with teachers and, on rare occasions, works with individual students. The work of the mental health team reduces severe behavior problems. The team also facilitates the work of the parent group.

Another important project element is the parent program. The parent program provides a parent assistant to a teacher in each classroom on a part-time basis. Parents working in this way serve as the core of a group of parents working to develop extracurricular activities in support of the academic program of the school. The combined effort of the governance and management group, the parents' group, and the mental health team serves to improve the school social climate and allows the staff to spend adequate time on planning the academic program, teaching, and evaluating.

The governance and management team focused first on the most urgent and disruptive behavior problems. As conditions improved, they turned to more subtle problems and opportunities which, in turn, led to even greater improvement. The governance and management group delegated the task of creating a good school climate to the parent-teacher group, which, in turn, devised a calendar of school support activities. All of the traditional holiday and seasonal activities— returning to school in the fall, leaving school in the spring, Halloween, Thanksgiving, Christmas, spring, and the like—were systematically and thoughtfully used to develop student appreciation of the arts and to create a good school climate. In response to a disruptive incident related to a transfer, the management group—with mental health team input—created a school orientation program for transfer students which greatly reduced the problems that often surround such events.

It took one teacher eight months to establish a trusting relationship with a child who was withdrawn and distrustful because of traumatic family conditions. The teacher was concerned about the fact that she was going to lose the child to the next grade in the next two months. After considering the problem of a high level of discontinuity in the lives of low-income children, the mental health team had a discussion with the entire staff. Out of this discussion evolved a program of keeping each classroom teacher with a class for two years. This greatly reduced much testing and acting out behavior. Some children, who had made no to little academic gain during the first year with a teacher, made two years of academic gain in the second year. A Discovery Room for "turned off" students was created. This program helped such students learn how to manage their feelings and express them appropriately. With the skill of appropriate expression, they were less fearful of involving themselves in academic and social activities; they were more likely to express their feelings appropriately rather than to turn them inward or outward in a way that harmed themselves or the system. This program also led to the creation of a "Crisis Unit," which did the same thing on an emergency basis.

Appreciation of the interplay among social skills, a sense of psychological well-being, and academic achievement brought about the creation of a "Social Skills Curriculum for Inner City Children." The curriculum was designed to provide low-income children with interactional skills, personal and situational, which children from better educated families obtain simply through living with their families. This program integrated the teaching of academic material, social skills, and the arts. Four units were developed based on the areas in which children will need performance skills to be successful adults—government and politics, business and economics, health and nutrition, and leisure-spiritual time. Parents work with teachers in planning and carrying out this program. The mental health team helped parents and staff to structure these activities so that they promoted student social, psychological and emotional, moral and cognitive growth. This collaboration is ongoing and includes periodic assessment and modification, elaboration, and development of new programs.

In short, the collaborative process at the building level is systematically managed in a way that permits all participants to contribute their skills and experience in an orderly, vital atmosphere. Successful interaction among administrator, teachers, and parents results in the kind of trust and hope that existed naturally in the pre-1940s school. This establishes a circle of improved teaching and learning, trust and hope and, in turn, even greater improvement in teaching and learning. As this process unfolds, a building program gradually improves.

The Urban Academy facilitates the building-level management and the teaching and learning process. This is possible because university administrative and mental health consultants, central office and building-level administrators, and teachers all serve on the Urban Academy Steering Committee. (The presence and leadership of the superintendent is the key to the effectiveness of this body.) With top-down, bottom-up communication through this mechanism, the central office is able to adjust and coordinate its personnel and services—subject-area supervisors, pupil personnel services, and so forth—with building level needs on an ongoing basis.

As Tier II schools improve, schools from the Tier I level can become a part of a more comprehensive program. The timing of involvement in the more comprehensive program can be regulated by the superintendent and the steering committee based on the availability of support personnel, system-level needs, and the readiness of schools to work in a collaborative way.

RESULTS

In 1969, students in the Martin Luther King, Jr., School (kindergarten to fourth grade)—the original project school—were nineteen and eighteen months behind in reading and mathematics respectively by the fourth grade. Since 1979, they have been at and above grade level in reading and mathematics with no apparent change in the socioeconomic level of the community.

End-of-the-year, 1983, test scores for the seven Tier II schools—all lower socioeconomic schools—were also very encouraging. Fourth graders in three of the seven schools were at or above grade level in their overall scores on the Iowa Test of Basic Skills. At three of the other Tier II elementary schools, the fourth graders were one, three, and four months below grade level respectively. All but one of the seven Tier II schools ranked higher among New Haven schools than they did the previous year. On the Base-3 criterion-referenced test taken by all third graders, three Tier II schools were among the top ten schools in the city on composite scores. Martin Luther King, Jr., School, our original project school, ranked fifth (out of twenty-five) in composite scores and fourth in mathematics scores, ahead of most middle-income schools.

Collaboration among staff members—principals, teachers, social workers, psychologists, special education teachers, aides—has been greatly improved in Urban Academy Tier II schools. Differences in the skill and style of building-level administrators may eventually prove to be a very important factor in collaboration, but this does not appear to be the case at this time. At the moment all of the governance and management teams are making satisfactory progress.

Parent participation has increased at all Tier II schools. The most reliable information is available from the initial Yale Child Study Center-New Haven School System collaboration project school (King) and the field test school (Brennan). In both schools, parents participated as classroom assistants on a regular basis and formed the core of an approximately thirty-person parent participation group which was responsible, with staff, for integrating the extracurricular program of the school with the academic program. Programs sponsored by parents and staff raised the average parent attendance for such affairs from fifteen to twenty in 1968 to 250 by 1976. Once involved with the program, at least eight parents from these low-income communities eventually obtained college degrees. Many eventually obtained jobs they would not have applied for prior to their work on the project.

The focus on prevention through applying mental health knowledge, skills, and perspectives to all activities developed by the governance and management group greatly reduced individual and interpersonal behavior problems. Attendance, an indication of the quality of relationships in a social system, improved dramatically among King and Brennan staff and students and to some degree in all of the Tier II schools. King students have been in the top five schools in attendance in New Haven in all of the last eight years, number one in attendance during three of these years. There have been no serious behavior problems at King in the past decade. Similar trends appear to be developing in most of the Tier II schools.

Summary and Conclusion

The demand for academic and social equity through excellence in education is stronger today than ever before. This appears to be the case because excellence in education and social equity appear to be inextricably linked as never before. For a number of reasons related largely to scientific, technological, and related social changes, the natural collaboration that existed between home, other community agencies, and school prior to the 1950s no longer exists. Students from all backgrounds, but particularly low-income and more often minority groups closed out of the socioeconomic mainstream in the past, need an educational program in which the skills and concerns of parents, teachers, administrators, college and university educators, and social and behavioral scientists are brought to bear, This can best be made possible through programs of collaboration at several levels.

We are not suggesting that the New Haven model is the only way to develop a collaborative process. Rather, we suggest that there are a number of issues involved and changes required in promoting excellence that cannot be simply identified and then mandated. Many of the issues are "human factors," what people are like under various social conditions. An educational program of excellence and equity requires a collaborative system that understands the "human factors" and facilitates interaction which results in optimal performance on the part of all involved.

FOOTNOTES

1. Colin Greer, *The Great School Legend* (New York: Viking Press, 1973).

2. James P. Comer, *Beyond Black and White* (New York: Quadrangle/New York Times Book Co., 1972), pp. 71-114.

3. Philip S. Foner, *Organized Labor and the Black Worker, 1619-1981* (New York: International Publishers, 1981).

4. *A Dream Deferred: The Economic Status of Black Americans* (Washington, D.C.: Center for the Study of Social Policy, 1983).

5. Urie Bronfenbrenner, *The Ecology of Human Development: Experiments by Nature and Design* (Cambridge: Harvard University Press, 1979).

6. James P. Comer, *School Power: Implications of an Intervention Project* (New York: Free Press, 1980).

7. Samuel Nash et al., "New Haven, Connecticut: New Haven Chose to Desegregate," in *The Integration of American Schools: Problems, Experience, and Solutions*, edited by Norene Harris, Nathaniel Jackson, and Carl E. Rydingsword (Boston: Allyn and Bacon, 1975), chap. 5.

8. Comer, *School Power*, pp. 57-212.

CHAPTER XIV

Linking School and Nonschool Education: Public Policy Considerations

MARIO D. FANTINI AND ROBERT L. SINCLAIR

This yearbook reaffirms that public schools are the major institutions for promoting learning. It also suggests that nonschool settings must now take on a greater share of the responsibilities that schools have too often faced alone. By reexamining school and nonschool education, this volume establishes a perspective for increasing constructive coordination among various environments for learning. It advances, we think, a powerful direction for reform and a compelling means for the delivery of education in our society during these challenging times.

In this closing chapter, we advance suggestions for a public policy that is intended to facilitate productive connections between school and nonschool settings. By doing so, we hope to contribute to the agenda for school reform needed to modernize our nation's public school system. We propose ideas to stimulate policymakers to utilize the current interest in educational reform as a means for moving sound ideas into constructive action.

Public policy becomes established through the political process. We urge that the formulation of public policy for school reform, whether at the federal, state, or local levels, transcend traditional party politics. To this end, policies for improved public education can be guided by four goals that are deeply rooted in our nation's ideals, traditions, and values. The first goal is to achieve *quality*—the accomplishment of the highest possible academic standards. The second is to create *equality*—the establishment of quality that is shared equally so that every individual has access to the best we can offer. The third is to insure *effectiveness*—the use of proven and productive approaches for promoting learning that are based on sound theory, research, and practice. And the fourth is to develop *efficiency*—the implementation of economical approaches that avoid unnecessary duplication of efforts and facilities while at the same time fully utilizing appropriate available learning resources. These four goals overlap, and their interdependent application to public policy, though difficult, is essential. Attention to these goals can facilitate a coordinated effort to stimulate desirable federal, state, and local legislative initiatives designed to assist schools and other institutions in the improvement of education.[1]

Public policy should not emphasize one of these goals at the expense of others. Yet, the call for reform does not always maintain a proper balance. For example, despite the assumption that the public schools exist as an agency of society to assure equality, the present school reform period seems to give increased emphasis and attention to quality. Past experience shows that policies aimed only at establishing higher standards in schools can lead to compromises that limit equal opportunity for learning. To achieve both quality and equality requires creative restructuring of the relationship between school and nonschool settings. Since public schools exist to guarantee equal access to quality services, policymakers and school leaders are responsible for providing services to improve learning environments for all people. They must take responsibility for assuring that every learner has access to broad opportunities for productive education in a variety of settings. Professional educators, in concert with other educative agencies, must play a major role. Policymakers can help foster connections between school and nonschool settings while also assessing the appropriateness of those arrangements.[2]

One major theme developing for some time in American education is that schools are central service agencies of the community. Underlying this idea is the assumption that, since schools belong to the community, the community can rightfully use their resources. This led to changes in the way schools were utilized. In many communities, schools are open in the evenings, on weekends, and during the summer. Adults, along with agencies such as Boy Scouts, Girl Scouts, and 4-H Clubs, are encouraged to meet on the school premises.

By the end of the 1970s, schools were viewed not only as agencies that should open their doors to the community, but as conduits for establishing relationships with other educative agencies. For example, in Flint, Michigan, the Charles Stewart Mott Foundation made public schools exemplars of community schools and community education. Community schools were central to the creation of partnerships between business and schools, between higher education and schools, between human service agencies and schools.

Public policy, which lagged behind some of these developments, is now starting to make major strides toward a recommitment to excellence in American education. Attention is focused once again upon the relationships between school and community. It is clear that as society changes the school is only one of the central settings in which learning can take place. Yet it has also become clear, particularly during the past two decades, that there is a growing disconnection between the schools and the communities they serve. The schools have too often become isolated and embattled institutions. Witness, for example, the deep dissatisfaction with the schools that was expressed through parental protests, school boycotts, and even riots in New York City during the 1960s. These acts of dissatisfaction were directed toward reclaiming control of the schools, achieving reforms, and reestablishing connection between the school and the community. Many proposals for school reform, then and now, center on the urgent need to connect schools constructively with their localities.[3] In order to promote this expanded system of *education* and not merely tinker with schooling, functional linkages between schools and many other learning environments in the community have to be fostered by proper public policy. New policies are beginning to emerge, enabling school and nonschool settings to connect in partnerships that are intended to provide quality and equal education while also addressing the goals of efficiency and effectiveness.

Policymakers must recognize that many professionals have long been urging a linkage of school and nonschool agencies. John Dewey, for example, recommended such connections early in this century. He observed that the school was an integral part of community life. It represented, however, only one of the environments through which the learner progressed. The home, the workplace, the neighborhood, and other settings also contributed to the broad process of education. Dewey also suggested that the schools play a mediating role in assuring that necessary interconnections among various settings were made in the best interests of the learner.[4] Later in the century,

Lawrence Cremin proposed an "ecology of education," in which the community would become the basic context for education, interlocking all of the educative agencies.[5] Recently, John I. Goodlad summarized his conclusions from an eight-year study of American schools with a concept of the community as the major educator of the people.[6] Many voices, then, call for a learning society,[7] and responsive public policy is necessary in order to move ideas for school and nonschool education into action.

Policymakers need to be more aware that all learning does not take place in one setting and that, while schooling is part of education, it should not be confused with the totality of education. Education is a lifelong process, taking place in a variety of settings, both formal and informal. Schooling is a formal procedure that is conducted within limits of time and place. The implications for compelling public policy for educational reform come from an understanding that varied learning environments can be linked in ways that promote improved education for all children and youth. Further, policymakers need to be reassured during this current reform period that professional educators, by virtue of their positions and their responsibilities, are in a key position to coordinate necessary relationships between the school and nonschool settings.

As functional linkages between various educative settings are established, a line of accountability is also essential. Today, accountability for excellence in education rests mainly with schools and with educators for assuring that proper concern for academic standards and a commitment to equality guide the effective delivery of services. Policy for educational reform needs to increase involvement and accountability of community leaders, parents, and other interested parties in the delivery of educational services.

While there is unity in the development of school and nonschool partnerships, there must also be a division of labor in the formulation and implementation of policies. We think the federal role is to inform the public and to establish consensus among the states so that national goals become the guiding criteria for continued examination and reform. At times, federal policy must provide financial assistance to address major educational issues. The states can devise more detailed policies to support reforms at the local level, with each state pursuing its own path, taking into account regional and local differences. The localities can then set their specific priorities and devise action plans for the actual implementation of desired policy. A combined federal, state, and local initiative would coordinate essential resources and focus them on the central issues of improving our nation's public system of education. Policies at the federal level must mesh with policies at the state and local levels. This will be no easy task, but it is one that must be given priority by our elected leaders if education is to improve.

Perhaps it may be useful to illustrate how federal, state, and local policy initiatives to build school and nonschool connections can be complementary and responsive to all levels of decision making involved in providing directions for better education.

At the national level. The Community Schools and Comprehensive Community Education Act of 1978 provides us with an example of specifics on the subject of creating partnerships. Under its statement of findings and policy, Congress found that (a) the school is an integral part of the local system for the delivery of human services, and (b) the school is a primary institution for the delivery of services, and may be the best instrument for the coordination of frequently fragmented services, including parental involvement in the delivery of such services. The statement of findings and policy indicates the following purposes of the act:

1. To provide educational, recreational, cultural, and other related community and human services, in accordance with the needs, interests, and concerns of the community agencies, through the expansion of community education programs;

2. To coordinate the delivery of social services to meet the needs and preferences of the residents of the community served by the school, and to provide for a research and development emphasis in community education which can contribute to the improved formulation of federal, state, and local policy.[8]

At the state level. The Massachusetts legislature has proposed that General Laws of that State be amended to include the following:

1. In order to promote school improvement activities at the school building level, to increase community involvement in the public schools, and to reaffirm the commitment of the Commonwealth to local control of the public schools, there shall be created a School Improvement Council at every public school.

2. Each School Improvement Council shall be broadly representative of the racial, ethnic, cultural, gender, and special needs populations of the school community.

3. The Board of Education shall promulgate regulations regarding the election of members to School Improvement Councils. In addition, the Board shall be authorized to award grants in support of the activities of School Improvement Councils.[9]

At the local level. National and state policies are ultimately justified by how well they are implemented at the local level. Thus, to be successful, policies linking school and nonschool learning environments must be translated into practice.

In Springfield, Massachusetts, the framework of a Partnership for Excellence provides an example for linking school and nonschool learning resources. The Partnership for Excellence developed a formal statement of its mission:

. . . to provide a permanent partnership of the public, private, and academic sectors to assist the Springfield Public Schools. Its purpose is to increase standards of excellence, to develop new resources, and to provide opportunities to help students achieve their standards in order to prepare them for employment, higher education, and social responsibility.[10]

Another example of a local attempt to implement policy exists in Boston, Massachusetts, where a major new initiative has been undertaken by the School Department, the city government, and the business community in an attempt to improve the public schools. The Boston Compact, as this initiative is called, represents an agreement between the school and businesses in which both sides commit themselves to identified and measurable objectives. In this broad-based compact, the community agrees upon a specific plan of action in concert with the School Department. (See chapter 3.) Under this five-year agreement, formalized in 1983, the School Department pledged to improve student attendance and performance, while more than two hundred businesses and forty cultural institutions in the Greater Boston area promised to provide permanent jobs for high school graduates.

The School Department, through the superintendent, agreed to initiate the following activities:

1. Issue a Policy Statement that embraces the Compact's goals and commits the Department to fulfilling them.

2. Require that all high schools promulgate annual reports that state publicly how the school is performing vis-à-vis attendance, achievement, and placement.

3. Assign School Department staff and allocate resources to continue planning in the eleven topic areas described in the Operational Plan: counseling, alternative education, job development, basic skills, arts, athletics, curriculum development, career education, computer literacy, research and evaluation, and school-based management.

4. Continue to implement and expand existing innovations that support the goals of the Compact, such as school-based management, the Job Collaborative, and new curricula for the high schools.

5. Assess individual high schools and their headmasters' performance on the basis of progress toward the Compact's goals and their involvement with external agencies.

6. Seek agreement with the Teachers Union on contract modifications that reflect the reality of the school system, provide stability for teachers, and focus on direct educational benefits.

7. Work with the city and the business community to implement graduated career preparation throughout the high schools and to expand the Job Collaborative to all high schools by 1985.

8. Allocate School Department resources toward activities that support the Boston Compact.[11]

Many more such examples of collaboration throughout the country could be cited indicating the participation of interested parties in the process of planning and developing initiatives at the level that mesh with state and federal policies for educational reform.

*   *   *

Education is too essential to our national well-being to fall victim to partisan politics. As some of the recent reports on American education dramatically indicated, the need for reform has reached the proportions of a major national priority.[12] We must ask that our makers of public policy rise above the interests and influences of party politics in a major bipartisan commitment to educational reform. Education must be elevated to a top-level priority on the national agenda, and we must find ways to support and maintain the current interest in education and educational reform. Meaningful and lasting reform is a long-term process. We will not benefit from the quick-fix or the shake-and-bake approach. Instead, we must engage in a fundamental and comprehensive restructuring of our educational system. To achieve this, we need not only a truly bipartisan approach, but also systematic cooperation between the federal and the state agencies and between the state and the local levels as well. Above all, policymakers must be guided by the goals of quality, equality, effectiveness, and efficiency as they work to achieve educational reform.

The ability of professional educators and other public leaders to meet present educational demands is being seriously challenged. There are no simple or universal solutions to the knotty problems that must be solved in order for school and nonschool settings to join in providing excellent education for all learners. Rather, the path to improvement will differ from community to community and from school to school. This underscores the need for federal and state policies that promote wise action on a local level and encourage rational school-based decision making. This yearbook will be of use to leaders at all levels who are determined to make constructive links between school and nonschool settings an integral part of improving American public education.

FOOTNOTES

1. See, for example, Douglas E. Mitchell and Dennis J. Encarnation, "Alternative State Policy Mechanisms for Influencing School Performance," *Educational Researcher* 13 (May 1984): 4-11.

2. Horace B. Reed and Elizabeth Lee Loughran, eds., *Beyond Schools: Education for Economic, Social, and Personal Development*, (Amherst, Mass.: Citizen Involvement Training Program and Community Education Resource Center, School of Education, University of Massachusetts, 1984).

3. McGeorge Bundy, *Reconnection for Learning: A Community School System for New York City*, Mayor's Advisory Panel on Decentralization of the New York City Schools (New York: Frederick A. Praeger, 1967).

4. John Dewey, *Democracy and Education* (New York: Macmillan Co., 1916).

5. Lawrence A. Cremin, *Public Education* (New York: Basic Books, 1976).

6. John I. Goodlad, *A Place Called School: Prospects for the Future* (New York: McGraw-Hill, 1984).

7. National Commission on Excellence in Education, *A Nation at Risk: The Imperative for Educational Reform* (Washington, D.C.: U. S. Government Printing Office, 1983).

8. Sections 801-815, Title VIII, *Community Schools* (PL 95-561), "Community Schools and Comprehensive Community Education Act, 1978."

9. Commonwealth of Massachusetts, House of Representatives, House No. 5704, 26 April 1984.

10. Public Schools of Springfield, Massachusetts, *Partnership for Excellence Plan*, 24 January 1984.

11. *The Boston Compact Executive Summary* (Boston, Mass.: The School Department, 1983), pp. 1-2.

12. *A Nation at Risk*; ABC's "To Save Our Schools, To Save Our Children," 4 September 1984.

Name Index

Adelson, Joseph, 15, 18, 26, 27, 28
Adler, Mortimer J., 38, 44
Ahmed, Durre-Sameed, 101
Ahmed, Manzoor, 243
Allen, Dwight W., 99
Anderson, Daniel, 189
Aries, Philippe, 13, 26
Aristotle, 195
Arnheim, Rudolf, 118, 139
Ashby, Eric, 23, 28
Axtell, James, 6, 25

Bach, Johann Sebastian, 198
Baer, Richard A., Jr., 158
Bailyn, Bernard, 5, 25
Baldick, Robert, 26
Balzac, Honoré de, 198
Banfield, Edward, 82, 99
Barbour, Ian G., 158
Barker, Robert G., 44
Barth, Richard, 244
Bazin, Germain, 116, 139
Beethoven, Ludwig von, 198
Bell, Daniel, 109
Bell, Norman W., 101
Bellah, Robert N., 27, 158
Benveniste, Guy, 27
Berger, Peter L., 143, 156
Berman, Paul, 244
Bernstein, Jeremy, 2
Bertram, Susan, 139
Blegin, Theodore C., 26
Bloom, Benjamin, 158, 242, 244
Boyer, Ernest L., 44, 63, 243
Branscomb, Lewis M., 109, 113
Bremer, Robert H., 27
Brim, Orville G., 99, 101
Bronfenbrenner, Urie, 99, 263
Bronowski, Jacob, 193
Brown, Richard D., 25
Brown, Stephen, 158
Brubacher, John, 256
Bruner, Jerome, 100
Bryce, Jennifer W., 101
Bundy, McGeorge, 271
Burgess, Charles, 26

Carter, Susan B., 28
Chazan, Barry, 157
Chopin, Frédéric François, 198
Church, Robert L., 26

Cicero, 195
Clark, Kenneth, 134, 156
Clifford, Geraldine Joncich, 4
Cohen, Burton, 140
Cohen, David K., 26
Coleman, James, 5, 6, 243
Comer, James P., 245, 262, 263
Commager, Henry Steele, 12, 26
Coombs, Philip H., 26, 243
Cooney, Joan Ganz, 71, 78, 187
Cowan, Ruth Schwartz, 100
Craig, Robert L., 27
Cremin, Lawrence, 5, 6, 15, 25, 26, 44,
  59, 63, 64, 66, 77, 78, 100, 101, 148,
  156, 158, 243, 267, 271
Cutler, Donald R., 156, 158

Dana, John Cotton, 138
Darwin, Charles, 57
David, Jacques Louis, 198
Davies, Don, 45
Davis, Dan, 78
Decker, Larry E., 48
DeMartino-Swyhart, Barbara Ann, 157
Democritus, 195
Dewey, John, 25, 28, 29, 38, 44, 51-52,
  62, 154, 158, 172, 239, 244, 266, 271
Dickens, Charles, 187, 198
Dolan, Lawrence, 244
Doyle, Denis, 104, 107, 113
Dunn, Kenneth, 63
Dunn, Rita, 63
Dykstra, Craig R., 157

Einstein, Albert, 57
Eliot, T. S., 3
Encarnation, Dennis J., 271
Erikson, Erik H., 156, 158
Evers, Christine J., 27

Fantini, Mario D., 46, 48, 49, 53, 59, 264
Faraday, Michael, 195
Feldman, Marvin, 102
Fenton, Edward, 223
Feshbach, Norma D., 45
Fishman, Joshua, 27
Flaubert, Gustave, 187
Fletcher, Donald W., 106
Foner, Philip S., 262
Ford, Henry, 102
Fowler, James W., 157

273

Frankfurter, Felix, 80
Freud, Sigmund, 156
Frickey, Edward L., 159, 173
Fuchs-Kreimer, Nancy, 158

Gartner, Alan, 182
Geertz, Clifford, 156
Ghory, Ward J., 230, 243
Gibson, James, 134, 139
Gilder, Richard W., 27
Gilmore, Paul, 109, 113
Goelman, Hillel, 100
Gold, Gerald G., 27
Goode, George Brown, 115
Goodlad, John I., 29, 44, 45, 59, 63, 267, 271
Goodman, Pau, 22
Goya, Francisco José de, 198
Graham, Patricia A., 27
Greco, El, 198
Greenburg, Daniel S., 139
Greer, Colin, 262
Groome, Thomas H., 156, 157
Gump, Paul V., 44

Hals, Frans, 198
Hamid-Buglione, Vera, 100
Harman, David, 99, 101
Harmin, Merrill, 157
Harris, Norene, 263
Haydn, Franz Joseph, 198
Heilman, Samuel, 155
Herberg, Will, 27
Herrick, Neil Q., 28
Hill, Clifford, 100
Hobbs, Nicholas, 45, 99
Holt, John, 22, 62
Howe, Leland, 157
Husén, Torsten, 26, 27
Hutchins, Robert Maynard, 194

Illich, Ivan, 4

Jackson, Nathaniel, 263
James, William, 31
Jencks, Christopher, 5, 6
Joffe, Carole E., 26
Johnson, David, 217
Johnson, Roger, 217
Jonas, Hans, 158
Joyce, Bruce, 244

Kareev, Yaakov, 78
Kathan, Boardman, 158
Keats, John, 198
Kennedy, John F., 161
Keppel, Frederick E., 115
Kerber, Linda, 26
Kirschenbaum, Howard, 157
Koss, Heinz, 27
Knowles, Malcolm S., 117, 139
Kohlberg, Lawrence, 146, 150, 157, 223
Kohler, Mary Conway, 159, 160, 182
Krathwohl, David R., 158

Labelle, Thomas J., 45
Lasch, Christopher, 243
Lazerson, Marvin, 26, 27
Lea, Dixie, 159, 173
Lee, James M., 157
Lefcowitz, Allen, 78
Leichter, Hope Jensen, 45, 65, 77, 81, 99, 100, 101
Lesser, Gerald S., 78
Levine, Marsha, 104, 107, 113
Lightfoot, Sara Lawrence, 26, 44, 244
Lippmann, Walter, 79
Lipsitz, Joan, 174, 182
Lockridge, Kenneth A., 26
Lombard, Avima, 45, 75, 78
Loughran, Elizabeth Lee, 271
Luckmann, Thomas, 156
Lukinsky, Joseph, 140, 158
Lusterman, Seymour, 113
Luther, Martin, 188
Lynton, Ernest, 20, 27

Maccoby, Michael, 28
McDermott, Raymond P., 100
Machiavelli, Niccolo, 195
McLaughlin, Milbrey, 244
McLuhan, Marshall, 2, 184, 187
McQuigg, Beverly, 107, 113
Maeroff, Gene I., 27
Mankiewicz, Frank, 189
Manno, Bruno V., 158
Marcus, Audrey Friedman, 157
Masia, Bertram B., 158
Mead, Margaret, 101, 156
Metz, Mary, 26
Meyer, Jack A., 113
Milton, John, 198
Mitchell, Douglas E., 271
Mitchell, William E., 101

Morison, Ann, 100
Morrisett, Lloyd, 71, 78
Mozart, Wolfgang Amadeus, 198
Mundy, Jennifer A., 26, 28
Munsey, Brenda, 157
Musgrove, Frank, 13, 26

Naisbitt, John, 62, 100
Nash, Samuel, 263
Neill, Shirley Boss, 28
Nelson, C. Ellis, 156
Neufeld, Barbara, 26
Newsom, Barbara Y., 78, 129, 139
Newton, Isaac, 57

Oakes, Jeannie, 44
Oberg, Antoinette, 100
O'Connell, Peter, 139
Olneck, Michael R., 27
Olson, David R., 25
Orwell, George, 79

Parsons, Talcott, 156
Passow, A. Harry, 64
Peters, R. S., 156
Peterson, Paul E., 25, 27
Petrillo, Robert, 168
Petrine, Macdonald, 27
Phenix, Philip H., 157
Piediscalzi, Nicholas, 157
Pitman-Gelles, Bonnie, 114, 139
Plato, 184, 185
Polanyi, Michael, 158
Postman, Neil, 21, 28, 183, 243
Price, Polly, 139
Purpel, David, 145, 157
Rather, Dan, 190
Raths, Louis E., 146, 157
Ravitch, Diane, 5, 25, 44
Reed, Horace B., 271
Riessman, Frank, 182
Ripley, Dillon, 114
Rodriguez, Richard, 27, 99
Ross, Wendy, 67, 68, 78
Rothblatt, Sheldon, 26
Rugg, Harold, 30, 44
Ryan, Devin, 145, 157
Rydingsword, Carl E., 263

Sagan, Carl, 190
Sarason, Seymour B., 44
Scheffler, Israel, 156

Schoeny, Donna Hager, 48
Schrag, Peter, 27
Schuster, Jack H., 27
Schwab, Joseph J., 156, 157
Sedlak, Michael W., 26
Seifman, Eli, 99
Senker, Peter, 27
Shakespeare, William, 198
Sheppard, Harold L., 28
Silberstein, Paula, 78
Silver, Adele Z., 78, 129, 139
Simon, Sidney B., 146, 157
Sinclair, Robert L., 230, 264
Sirotnik, Kenneth A., 44
Sizer, Theodore 38, 44, 63
Skinner, B. F., 57
Slater, Philip E., 156
Sloan, Douglas M., 157
Smith, Frank, 100
Smith, Timothy, 16, 27
Socrates, 184, 185
Sprinthall, Norman, 169
Stephenson, Grace, 68
Stewart, John S., 157
Suppes, Patrick, 8, 25

Taylor, Marvin J., 156
Thucydides, 195
Tirozzi, Gerald, 255
Tolstoy, Leo, 198
Toynbee, Arnold, 195
Tsongas, Paul, 54, 63
Tye, Barbara Benham, 45
Tye, Kenneth A., 45
Tyler, Ralph W., 203

Varenne, Herve, 100
Verhine, Robert E., 45
Vogel, Ezra F., 101

Waller, Willard, 26
Wallwork, Ernest, 157
Weinberger, Kay, 78
Whipple, Guy M., 44
Whiston, Tom, 27
Whitehead, Alfred N., 44
Will, Paul J., 157
Wright, Orville, 187
Wright, Wilbur, 187

Yin, Robert K., 78

Subject Index

Aetna Life and Casualty, 106
Affective education: learning conditions for, 226-228; overall objectives of, 227; religious institutions as providers of, 144
American Council on Education, 104
American Enterprise Institute, 104
American Institutes for Research, 222
Americanization: promotion of, as function of schools, 15-16, 154
American Museum of Natural History, 115, 126
American Society for Training and Development, 104
A. T. and T., 104, 106, 107
A Nation at Risk (National Commission on Excellence in Education), 31, 84
A Place Called School (Goodlad), 35, 42, 59
Apprenticeship programs, 236
Arthur D. Little Co., 104

Back-to-basics movement, 31, 207
Barefoot Doctors program (New York City), 171-72
Boston Compact, 54, 269
Boy Scouts, 265
Brooklyn Public Library, 73-74
Burroughs Corporation, 106
Business Week, 110

Career Center (Berkeley, Calif.), 170
Carnegie Foundation, report of, 231
Charles Stewart Mott Foundation, 266
Charleston Museum, 115
Childhood, effects of changes in understanding of, on schools, 13-14
Children's Experimental Workshop. See Glen Echo Park Children's Experimental Workshop.
Children's Museum (Boston), 126, 129
Children's Television Workshop, 69-72
Citizenship: conditions for learning of, 222-24; requirements of, as cause of ascendance of public schools, 10
Class, Bureaucracy, and Schools (1971), 5
Class consciousness, as challenge to hegemony of schools, 18-20
Collaboration among educational institu-
tions: New Haven model as example of, 255-62; requirements for, 254-55. *See also*, School and nonschool environments.
Collaboration, between school and nonschool environments: guiding principles for, 76-77; need for cooperation in establishing policies for, 267-70. *See also*, School and nonschool environments.
Community Schools and Comprehensive Community Education Act of 1978, 53, 268
Computer and electronic literacy, need for education for, 56, 236
Cooperation and altruism, as conditions for learning, 216-19
Cultural Education Collaborative (Boston), 130-31

Day Care Youth Helpers, 165-67, 218, 219, 228
Demographic shifts, effects of, on schools, 21
Detroit College of Business, 106

Economic change, effects of, on schools, 11-13
Education and educating: definitions of, 6-7, 64, 80, 88, 91, 193-94; definition of, as different from schooling, 29-39, 267
Elbenwood Center for the Study of the Family as Educator, 85, 88, 94
"Electric Company." See Children's Television Workshop.
Equality of Educational Opportunity (Coleman), 5
Evaluation, effect of, by family members, 95-96
Expectations, for schools: degree to which schools meet, 36-39; parental assumptions about, 35-36; sociopolitical assumptions concerning, 33-35
Exploratorium (San Francisco), 125

Family: concepts about, as educator, 85-90; distinctive features of, in educational functions, 86-88; kinds of educational activities taking place in, 86-90, 208; outcomes of education in and by, 92; personal biases in thinking about, 82; questions of educational role of, 83-84; relation of, to other educational institutions, 97-98

Fashion Institute of Technology (New York City), 106

Field trips, as method of combining environments for learning, 234-35

First Pennsylvania Bank, 106

4-H: educational activities in, 177-79; origin and development of, 174-75; problems of, 180-182; volunteer leaders in, 179-80

General Electric, 104-106

General Motors Institute, 104

Girl Scouts, 167, 265

Glen Echo Park Children's Experimental Workshop, 67-69

Harris Corporation, 106

Hartford, University of, 106

Headstart, 31

Home education, 52

Home Instruction Program for Preschool Youngsters (HIPPY), 74-76

Immigration, relation of, to standardization of schooling, 50

Inequality: A Reassessment of the Effect of Family and Schooling in America (Jencks), 5

IBM, 104, 109

International Evaluation of Educational Achievement, 220, 222

John Wood Community College, 106

Learning, conditions for, 204-8

Literacy: changes in definition of, 9; need for educating for, in computers and electronics, 56, 236; role of family in development of, 88-90, 96

Literature, conditions for learning, 225-26

Localism: dominant pattern of, in organization of schools, 16-17; federal challenges to, 17-18

Lowell Model for Educational Excellence, 54

Manchester Community College, 106

Mass schooling, emergence of concept of, 50

Mathematics, conditions for learning, 219-20

Memorial Art Gallery (University of Rochester), 72-73

Metropolitan Museum of Art, 115

Morrill Act, 12

Motivation for learning, 204, 242

Museum of Fine Arts (Boston), 115

Museum of Science and Industry (Chicago), 116, 123

Museum-school programs: components for learning in, 132-34; recommendations for, 135-38

Museums: collaboration of, with teachers, in programming, 130-32; programs of, for credit, 125; programs of, for training teachers, 127-29; services of, to schools, 123-25; value of, as learning environment, 117-20; visits of, to schools, 125-27

Museums Collaborative (New York), 131

Museums for children, 115, 126

National Assessment of Educational Progress, 207, 215, 219-20, 221, 222

National Commission for Cooperative Education, 105

National Commission on Excellence in Education, 40

National Commission on Resources for Youth, 218, 223; experimental programs of, 163-72; origin and mission of, 161-62

National Gallery of Art (Washington, D.C.) 126

National Industrial Conference Board, 105

National Institute for Work and Learning (Manpower Institute), 105

National Zoological Park (Washington, D.C.), 124

New Haven Model, 255-62

Old Sturbridge Village, 128-29

Oral language development, conditions for fostering, 211-14

Partnership for Excellence (Springfield, Mass.), 54-269

Peabody Museum of Salem, 124

Peer co-counseling, 167-69

Polaroid, 107

Popular culture, effects of, on schools, 20-21

Pratt and Whitney Aircraft Group (United Technologies), 106

President's Science Advisory Committee, Youth Panel of, 159

Protestant Revolution, effects of, on schools, 9-10

Public Education (Cremin), 59

Public schooling: ascendance of, as consequence of modernism, 8-14; causes of divergence of, from Western Europe, 16; challenges to hegemony of, 18-21; citizenship requirements as cause of ascendance of, 10; functions of, to be conserved, 24; goals for guiding policies for improving, 264-65. *See also*, Schools.

Reading, conditions for learning, 214-16

Religious institutions: as providers of affective experiences, 144; as providers of moral education, 145-47; as teachers of a world view, 141-43

Religious teachings and schools, conflicts between, 151-52

Religion: need for schools to relate to education provided by, 148-51; teaching about, in schools, 147-48, 198-99

Remedial education, corporate offerings of, 107

Rights, individual and family, as challenge to hegemony of schools, 22-23

Schempp decision (1963), 147-48

School and nonschool environments: need for coordination among, 228-29; need for leadership role for teacher in promoting connections among, 234-36; points for connecting, 233-36; stages in the evolution of, 47-54; viewpoints that block progress toward building connections among, 237-42

Schooling, definition of, 29, 39, 46, 61-62

Schools: ascent of humanity as unifying theme in determining functions of, 193-99; basic goals of, to be conserved, 24, 60; guiding postulates in thinking about, 43; need for overarching postulate to determine functions of, 40

Science, conditions for learning, 220-22

Self-discipline, conditions for learning, 209-11

Self-instruction systems, 111

"Sesame Street," 187, 191. *See also*, Children's Television Workshop.

Skills of community, schools as developers of, 153

Smith-Hughes Act, 12

Smithsonian Institution, 115

Social studies, conditions for learning, 222

Sputnik, effects of, on schooling, 30-31

Switching Yard (Marin County), 170

Technological change: effects of, on schools, 8-9, 20-21, 248-52; major problems posed by, 185-86

Television: direct opposition of, to curriculum of schools, 189-93; effects of, on schools, 21, 186-89; family as mediators in impact of, on children, 97-98; possibilities of, as potential ally of schooling, 199-200; ways for schools to combat effects of, 193-98

Temple University, 106

Textronix, Inc., 105

The Imperfect Panacea (1968), 5

The Sorting Machine (1976), 5

Union College (Schenectady), 106

Vocational education, as component of general education, 42

Wang Laboratories, 104

Workplace as educator, ethical questions raised as a result of, 108-9

Xerox Residential Corporate Education Center, 103, 104

Yale Child Study Center, 257, 261

Youth participation programs: definition of, 172-73; examples of, 162-72

Youth Tutoring programs, 163-65, 218, 219

INFORMATION ABOUT MEMBERSHIP IN THE SOCIETY

From its small beginnings in the early 1900s, the National Society for the Study of Education has grown to a major educational organization with more than 3,000 members in the United States, Canada, and overseas. Members include professors, researchers, graduate students, and administrators in colleges and universities; teachers, supervisors, curriculum specialists, and administrators in elementary and secondary schools; and a considerable number of persons who are not formally connected with an educational institution. Membership in the Society is open to all persons who desire to receive its publications.

Since its establishment the Society has sought to promote its central purpose—the stimulation of investigations and discussions of important educational issues—through regular publication of a two-volume yearbook that is sent to all members. Many of these volumes have been so well received throughout the profession that they have gone into several printings. A recently inaugurated series of substantial paperbacks on Contemporary Educational Issues supplements the series of yearbooks and allows for treatment of a wider range of educational topics than can be addressed each year through the yearbooks alone.

Through membership in the Society one can add regularly to one's professional library at a very reasonable cost. Members also help to sustain a publication program that is widely recognized for its unique contributions to the literature of education.

The categories of membership, and the current dues in each category, are as follows:

Regular. The member receives a clothbound copy of each part of the two-volume yearbook (approximately 300 pages per volume). Annual dues, $20.

Comprehensive. The member receives clothbound copies of the two-volume yearbook and the two volumes in the current paperback series. Annual dues, $35.

Retirees and Graduate Students. Reduced dues—Regular, $16; Comprehensive, $31.
The above reduced dues are available to (a) those who have retired or are over sixty-five years of age and who have been members of the Society for at least ten years, and (b) graduate students in their first year of membership.

279

Life Membership. Persons sixty years of age or over may hold a Regular Membership for life upon payment of a lump sum based upon the life expectancy for their age group. Consult the Secretary-Treasurer for further details.

New members are required to pay an entrance fee of $1, in addition to the dues, in their first year of membership.

Membership is for the calendar year and dues are payable on or before January 1. A reinstatement fee of $.50 must be added to dues payments made after January 1.

In addition to receiving the publications of the Society as described above, members participate in the nomination and election of the six-member Board of Directors, which is responsible for managing the business and affairs of the Society, including the authorization of volumes to appear in the yearbook series. Two members of the Board are elected each year for three-year terms. Members of the Society who have contributed to its publications and who indicate a willingness to serve are eligible for election to the Board.

Members are urged to attend the one or more meetings of the Society that are arranged each year in conjunction with the annual meetings of major educational organizations. The purpose of such meetings is to present, discuss, and critique volumes in the current yearbook series. Announcements of meetings for the ensuing year are sent to members in December.

Upon written request from a member, the Secretary-Treasurer will send the current directory of members, synopses of meetings of the Board of Directors, and the annual financial report.

Persons desiring further information about membership may write to

KENNETH J. REHAGE, Secretary-Treasurer
National Society for the Study of Education

5835 Kimbark Ave.
Chicago, Ill. 60637

PUBLICATIONS OF THE NATIONAL SOCIETY FOR THE STUDY OF EDUCATION

1. The Yearbooks

NOTICE: Many of the early yearbooks of this series are now out of print. In the following list, those titles to which an asterisk is prefixed are not available for purchase.

*First Yearbook, 1902, Part I—*Some Principles in the Teaching of History.* Lucy M. Salmon.
*First Yearbook, 1902, Part II—*The Progress of Geography in the Schools.* W. M. Davis and H. M. Wilson.
*Second Yearbook, 1903, Part I—*The Course of Study in History in the Common School.* Isabel Lawrence, C. A. McMurry, Frank McMurry, E. C. Page, and E. J. Rice.
*Second Yearbook, 1903, Part II—*The Relation of Theory to Practice in Education.* M. J. Holmes, J. A. Keith, and Levi Seeley.
*Third Yearbook, 1904, Part I—*The Relation of Theory to Practice in the Education of Teachers.* John Dewey, Sarah C. Brooks, F. M. McMurry, et al.
*Third Yearbook, 1904, Part II—*Nature Study.* W. S. Jackman.
*Fourth Yearbook, 1905, Part I—*The Education and Training of Secondary Teachers.* E. C. Elliott, E. G. Dexter, M. J. Holmes, et al.
*Fourth Yearbook, 1905, Part II—*The Place of Vocational Subjects in the High-School Curriculum.* J. S. Brown, G. B. Morrison, and Ellen Richards.
*Fifth Yearbook, 1906, Part I—*On the Teaching of English in Elementary and High Schools.* G. P. Brown and Emerson Davis.
*Fifth Yearbook, 1906, Part II—*The Certification of Teachers.* E. P. Cubberley.
*Sixth Yearbook, 1907, Part I—*Vocational Studies for College Entrance.* C. A. Herrick, H. W. Holmes, T. deLaguna, V. Prettyman, and W. J. S. Bryan.
*Sixth Yearbook, 1907, Part II—*The Kindergarten and Its Relation to Elementary Education.* Ada Van Stone Harris, E. A. Kirkpatrick, Marie Kraus-Boelté, Patty S. Hill, Harriette M. Mills, and Nina Vandewalker.
*Seventh Yearbook, 1908, Part I—*The Relation of Superintendents and Principals to the Training and Professional Improvement of Their Teachers.* Charles D. Lowry.
*Seventh Yearbook, 1908, Part II—*The Co-ordination of the Kindergarten and the Elementary School.* B. C. Gregory, Jennie B. Merrill, Bertha Payne, and Margaret Giddings.
*Eighth Yearbook, 1909, Part I—*Education with Reference to Sex: Pathological, Economic, and Social Aspects.* C. R. Henderson.
*Eighth Yearbook, 1909, Part II—*Education with Reference to Sex: Agencies and Methods.* C. R. Henderson and Helen C. Putnam.
*Ninth Yearbook, 1910, Part I—*Health and Education.* T. D. Wood.
*Ninth Yearbook, 1910, Part II—*The Nurses in Education.* T. D. Wood, et al..
*Tenth Yearbook, 1911, Part I—*The City School as a Community Center.* H. C. Leipziger, Sarah E. Hyre, R. D. Warden, C. Ward Crampton, E. W. Stitt, E. J. Ward, Mrs. E. C. Grice, and C. A. Perry.
*Tenth Yearbook, 1911, Part II—*The Rural School as a Community Center.* B. H. Crocheron, Jessie Field, F. W. Howe, E. C. Bishop, A. B. Graham, O. J. Kern, M. T. Scudder, and B. M. Davis.
*Eleventh Yearbook, 1912, Part I—*Industrial Education: Typical Experiments Described and Interpreted.* J. F. Barker, M. Bloomfield, B. W. Johnson, P. Johnston, L. M. Leavitt, G. A. Mirick, M. W. Murray, C. F. Perry, A. L. Safford, and H. B. Wilson.
*Eleventh Yearbook, 1912, Part II—*Agricultural Education in Secondary Schools.* A. C. Monahan, R. W. Stimson, D. J. Crosby, W. H. French, H. F. Button, F. R. Crane, W. R. Hart, and G. F. Warren.
*Twelfth Yearbook, 1913, Part I—*The Supervision of City Schools.* Franklin Bobbitt, J. W. Hall, and J. D. Wolcott.
*Twelfth Yearbook, 1913, Part II—*The Supervision of Rural Schools.* A. C. Monahan, L. J. Hanifan, J. E. Warren, Wallace Lund, U. J. Hoffman, A. S. Cook, E. M. Rapp, Jackson Davis, J. D. Wolcott.
*Thirteenth Yearbook, 1914, Part I—*Some Aspects of High-School Instruction and Administration.* H. C. Morrison, E. R. Breslich, W. A. Jessup, and L. D. Coffman.
*Thirteenth Yearbook, 1914, Part II—*Plans for Organizing School Surveys, with a Summary of Typical School Surveys.* Charles H. Judd and Henry L. Smith.
*Fourteenth Yearbook, 1915, Part I—*Minimum Essentials in Elementary School Subjects— Standards and Current Practices.* H. B. Wilson, H. W. Holmes, F. E. Thompson, R. G. Jones, S. A. Courtis, W. S. Gray, F. N. Freeman, H. C. Pryor, J. F. Hosic, W. A. Jessup, and W. C. Bagley.
*Fourteenth Yearbook, 1915, Part II—*Methods for Measuring Teachers' Efficiency.* Arthur C. Boyce.

282   PUBLICATIONS

*Fifteenth Yearbook, 1916, Part I—*Standards and Tests for the Measurement of the Efficiency of Schools and School Systems.* G. D. Strayer, Bird T. Baldwin, B. R. Buckingham, F. W. Ballou, D. C. Bliss, H. G. Childs, S. A. Courtis, E. P. Cubberley, C. H. Judd, George Melcher, E. E. Oberholtzer, J. B. Sears, Daniel Starch, M. R. Trabue, and G. M. Whipple.
*Fifteenth Yearbook, 1916, Part II—*The Relationship between Persistence in School and Home Conditions.* Charles E. Holley.
*Fifteenth Yearbook, 1916, Part III—*The Junior High School.* Aubrey A. Douglass.
*Sixteenth Yearbook, 1917, Part I—*Second Report of the Committee on Minimum Essentials in Elementary-School Subjects.* W. C. Bagley, W. W. Charters, F. N. Freeman, W. S. Gray, Ernest Horn, J. H. Hoskinson, W. S. Monroe, C. F. Munson, H. C. Pryor, L. W. Rapeer, G. M. Wilson, and H. B. Wilson.
*Sixteenth Yearbook, 1917, Part II—*The Efficiency of College Students as Conditioned by Age at Entrance and Size of High School.* B. F. Pittenger.
*Seventeenth Yearbook, 1918, Part I—*Third Report of the Committee on Economy of Time in Education.* W. C. Bagley, B. B. Bassett, M. E. Branom, Alice Camerer, J. E. Dealey, C. A. Ellwood, E. B. Greene, A. B. Hart, J. F. Hosic, E. T. Housh, W. H. Mace, L. R. Marston, H. C. McKown, A. E. Mitchell, W. C. Reavis, D. Snedden, and H. B. Wilson.
*Seventeenth Yearbook, 1918, Part II—*The Measurement of Educational Products.* E. J. Ashbaugh, W. A. Averill, L. P. Ayers, F. W. Ballou, Edna Bryner, B. R. Buckingham, S. A. Courtis, M. E. Haggerty, C. H. Judd, George Melcher, W. S. Monroe, E. A. Nifenecker, and E. L. Thorndike.
*Eighteenth Yearbook, 1919, Part I—*The Professional Preparation of High-School Teachers.* G. N. Cade, S. S. Colvin, Charles Fordyce, H. H. Foster, T. S. Gosling, W. S. Gray, L. V. Koos, A. R. Mead, H. L. Miller, F. C. Whitcomb, and Clifford Woody.
*Eighteenth Yearbook, 1919, Part II—*Fourth Report of Committee on Economy of Time in Education.* F. C. Ayer, F. N. Freeman, W. S. Gray, Ernest Horn, W. S. Monroe, and C. E. Seashore.
*Nineteenth Yearbook, 1920, Part I—*New Materials of Instruction.* Prepared by the Society's Committee on Materials of Instruction.
*Nineteenth Yearbook, 1920, Part II—*Classroom Problems in the Education of Gifted Children.* T. S. Henry.
*Twentieth Yearbook, 1921, Part I—*New Materials of Instruction.* Second Report by Society's Committee.
*Twentieth Yearbook, 1921, Part II—*Report of the Society's Committee on Silent Reading.* M. A. Burgess, S. A. Courtis, C. E. Germane, W. S. Gray, H. A. Greene, Reginia R. Heller, J. H. Hoover, J. A. O'Brien, J. L. Packer, Daniel Starch, W. W. Theisen, G. A. Yoakum, and representatives of other school systems.
*Twenty-first Yearbook, 1922, Parts I and II—*Intelligence Tests and Their Use,* Part I—*The Nature, History, and General Principles of Intelligence Testing.* E. L. Thorndike, S. S. Colvin, Harold Rugg, G. M. Whipple, Part II—*The Administrative Use of Intelligence Tests.* H. W. Holmes, W. K. Layton, Helen Davis, Agnes L. Rogers, Rudolf Pintner, M. R. Trabue, W. S. Miller, Bessie L. Gambrill, and others. The two parts are bound together.
*Twenty-second Yearbook, 1923, Part I—*English Composition: Its Aims, Methods and Measurements.* Earl Hudelson.
*Twenty-second Yearbook, 1923, Part II—*The Social Studies in the Elementary and Secondary School.* A. S. Barr, J. J. Coss, Henry Harap, R. W. Hatch, H. C. Hill, Ernest Horn, C. H. Judd, L. C. Marshall, F. M. McMurry, Earle Rugg, H. O. Rugg, Emma Schweppe, Mabel Snedaker, and C. W. Washburne.
*Twenty-third Yearbook, 1924, Part I—*The Education of Gifted Children.* Report of the Society's Committee, Guy M. Whipple, Chairman.
*Twenty-third Yearbook, 1924, Part II—*Vocational Guidance and Vocational Education for Industries.* A. H. Edgerton and others.
*Twenty-fourth Yearbook, 1925, Part I—*Report of the National Committee on Reading.* W. S. Gray, Chairman, F. W. Ballou, Rose L. Hardy, Ernest Horn, Francis Jenkins, S. A. Leonard, Estaline Wilson, and Laura Zirbes.
*Twenty-fourth Yearbook, 1925, Part II—*Adapting the Schools to Individual Differences.* Report of the Society's Committee. Carleton W. Washburne, Chairman.
*Twenty-fifth Yearbook, 1926, Part I—*The Present Status of Safety Education.* Report of the Society's Committee. Guy M. Whipple, Chairman.
*Twenty-fifth Yearbook, 1926, Part II—*Extra-Curricular Activities.* Report of the Society's Committee. Leonard V. Koos, Chairman.
*Twenty-sixth Yearbook, 1927, Part I—*Curriculum-making: Past and Present.* Report of the Society's Committee. Harold O. Rugg, Chairman.
*Twenty-sixth Yearbook, 1927, Part II—*The Foundations of Curriculum-making.* Prepared by individual members of the Society's Committee. Harold O. Rugg, Chairman.
*Twenty-seventh Yearbook, 1928, Part I—*Nature and Nurture: Their Influence upon Intelligence.* Prepared by the Society's Committee. Lewis M. Terman, Chairman.
*Twenty-seventh Yearbook, 1928, Part II—*Nature and Nurture: Their Influence upon Achievement.* Prepared by the Society's Committee. Lewis M. Terman, Chairman.

*Twenty-eighth Yearbook, 1929, Parts I and II—*Preschool and Parental Education.* Part I—*Organization and Development.* Part II—*Research and Method.* Prepared by the Society's Committee. Lois H. Meek, Chairman. Bound in one volume. Cloth.
*Twenty-ninth Yearbook, 1930, Parts I and II—*Report of the Society's Committee on Arithmetic.* Part I—*Some Aspects of Modern Thought on Arithmetic.* Part II—*Research in Arithmetic.* Prepared by the Society's Committee. F. B. Knight, Chairman. Bound in one volume.
*Thirtieth Yearbook, 1931, Part I—*The Status of Rural Education.* First Report of the Society's Committee on Rural Education. Orville G. Brim, Chairman.
Thirtieth Yearbook, 1931, Part I—*The Textbook in American Education.* Report of the Society's Committee on the Textbook. J. B. Edmonson, Chairman. Cloth. Paper.
*Thirty-first Yearbook, 1932, Part I—*A Program for Teaching Science.* Prepared by the Society's Committee on the Teaching of Science. S. Ralph Powers, Chairman.
*Thirty-first Yearbook, 1932, Part II—*Changes and Experiments in Liberal-Arts Education.* Prepared by Kathryn McHale, with numerous collaborators.
*Thirty-second Yearbook, 1933—*The Teaching of Geography.* Prepared by the Society's Committee on the Teaching of Geography. A. E. Parkins, Chairman.
*Thirty-third Yearbook, 1934, Part I—*The Planning and Construction of School Buildings.* Prepared by the Society's Committee on School Buildings. N. L. Engelhardt, Chairman.
*Thirty-third Yearbook, 1934, Part II—*The Activity Movement.* Prepared by the Society's Committee on the Activity Movement, Lois Coffey Mossman, Chairman.
Thirty-fourth Yearbook, 1935—*Educational Diagnosis.* Prepared by the Society's Committee on Educational Diagnosis. L. J. Brueckner, Chairman. Paper.
*Thirty-fifth Yearbook, 1936, Part I—*The Grouping of Pupils.* Prepared by the Society's Committee. W. W. Coxe, Chairman.
*Thirty-fifth Yearbook, 1936, Part II—*Music Education.* Prepared by the Society's Committee. W. L. Uhl, Chairman.
*Thirty-sixth Yearbook, 1937, Part I—*The Teaching of Reading.* Prepared by the Society's Committee. W. S. Gray, Chairman.
*Thirty-sixth Yearbook, 1937, Part II—*International Understanding through the Public-School Curriculum.* Prepared by the Society's Committee. I. L. Kandel, Chairman.
*Thirty-seventh Yearbook, 1938, Part I—*Guidance in Educational Institutions.* Prepared by the Society's Committee. G. N. Kefauver, Chairman.
*Thirty-seventh Yearbook, 1938, Part II—*The Scientific Movement in Education.* Prepared by the Society's Committee. F. N. Freeman, Chairman.
*Thirty-eighth Yearbook, 1939, Part I—*Child Development and the Curriculum.* Prepared by the Society's Committee. Carleton Washburne, Chairman.
*Thirty-eighth Yearbook, 1939, Part II—*General Education in the American College.* Prepared by the Society's Committee. Alvin Eurich, Chairman. Cloth.
*Thirty-ninth Yearbook, 1940, Part I—*Intelligence: Its Nature and Nurture. Comparative and Critical Exposition.* Prepared by the Society's Committee. G. D. Stoddard, Chairman.
*Thirty-ninth Yearbook, 1940, Part II—*Intelligence: Its Nature and Nurture. Original Studies and Experiments.* Prepared by the Society's Committee. G. D. Stoddard, Chairman.
*Fortieth Yearbook, 1941—*Art in American Life and Education.* Prepared by the Society's Committee. Thomas Munro, Chairman.
Forty-first Yearbook, 1942, Part I—*Philosophies of Education.* Prepared by the Society's Committee. John S. Brubacher, Chairman. Paper.
Forty-first Yearbook, 1942, Part II—*The Psychology of Learning.* Prepared by the Society's Committee. T. R. McConnell, Chairman. Cloth.
*Forty-second Yearbook, 1943, Part I—*Vocational Education.* Prepared by the Society's Committee. F. J. Keller, Chairman.
*Forty-second Yearbook, 1943, Part II—*The Library in General Education.* Prepared by the Society's Committee. L. R. Wilson, Chairman.
Forty-third Yearbook, 1944, Part I—*Adolescence.* Prepared by the Society's Committee. Harold E. Jones, Chairman. Paper.
*Forty-third Yearbook, 1944, Part II—*Teaching Language in the Elementary School.* Prepared by the Society's Committee. M. R. Trabue, Chairman.
*Forty-fourth Yearbook, 1945, Part I—*American Education in the Postwar Period: Curriculum Reconstruction.* Prepared by the Society's Committee. Ralph W. Tyler, Chairman.
*Forty-fourth Yearbook, 1945, Part II—*American Education in the Postwar Period: Structural Reorganization.* Prepared by the Society's Committee. Bess Goodykoontz, Chairman. Paper.
*Forty-fifth Yearbook, 1946, Part I—*The Measurement of Understanding.* Prepared by the Society's Committee. William A. Brownell, Chairman.
*Forty-fifth Yearbook, 1946, Part II—*Changing Conceptions in Educational Administration.* Prepared by the Society's Committee. Alonzo G. Grace, Chairman.
*Forty-sixth Yearbook, 1947, Part I—*Science Education in American Schools.* Prepared by the Society's Committee. Victor H. Noll, Chairman.

*Forty-sixth Yearbook, 1947, Part II—*Early Childhood Education.* Prepared by the Society's Committee. N. Searle Light, Chairman. Paper.

Forty-seventh Yearbook, 1948, Part I—*Juvenile Delinquency and the Schools.* Prepared by the Society's Committee. Ruth Strang, Chairman. Cloth.

Forty-seventh Yearbook, 1948, Part II—*Reading in the High School and College.* Prepared by the Society's Committee. William S. Gray, Chairman. Cloth. Paper.

*Forty-eighth Yearbook, 1949, Part I—*Audio-visual Materials of Instruction.* Prepared by the Society's Committee. Stephen M. Corey, Chairman. Cloth.

*Forty-eighth Yearbook, 1949, Part II—*Reading in the Elementary School.* Prepared by the Society's Committee. Arthur I. Gates, Chairman.

*Forty-ninth Yearbook, 1950, Part I—*Learning and Instruction.* Prepared by the Society's Committee. G. Lester Anderson, Chairman.

*Forty-ninth Yearbook, 1950, Part II—*The Education of Exceptional Children.* Prepared by the Society's Committee. Samuel A. Kirk, Chairman.

Fiftieth Yearbook, 1951, Part I—*Graduate Study in Education.* Prepared by the Society's Board of Directors. Ralph W. Tyler, Chairman. Paper.

Fiftieth Yearbook, 1951, Part II—*The Teaching of Arithmetic.* Prepared by the Society's Committee. G. T. Buswell, Chairman. Cloth, Paper.

Fifty-first Yearbook, 1952, Part I—*General Education.* Prepared by the Society's Committee. T. R. McConnell, Chairman. Cloth, Paper.

Fifty-first Yearbook, 1952, Part II—*Education in Rural Communities.* Prepared by the Society's Committee. Ruth Strang, Chairman. Cloth, Paper.

*Fifty-second Yearbook, 1953, Part I—*Adapting the Secondary-School Program to the Needs of Youth.* Prepared by the Society's Committee: William G. Brink, Chairman.

Fifty-second Yearbook, 1953, Part II—*The Community School.* Prepared by the Society's Committee. Maurice F. Seay, Chairman. Cloth.

Fifty-third Yearbook, 1954, Part I—*Citizen Cooperation for Better Public Schools.* Prepared by the Society's Committee. Edgar L. Morphet, Chairman. Cloth, Paper.

*Fifty-third Yearbook, 1954, Part II—*Mass Media and Education.* Prepared by the Society's Committee. Edgar Dale, Chairman.

*Fifty-fourth Yearbook, 1955, Part I—*Modern Philosophies and Education.* Prepared by the Society's Committee. John S. Brubacher, Chairman.

Fifty-fourth Yearbook, 1955, Part II—*Mental Health in Modern Education.* Prepared by the Society's Committee. Paul A. Witty, Chairman. Paper.

*Fifty-fifth Yearbook, 1956, Part I—*The Public Junior College.* Prepared by the Society's Committee. B. Lamar Johnson, Chairman.

*Fifty-fifth Yearbook, 1956, Part II—*Adult Reading.* Prepared by the Society's Committee. David H. Clift, Chairman.

*Fifty-sixth Yearbook, 1957, Part I—*In-service Education of Teachers, Supervisors, and Administrators.* Prepared by the Society's Committee. Stephen M. Corey, Chairman. Cloth.

Fifty-sixth Yearbook, 1957, Part II—*Social Studies in the Elementary School.* Prepared by the Society's Committee. Ralph C. Preston, Chairman. Cloth, Paper.

*Fifty-seventh Yearbook, 1958, Part I—*Basic Concepts in Music Education.* Prepared by the Society's Committee. Thurber H. Madison, Chairman. Cloth.

*Fifty-seventh Yearbook, 1958, Part II—*Education for the Gifted.* Prepared by the Society's Committee. Robert J. Havighurst, Chairman.

*Fifty-seventh Yearbook, 1958, Part III—*The Integration of Educational Experiences.* Prepared by the Society's Committee. Paul L. Dressel, Chairman. Cloth.

Fifty-eighth Yearbook, 1959, Part I—*Community Education: Principles and Practices from World-wide Experience.* Prepared by the Society's Committee. C. O. Arndt, Chairman. Cloth, Paper.

Fifty-eighth Yearbook, 1959, Part II—*Personnel Services in Education.* Prepared by the Society's Committee. Melvene D. Hardee, Chairman. Paper.

*Fifty-ninth Yearbook, 1960, Part I—*Rethinking Science Education.* Prepared by the Society's Committee. J. Darrell Barnard, Chairman.

*Fifty-ninth Yearbook, 1960, Part II—*The Dynamics of Instructional Groups.* Prepared by the Society's Committee. Gale E. Jensen, Chairman.

Sixtieth Yearbook, 1961, Part I—*Development in and through Reading.* Prepared by the Society's Committee. Paul A. Witty, Chairman. Cloth.

Sixtieth Yearbook, 1961, Part II—*Social Forces Influencing American Education.* Prepared by the Society's Committee. Ralph W. Tyler, Chairman. Cloth, Paper.

Sixty-first Yearbook, 1962, Part I—*Individualizing Instruction.* Prepared by the Society's Committee. Fred T. Tyler, Chairman. Cloth.

Sixty-first Yearbook, 1962, Part II—*Education for the Professions.* Prepared by the Society's Committee. G. Lester Anderson, Chairman. Cloth.

Sixty-second Yearbook, 1963, Part I—*Child Psychology.* Prepared by the Society's Committee. Harold W. Stevenson, Editor. Cloth.

Sixty-second Yearbook, 1963, Part II—*The Impact and Improvement of School Testing Programs.* Prepared by the Society's Committee. Warren G. Findley, Editor. Cloth.

Sixty-third Yearbook, 1964, Part I—*Theories of Learning and Instruction.* Prepared by the Society's Committee. Ernest R. Hilgard, Editor. Paper, Cloth.

Sixty-third Yearbook, 1964, Part II—*Behavioral Science and Educational Administration.* Prepared by the Society's Committee. Daniel E. Griffiths, Editor. Paper.

Sixty-fourth Yearbook, 1965, Part I—*Vocational Education.* Prepared by the Society's Committee. Melvin L. Barlow, Editor. Cloth.

*Sixty-fourth Yearbook, 1965, Part II—*Art Education.* Prepared by the Society's Committee. W. Reid Hastie, Editor.

Sixty-fifth Yearbook, 1966, Part I—*Social Deviancy among Youth.* Prepared by the Society's Committee. William W. Wattenberg, Editor. Cloth.

Sixty-fifth Yearbook, 1966, Part II—*The Changing American School.* Prepared by the Society's Committee. John I. Goodlad, Editor. Cloth.

*Sixty-sixth Yearbook, 1967, Part I—*The Educationally Retarded and Disadvantaged.* Prepared by the Society's Committee. Paul A. Witty, Editor. Cloth.

*Sixty-sixth Yearbook, 1967, Part II—*Programed Instruction.* Prepared by the Society's Committee. Phil C. Lange, Editor. Cloth.

Sixty-seventh Yearbook, 1968, Part I—*Metropolitanism: Its Challenge to Education.* Prepared by the Society's Committee. Robert J. Havighurst, Editor. Cloth.

Sixty-seventh Yearbook, 1968, Part II—*Innovation and Change in Reading Instruction.* Prepared by the Society's Committee. Helen M. Robinson, Editor. Cloth.

Sixty-eighth Yearbook, 1969, Part I—*The United States and International Education.* Prepared by the Society's Committee. Harold G. Shane, Editor. Cloth.

Sixty-eighth Yearbook, 1969, Part II—*Educational Evaluation: New Roles, New Means.* Prepared by the Society's Committee. Ralph W. Tyler, Editor. Paper.

*Sixty-ninth Yearbook, 1970, Part I—*Mathematics Education.* Prepared by the Society's Committee. Edward G. Begle, Editor. Cloth.

Sixty-ninth Yearbook, 1970, Part II—*Linguistics in School Programs.* Prepared by the Society's Committee. Albert H. Marckwardt, Editor. Cloth.

*Seventieth Yearbook, 1971, Part I—*The Curriculum: Retrospect and Prospect.* Prepared by the Society's Committee. Robert M. McClure, Editor. Paper.

Seventieth Yearbook, 1971, Part II—*Leaders in American Education.* Prepared by the Society's Committee. Robert J. Havighurst, Editor. Cloth.

Seventy-first Yearbook, 1972, Part I—*Philosophical Redirection of Educational Research.* Prepared by the Society's Committee. Lawrence G. Thomas, Editor. Cloth.

Seventy-first Yearbook, 1972, Part II—*Early Childhood Education.* Prepared by the Society's Committee. Ira J. Gordon, Editor. Paper.

*Seventy-second Yearbook, 1973, Part I—*Behavior Modification in Education.* Prepared by the Society's Committee. Carl E. Thoresen, Editor. Cloth.

Seventy-second Yearbook, 1973, Part II—*The Elementary School in the United States.* Prepared by the Society's Committee. John I. Goodlad and Harold G. Shane, Editors. Cloth.

Seventy-third Yearbook, 1974, Part I—*Media and Symbols: The Forms of Expression, Communication and Education.* Prepared by the Society's Committee. David R. Olson, Editor. Cloth.

Seventy-third Yearbook, 1974, Part II—*Uses of the Sociology of Education.* Prepared by the Society's Committee. C. Wayne Gordon, Editor. Cloth.

Seventy-fourth Yearbook, 1975, Part I—*Youth.* Prepared by the Society's Committee. Robert J. Havighurst and Phillip H. Dreyer, Editors. Cloth.

Seventy-fourth Yearbook, 1975, Part II—*Teacher Education.* Prepared by the Society's Committee. Kevin Ryan, Editor. Cloth.

Seventy-fifth Yearbook, 1976, Part I—*Psychology of Teaching Methods.* Prepared by the Society's Committee. N. L. Gage, Editor. Paper.

*Seventy-fifth Yearbook, 1976, Part II—*Issues in Secondary Education.* Prepared by the Society's Committee. William Van Til, Editor. Cloth.

Seventy-sixth Yearbook, 1977, Part I—*The Teaching of English.* Prepared by the Society's Committee. James R. Squire, Editor. Cloth.

Seventy-sixth Yearbook, 1977, Part II—*The Politics of Education.* Prepared by the Society's Committee. Jay D. Scribner, Editor. Paper.

Seventy-seventh Yearbook, 1978, Part I—*The Courts and Education,* Clifford P. Hooker, Editor. Cloth.

*Seventy-seventh Yearbook, 1978, Part II—*Education and the Brain,* Jeanne Chall and Allan F. Mirsky, Editors. Paper.

Seventy-eighth Yearbook, 1979, Part I—*The Gifted and the Talented: Their Education and Development,* A. Harry Passow, Editor. Paper.

Seventy-eighth Yearbook, 1979, Part II—*Classroom Management,* Daniel L. Duke, Editor. Paper.

Seventy-ninth Yearbook, 1980, Part I—*Toward Adolescence: The Middle School Years.* Mauritz Johnson, Editor. Cloth.

Seventy-ninth Yearbook, 1980, Part II—*Learning a Second Language,* Frank M. Grittner, Editor. Cloth.

Eightieth Yearbook, 1981, Part I—*Philosophy and Education*, Jonas F. Soltis, Editor. Cloth.

Eightieth Yearbook, 1981, Part II—*The Social Studies*, Howard D. Mehlinger and O. L. Davis, Jr., Editors. Cloth.

Eighty-first Yearbook, 1982, Part I—*Policy Making in Education*, Ann Lieberman and Milbrey W. McLaughlin, Editors. Cloth.

Eighty-first Yearbook, 1982, Part II—*Education and Work*, Harry F. Silberman, Editor. Cloth.

Eighty-second Yearbook, 1983, Part I—*Individual Differences and the Common Curriculum*, Gary D Fenstermacher and John I. Goodlad, Editors. Cloth.

Eighty-second Yearbook, 1983, Part II—*Staff Development*, Gary Griffin, Editor. Cloth.

Eighty-third Yearbook, 1984, Part I—*Becoming Readers in a Complex Society*, Alan C. Purves and Olive S. Niles, Editors. Cloth.

Eighty-third Yearbook, 1984, Part II—*The Humanities in Precollegiate Education*, Benjamin Ladner, Editor. Cloth.

Eighty-fourth Yearbook, 1985, Part I—*Education in School and Nonschool Settings*, Mario D. Fantini and Robert L. Sinclair, Editors. Cloth.

Eighty-fourth Yearbook, 1985, Part II—*Learning and Teaching the Ways of Knowing*, Elliot Eisner, Editor. Cloth.

Yearbooks of the National Society are distributed by

UNIVERSITY OF CHICAGO PRESS, 5801 ELLIS AVE., CHICAGO, ILLINOIS 60637

Please direct inquiries regarding prices of volumes still available to the University of Chicago Press. Orders for these volumes should be sent to the University of Chicago Press, not to the offices of the National Society.

2. The Series on Contemporary Educational Issues

In addition to its Yearbooks the Society now publishes volumes in a series on Contemporary Educational Issues. These volumes are prepared under the supervision of the Society's Commission on an Expanded Publication Program.

The 1985 Titles

Adapting Instruction to Student Differences (Margaret C. Wang and Herbert J. Walberg, eds.)

Colleges of Education: Perspectives on Their Future (Charles W. Case and William A. Matthes, eds.)

The 1984 Titles

Women and Education: Equity or Equality? (Elizabeth Fennema and M. Jane Ayer, eds.)

Curriculum Development: Problems, Processes, and Programs (Glenys G. Unruh and Adolph Unruh, eds.)

The 1983 Titles

The Hidden Curriculum and Moral Education (Henry A. Giroux and David Purpel, eds.)

The Dynamics of Organizational Change in Education (J. Victor Baldridge and Terrance Deal, eds.)

The 1982 Titles

Improving Educational Standards and Productivity: The Research Basis for Policy (Herbert J. Walberg, ed.)

Schools in Conflict: The Politics of Education (Frederick M. Wirt and Michael W. Kirst)

The 1981 Titles

Psychology and Education: The State of the Union (Frank H. Farley and Neal J. Gordon, eds.)

Selected Issues in Mathematics Education (Mary M. Lindquist, ed.)

The 1980 Titles

Minimum Competency Achievement Testing: Motives, Models, Measures, and Consequences (Richard M. Jaeger and Carol K. Tittle, eds.)

Collective Bargaining in Public Education (Anthony M. Cresswell, Michael J. Murphy, with Charles T. Kerchner)

The 1979 Titles

Educational Environments and Effects: Evaluation, Policy, and Productivity (Herbert J. Walberg, ed.)

Research on Teaching: Concepts, Findings, and Implications (Penelope L. Peterson and Herbert J. Walberg, eds.)

The Principal in Metropolitan Schools (Donald A. Erickson and Theodore L. Reller, eds.)

The 1978 Titles

Aspects of Reading Education (Susanna Pflaum-Connor, ed.)

History, Education, and Public Policy: Recovering the American Educational Past (Donald R. Warren, ed.)

From Youth to Constructive Adult Life: The Role of the Public School (Ralph W. Tyler, ed.)

The 1977 Titles

Early Childhood Education: Issues and Insights (Bernard Spodek and Herbert J. Walberg, eds.)

The Future of Big City Schools: Desegregation Policies and Magnet Alternatives (Daniel U. Levine and Robert J. Havighurst, eds.)

Educational Administration: The Developing Decades (Luvern L. Cunningham, Walter G. Hack, and Raphael O. Nystrand, eds.)

The 1976 Titles

Prospects for Research and Development in Education (Ralph W. Tyler, ed.)

Public Testimony on Public Schools (Commission on Educational Governance)

Counseling Children and Adolescents (William M. Walsh, ed.)

The 1975 Titles

Schooling and the Rights of Children (Vernon Haubrich and Michael Apple, eds.)

Systems of Individualized Education (Harriet Talmage, ed.)

Educational Policy and International Assessment: Implications of the IEA Assessment of Achievement (Alan Purves and Daniel U. Levine, eds.)

The 1974 Titles

Crucial Issues in Testing (Ralph W. Tyler and Richard M. Wolf, eds.)

Conflicting Conceptions of Curriculum (Elliot Eisner and Elizabeth Vallance, eds.)

Cultural Pluralism (Edgar G. Epps, ed.)

Rethinking Educational Equality (Andrew T. Kopan and Herbert J. Walberg, eds.)

All of the preceding volumes may be ordered from

McCutchan Publishing Corporation
P.O. Box 774
Berkeley, California 94701

The 1972 Titles

Black Students in White Schools (Edgar G. Epps, ed.)

Flexibility in School Programs (W. J. Congreve and G. L. Rinehart, eds.)

Performance Contracting—1969-1971 (J. A. Mecklenburger)

The Potential of Educational Futures (Michael Marien and W. L. Ziegler, eds.)

Sex Differences and Discrimination in Education (Scarvia Anderson, ed.)

The 1971 Titles

Accountability in Education (Leon M. Lessinger and Ralph W. Tyler, eds.)

Farewell to Schools??? (D. U. Levine and R. J. Havighurst, eds.)

Models for Integrated Education (D. U. Levine, ed.)

PYGMALION *Reconsidered* (J. D. Elashoff and R. E. Snow)

Reactions to Silberman's CRISIS IN THE CLASSROOM (A. Harry Passow, ed.)

The 1971 and 1972 titles in this series are now out of print.